BUSINESS ETHICS:
A EUROPEAN CASEBOOK

Principles ❑ *Examples* ❑ *Cases* ❑ *Codes*

John Donaldson
Centre for Service Management Studies
Twyford, UK

Guest Contributors:

Peter Davis (UK)

David Huddy (UK)

Dirk Lindenbergh (Netherlands)

Diana Robertson (USA)

Rob van Es (Netherlands)

Academic Press
Harcourt Brace Jovanovich, Publishers
London   San Diego   New York
Boston   Sydney   Tokyo   Toronto

This book is printed on acid-free paper

ACADEMIC PRESS LIMITED
24–28 Oval Road
LONDON NW1 7DX

United States Edition published by
ACADEMIC PRESS INC.
San Diego, CA 92101

A catalogue record for this book is available from the British Library

ISBN 0-12-220542-1
ISBN 0-12-220543-X (pbk)

Typeset by Columns Design and Production Services Limited
Printed and bound in Great Britain by TJ Press Ltd.,
Padstow, Cornwall

Contents

Foreword

Business is driven by values. Much business activity is directed at achieving the results required by the prevailing values. Mostly these values are impeccable, and are generally accepted as proper and are achieved. Some business values are commercial and technical, such as those that relate to the rates of profit that will keep a business in operation, or those that demand the efficient and skilled operation of plant or administrative systems. Some values are prudential, as when companies set up reserves, or insure against legal action. Often the values are clearly moral values, as when companies declare their policy to be 'responsible', or as fulfilling a duty to produce wholesome and safe products safely. Firms are expressing ethical values when they aspire to be enlightened employers, or when they set standards that reject bribery and honour contracts and obligations according to the spirit as well as to the letter.

Firms employ a language of ethics when they establish the responsibilities of the company or its employees. These responsibilities both imply and demand duties, such as obedience of lawful orders. Unions demand fair and equitable rewards. Firms state or imply that their advertising claims are accurate and true.

Some business values are mixed, in that what is ethically right is often also skilled and prudent practice. Sometimes values may be incompatible, as when observing safe working practices is so expensive as to threaten the stability of the firm, or its return to investors. Sometimes firms in a monopoly position can achieve greater returns to their investors by raising prices at the expense of customers. Sometimes products of great potential welfare value are not produced because the estimated commercial demand is deemed insufficient to make production profitable, so that opportunities to 'add value' are restricted by the rules of the market that reduce the definition of value to cash terms only.

While values such as these drive business and are generally achieved, fully or to the extent of an acceptable compromise, the practical results are increasingly being called into question. The tide of legal and quasi-legal activity in and around business is rising, even though some legislation is aimed at reducing legislative control. More areas of business behaviour are falling within the ambit of codes of practice and codes of ethics. The results of such codes are often disappointing, or are viewed with scepticism as mere public relations exercises.

This book is offered as a contribution to the search for improvement in business performance. Traditionally, 'efficiency' and 'success' have been sought with the mistaken assumption that they are value-free, and achievable by technical means, or by formulae or inspired insights as to how businesses work 'in the market-place'. This view is now widely recognized to be inadequate, and increasingly attention is turning to business ethics in general, and to the development of codes of practice in particular. There have been many achievements on these lines. They are illustrated in the studies that follow.

The main arguments offered can be summarized as follows:

1 The 'official' values that drive business are usually impeccable and are widely accepted.
2 There is a gap between these values and aspirations and industrial reality. This gap is variable over time and place and between industries and firms, and can most plausibly be explained in terms other than a resigned acceptance that the imperfections of individual people prevent the gap from closing.
3 The rising tide of legal action and the explosive growth of codes of practice, and of disappointment with them, point to some missing factors in the standard outlooks that explain business and prescribe for it.

These missing factors are identified here as including an imbalance between technical (efficiency) values and equity (ethical) values. Much emphasis, training, development of technique and advice are given to the former, while the latter are usually allowed to look after themselves, with codes and edicts appearing when problems arise. The second missing factor is the underdevelopment of an adequate language with which to describe and analyse business behaviour in terms of the values that drive it. In other words the systematic handling of values in business is hampered by inadequate means of expressing it in ways that business people find congenial. The third missing factor is the scarcity of detailed research evidence on the operation of values in business.

Taken together, these factors suggest that the drive to produce effective codes and legislation is likely to continue to be disappointing to the authors and subjects alike until the three missing factors are developed more and used more.

This book presents some forty-eight cases in business ethics, of varying length. Some methods of analysing the meaning of the cases in terms of the principles involved and the practical results are offered. As the book progresses, the emphasis shifts from illustrating arguments and issues, to providing evidence upon which readers can test their own explanations and analyses against those offered in the book. The kind of evidence gathered, and the quality of analysis used, are crucial to the continued acceptable improvement of business in a way that balances equity and efficiency.

Much evidence in support of prescriptions for business success in the popular management literature is of an anecdotal kind. While this can often provide easy-to-understand illustrations or insights, it has the disadvantage of being virtually uncheckable, since the evidence is not available to the reader except through the primary filter of what companies will allow to be said about them, and the secondary filter of the authors of the prescriptive (and usually inspirational) texts. It could be that many busy managers can only make time for taking in arguments about business in small, predigested pieces. This is unlikely to be true for all, however. This collection contains a mixture of short cases, of the anecdotal kind, and of sustained arguments and discussions about ethical matters from managers at various levels and from researchers with long experience of the practical application of values.

At the core of ethical issues in business is the fact that different 'players' often have different perspectives. They have some values in common, as well as some conflicting ones. From a methodological point of view, the ideal, or 'paradigm' for case material requires authentic statements from the various 'players'. This presents difficulties, in that much published material is supplied through the filters described above, or from 'negative' cases in which companies are accused in the press or in the courts of conduct that is thought to fall short of what are believed to be 'proper' values or obligations.

The bulk of the material in this collection is from published sources, and is thus limited by these factors. Despite this, most of the cases represent defensible and responsible efforts to improve business standards and behaviour. Several firms and institutions have generously agreed to publication of longer documents that express well thought-out approaches by different people to issues involving important values. Some, as is the case with the European Community, give general permission for their value-setting and value-related publications to be reproduced.

The development of more prescriptive and lasting 'how to do it' work on achieving aspirations in business seems to me to be dependent upon the willingness of companies and institutions on the one hand, and of researchers on the other, to undertake detailed studies of the operation of the values and codes. These could usefully include their approaches to dilemmas and to the issues surrounding the balance (and possible mutual support) between efficiency and equity. Work is in progress at the Centre for Service Management Studies on these lines. As it happens, companies do seem to need much time and discussion and reassurance, as the notion of 'ethics' in the business context even now seems to raise the incompatible expectations of either being hopelessly idealistic, a cynical whitewashing operation, or as somehow striking at the legitimacy of business by parading (real or alleged) misdemeanours.

Business ethics is capable of providing methods of improving equity and efficiency together, and of facing up to real, as opposed to imaginary trade-offs and dilemmas. In collecting the material I have tried to provide authentic illustrations in which this has been so, as well as illustrations in which it has not.

Much, though by no means all of the material is of European origin or from European-based multinationals. Where this is so, it is more specifically related to the countries of the European Community, with British cases occupying rather more space than the relative size of the population (or of the economy) would perhaps warrant. There are several reasons for this. Firstly, there has hitherto been a relative shortage of European case material in business ethics, as opposed to American material. There is a longer tradition in America than elsewhere of tackling ethical issues in business, and a much more developed teaching effort.

The philosophical elements of the book are in the Anglo-American tradition. The American literature and example were drawn upon in my earlier book, *Key Issues in Business Ethics* (1989). The material and perspectives and issues in the book owe a great deal to discussion with American colleagues, some of whom have contributed to the collection (and especially to the dialogue in Chapter 14). The role of the law has been much greater in America than in Europe. The development of a more unified Europe is likely to raise some similar issues of regulation to those already faced across the Atlantic.

The relative shortage hitherto of published European material in a self-consciously 'business ethics' format is part of the explanation for the choices eventually made: there is no shortage of ethically-related European material on the operation of business. The influence on the rest of the world of the European

Community is likely to rise. The exclusion from the text of the newly opened-up countries of Eastern Europe is explained by the shortage of material from those sources so soon after the opening up.

There are major ethical issues facing trade and economic relations with the Third World and with countries whose regimes are out of favour with governments or with sections of the population. These have not been covered in much detail in this volume. This is not because I do not think they matter: they obviously do matter. Their detailed inclusion has its own problems of data-gathering, and would be a different project from the current one. Similarly, the detailed discussion of multinational corporations is a separate project. Distinguished work has been done in the area, for example by Tom Donaldson (1989). This has been drawn upon.

If, as I maintain, the key issues of business ethics are more to do with *how* rules are made, than with *what* rules are made, the cases in the collections should be representative enough. This is not to imply that means are more important than ends, but that, at least in terms of the moral claims that people make, there is a good deal more consensus than is usually supposed on the ends, and the means provide the keys to their acceptable achievement.

JOHN DONALDSON
Centre for Service Management Studies
Twyford, UK

Acknowledgements

Many people have discussed with me the ideas that led to the preparation of this casebook. Their contributions are acknowledged and appreciated as much for the matters on which they have been sceptical as for those where we have agreed. It is impossible to identify the sources of all the ideas and evidence. The most frequent discussions have been with Pauline Donaldson, Peter Davis, Mike Waller, John Sheldrake, Derek Burton, Frank Edwards, Hyder Al-Hassan and Basil Garoufalidis, sometimes over long distances.

A number of companies and industrialists have been willing to provide or discuss information on their own attitudes and work in a subject area which is still generally regarded as taboo, or impossible to treat rationally. Without their contributions the casebook would have been impossible: Errel Holding of Groningen, British Rail Engineering Limited, Commercial Science Ltd, The Sedgwick Group plc and especially David Patterson.

The two companies with which I am connected, the Centre for Service Management Studies and TCAS Limited agreed to my part-time commitment. Nigel O'Neill of Moores Rowland, Chartered Accountants provided encouragement and some well-focused questions.

Leo Ryan of De Paul University, Chicago, Laura Nash, of the Boston University Graduate School of Management, David Mathison of Loyola Marymount University, Los Angeles, and Diana King, a freelance editor, have made helpful comments, not all of which could be fully incorporated.

Jennifer Pegg, senior editor at Academic Press, encouraged the project from the start, and I am grateful for her support.

The guest contributors, Peter Davis, Diana C. Robertson, David Huddy, Dirk Lindenbergh and Rob van Es, provided essential correctives to the inevitable biases of time, place and limited experience that beset any author's attempts to provide objective work in business ethics.

The purpose of the work has been constructive, to show that business ethics can be and often is discussed rationally, and its conclusions acted upon to the mutual benefit of those affected by what is done by, within and for business. I take responsibility for remaining errors, omissions, or biases, of which some are inevitable. It is my hope that the book will encourage more open discussion and greater willingness to try out new ideas, and recognition and removal of obstacles in the way of continued, ethically-based business growth and development.

Contributors

John Donaldson, is chairman of the British-based Centre for Service Management Studies, an independent, not-for-profit business research company. He graduated in philosophy, politics and economics at Oxford. He is a director of the robotics company TCAS Limited, and has taught business ethics and economics at several universities and business schools. He is a member of the Institute of Training and Development, and the author of *Key Issues in Business Ethics* (1989, Academic Press).

Guest contributors

Peter Davis joined the International Management Centre at Leicester University in 1991. His specialist interests cover all aspects of employment law, human resource management and business ethics. He has published widely and undertaken many consultancy and training assignments in these fields. He made a special study of the cooperative movement for his PhD.

David Huddy, graduated as a mathematician at Cambridge University, and has since been employed in industrial accounting and bank lending in the City of London. He is presently active in technology transfer as managing director of his own company, Commercial Science Ltd.

Dirk Lindenbergh, is managing director of Errel, a Dutch holding of companies in the gaming machine business, and is treasurer of Euromat, the European Association of slot machine companies and has an MBA.

Diana C. Robertson is Assistant Professor of Legal Studies at The Wharton School, University of Pennsylvania, where she teaches courses on social responsibility and business ethics. She has also been a visiting assistant professor at the London Business School.

Rob van Es, is a scientific researcher in ethics at Nijenrode University of Management, in the Netherlands. He is working on a doctoral thesis on negotiation ethics and is a part-time adviser in business ethics.

List of cases

Chapter 13

Glossary

The expressions listed below summarize the concepts and ideas which I consider to be basic to constructive debate on business ethics. Most of the words have several levels of meaning, and many uses – descriptive, emotional, prescriptive, persuasive (for example) – and many overtones. They are thus theory-loaded, and can give rise to much argument at cross purposes, and to much wandering from the points at issue. This is in the nature of the subject. The uses in the text are, unless otherwise stated, those of the Concise Oxford Dictionary (*COD*), and non-technical uses are preferred to technical ones. Where the words have many meanings, such as the word 'key' or the word 'issue', it should be clear from the context which one is intended. In some cases the expressions are used in a way that is inclusive of several shades of meaning. The definitional precision often sought in arguments on moral issues is not always appropriate. It is not easy to achieve consistently, and in my experience least often achieved by those who tend to be most insistent upon it. Using words carefully is always a better alternative than spurious precision or fake hard-headedness.

Further details of usage can be found in any general dictionary or dictionary of philosophy, for example Flew (1984).

agapism An influential notion often neglected in theoretical work, agapism is the idea that there is only one truly general ethical imperative: to love (God, one's fellows, or the whole of nature, etc.).

analysis/analytical Generally taken to mean breaking down complex ideas into simple ones. Can be used more generally to refer to drawing out the implications of ideas, doctrines or situations.

analytic A technical term used in logical theory to refer to the idea that some truths are independent of the state of the universe. An example is $2 + 2 = 4$. Often means 'true (or false) by definition'. An essential element in the doctrine of logical positivism, which is discussed in the text. The whole of mathematics would usually be taken to be analytic. The notion usually forms one part of a dichotomy. Its partner is 'synthetic', which means that a proposition is true (or false) if it is supported (or not supported) by the evidence. Analysis is usually opposed to description and sometimes to prescription. Though attempts to make hard-and-fast distinctions between these concepts are fraught with difficulties, the concepts remain useful.

autonomy   The right of self-government, extended to mean that people are, or ought to be placed in, a position to be able to make up their own minds about moral issues. It implies an appropriate level of knowledge, and a supportive institutional framework.

business ethics   Explained in detail in the text. In short it can be described as the systematic study of moral (ethical) matters pertaining to business, industry or related activities, institutions, or practices and beliefs. Can also refer to the actual standards, values or practices – or beliefs. An example of the latter use is seen in the title of Max Weber's book, *The Protestant Ethic and the Spirit of Capitalism.*

casuistry   Sometimes used in a derogatory sense to refer to an alleged quibbler or sophist, with the implication that the casuistry is insincere, or ignores major matters in favour of trivial ones. In the text the expression is used to refer to the systematic discussion of the application of general moral laws to particular courses of conduct, or to accommodation of new ideas that enter and challenge the social order (Flew, 1984).

collective bargaining   The practice in industrial relations of negotiating pay and conditions by representatives on behalf of an indefinite number of employers and employees, usually members of the organizations to which the bargainers belong.

collective rights   A term used in industrial relations, implying the belief that some rights are attributable to groups as opposed to individuals. The concept is not recognized in law.

definition   A process or expression that provides the precise meaning of a word or phrase (Flew, 1984). Much has been written on the nature and value of definitions, occupying much time in formal and informal logic. In moral matters, the precision of definitions can be preserved at the cost of rendering them worthless in practice, or of making them so broad that they are hopelessly ambiguous. Three kinds of definitions are worth noting:

lexical   reporting on how expressions are in fact used.

prescriptive   recommending a use for an expression (a procedure that is often difficult to maintain consistently).

persuasive   a definition in which emotive overtones dominate the logical or factual content.

Much moral reasoning is at cross purposes as a result of confusion between those forms of definition, and as a result of popular misconceptions such as that the moral argument must begin with definitions.

deontology The doctrine that ethics is grounded in notions of duty; that some acts are morally obligatory, regardless of consequences in terms of practice. One of the major doctrines in ethics.

democracy A notoriously ambiguous expression. Broadly refers to the idea that people affected by a decision, government, practice or institution should have an equitable say in the processes leading to the decisions, etc. Various theorists of democracy use different principles on which to ground their conclusions. In general it should be recognized that people can appeal to different principles and to different institutional arrangements in referring to democracy. Its emotive appeal often obscures the fact that, democratic states, businesses and processes can be very different, with very little in common. The principles and the arrangements both need to be specified in constructive discussion on the topic.

descriptivism The notion that moral judgments are derivable from facts. Sometimes referred to as naturalism.

determinism The doctrine that human action is not free, but determined by motives regarded as external forces acting on the will (*COD*).

Deus ex machina Power or event that comes in the nick of time to solve a difficulty. More loosely can refer to an unexplained method of solving a perplexing problem.

egoism The belief that self interest is the foundation of morality.

empirical Another word for evidence.

ethics Moral philosophy (q.v.) can also refer to the customs or standards which a particular group or community acts upon (or is supposed to act upon). Thus it refers to the codes and practices and to the principles to which they can be analysed or criticized, positively or negatively. Derived from the classical Greek, meaning the characteristic beliefs of a people. It is useful to distinguish between 'ethics 1', referring to the actions that are considered 'good' or 'bad', 'right' or 'wrong', etc., and 'ethics 2', referring to the reasons why ethical statements are accepted or rejected. Much argument at cross purposes occurs as a result of confusing the two. Both are amenable to reasoned argument, but the (real or alleged) 'subjectivity' of ethics and values is more relevant to ethics 1 than to ethics 2.

essentialism A variety of doctrines. In ethics, generally taken to mean the idea that concepts have an indispensable or fundamental element, which is necessary to establish the presence of a concept or its use. For instance, in economics, inflation is sometimes thought (mistakenly) to be 'essentially a monetary phenomenon'.

first order (and higher order)   A logical distinction. A first order proposition would be: 'management has a right to manage'. For the second order we might say: 'The idea that management has the right to manage is ambiguous'. At the third order we might say: 'The ambiguity of it is not in question'. At the fourth order we could say: 'Your statement that the ambiguity is not in question is misleading'. There is no limit to the number of orders of analysis. In practice the distinction between first order and second order is sufficient.

freedom   An ambiguous concept. It broadly means the same as liberty. It is usual to follow Sir Isaiah Berlin and distinguish between positive freedom, e.g. to do things, and negative freedom, to be free not to do them.

free will   Sometimes called libertarianism. It broadly means that people are able to decide for themselves what they believe and what they do. The doctrine can be modified to hold that the freedom operates within the laws of nature.

golden rule   Do as you would be done by. Various expressions for this fundamental rule are to be found in most religions and creeds through the ages, testifying to its universal applicability (Flew, 1984).

groupthink   The idea originated in George Orwell's novel *Nineteen Eighty-Four*. In general it refers to what are called group norms, which do not admit challenge or amendment. Individuals are required to believe what the group thinks, suppressing or exchanging their own views in favour of the official view of the group. Very widespread.

ideology   Manner of thinking of a class or individual. Set of ideas as a basis for a political or economic system (*COD*). Sometimes, apparently, believed to be (i) essential to any system (ii) beyond rational debate between systems or (iii) rendering ethics impossible.

improvement   Making something better or adding something to it. Views differ as to whether a change is an improvement or not, hence the need for agreed criteria for judging.

inflation   Any tendency for prices on the average to rise. Its ethical, political and economic significance, causes and possible acceptable cures are subject to much opinion and much measurement. Discussions of inflation provide ample evidence of the influences of emotion, preference and prejudice on attempts at detached analysis and measurement.

intuitionism   Doctrine that the perception of truth is by intuition;

doctrine that in perception external objects are known immediately by intuition (*COD*). A major doctrine in meta-mathematics. Many philosophers, mathematicians and logicians have been intuitionists, including Lewis Carroll. G. E. Moore (1903) and Sir David Ross (1939) wrote influential works from an intuitionist viewpoint.

issue Any affair in question, or any topic for discussion.

jargon Mode of speech familiar only to a group or profession. Often used derogatorily to indicate that expressions are meaningless, worthless or unnecessarily obscure.

kangaroo court Improperly constituted illegal court, held by strikers, etc. Increasingly found in industry and in other institutions.

labelling Literally, attaching labels. Figuratively, it refers to the use of classifying phrases with intent to persuade self or others to accept a description that may not be accurate. For example 'freedom fighter' or 'terrorist' are labels that purport to describe the same activist. Labelling is a subtle process with many moral overtones and implications.

meta-ethics Any higher-order statement concerning ethics, e.g. 'all ethical theories are incomplete' is a meta-ethical statement.

metaphysics Branch of learning, currently unfashionable, that is taken to refer to attempts to identify the fundamental realities, or 'God', 'freedom' and 'immortality' (Kant); or the absolute presuppositions of our (or any other) age.

methodology Refers to (i) the list of methods used in an enquiry and/or (ii) the analysis or critique of the methods that are, or can be, used in an enquiry.

moral Synonymous with 'ethical'. Refers to the customs, values, standards, practices of a group, age, or of a theory intended to be timeless. Refers also to the way in which they are, or can be criticized constructively or destructively. From the Latin *mores*, meaning customs. (See also *ethics*.)

moral concepts Key concepts include (for example) 'good', 'bad', 'right', 'wrong', 'just', 'unjust', 'improper'. Their meaning and importance are viewed differently by the different theories of ethics, such as those discussed in the text. As concepts they are interrelated and in part, often take their meaning from each other.

normative Intended, inadvertent, or *de facto* laying down or prescribing of rules.

normal values The values that hold a practice in place. They include the ethical, prudential and technical values that justify an event, practice, state or process. Deviation from them may be either deliberate, offering a different set of values, inadvertent, or denied.

objectivism The belief that there are at least some moral truths that would remain true whatever anyone or everyone thought. A version is the idea that at least some moral arguments are capable of proof or refutation in the same way as mathematical or scientific arguments are. Objectivists do not necessarily claim certainty or infallibility, only that some ethical issues are decidable. Objectivists differ in their use of the term and in the extent to which they are willing to qualify the doctrine.

ombudsman Official appointed to investigate complaints, usually against public authorities.

pathology Adapted from the medical use. In the context of business, often used to refer to systems or practices that deteriorate or cause deterioration in performance.

pluralism The view that the world contains many kinds of existent, which in their uniqueness cannot be reduced to just one (Flew, 1984). In moral and political theory it is the view that there can be more than one focus of loyalty for an individual, and that different institutions with opposing views and different opposing theories or beliefs are permissible or desirable.

positivism The philosophical system of Auguste Comte, recognizing only positive facts and observable phenomena, and rejecting metaphysics and theism (*COD*). The doctrine predates Comte. Despite its rejection of metaphysics, positivism is a metaphysical doctrine.

prescriptivism The view that the primary function of moral judgment is to prescribe courses of action (Flew, 1984). The term was coined by the contemporary British philosopher, R.M. Hare.

profit A key concept in business literature and practice. Surrounded by much myth and emotion, attitudes to it are often taken as being indicative of a person's general economic and political outlook. Definitive statements of its role and ethical status have proved to be elusive through the ages.

progress Move forward or onward, advance to a better state (*COD*).

relativism See *subjectivism*.

rights A person's entitlements as a member of society (or the 'body politic') and including liberties such as the right to use a public highway, and 'claim rights', such as the right to a defence counsel (Flew, 1984). Few people would deny that rights exist; but the sources are in dispute. Views range from rights as grants from the sovereign or from the law, to natural rights upon which the law is thought to be based.

science A general term whose use has varied in different historical periods. In contemporary thought, generally taken to refer to organized studies or research in physics, chemistry and other disciplines where principles and evidence are thought to be capable of rigorous proof and testing. There is no single theory of science. The expression is sometimes used to mean organized knowledge of any kind. The social sciences are often referred to as though they are not really sciences at all. On the whole it is probably more defensible to distinguish between high-grade rational enquiry, some of which is scientific, and other forms of activity. On this view, not all science is high-grade or rationally defensible.

scientism Method or doctrine deemed to be characteristic of scientists. Often used pejoratively to indicate a belief that scientific modes of thought in a particular case are being applied, though inappropriate to the question in hand.

sciolism Superficial pretence at knowledge.

social/society The words are notoriously ambiguous. 'Society' can mean the rich at play, or be taken to refer to the people within a national boundary. Following Russell, we can refer to a society as a logical construction out of individuals. This implies that society is an abstraction with no claims over individuals. At a more neutral level it is perhaps best to treat 'society' in the same way as 'democracy' or 'freedom', and regard it as a weasel word (q.v.) until a defensible use is offered.

stakeholder Any person who can be identified as having a legitimate interest in the processes or outcomes of business activity, or as having a right (formal or informal) to a say in it.

subjectivism In its simplest form, the position held by someone who believes that all moral attitudes are merely a matter of personal taste (Flew, 1984). Generally held to be the antithesis of objectivism. Cognate forms include relativism, the idea that moral values are valid, if at all, only for the groups who hold them or for a particular epoch.

truth There are many theories of truth, none of which is satisfactory. Theories include the correspondence theory, the pragmatic theory and the coherence theory. Particular truths are less problematic than truth in general. It is probably advisable to discover the particular requirements that people have for the concept in a particular context. Some require truth to be certain and infallible; others are prepared to settle for probability. It is usually possible to tell whether people are lying or reporting accurately. The problem is not, in my view, that of discovering what truth is, but of why we should feel the need for a single word to cover such a wide variety of matters.

utilitarianism In general the notion that an action, state, process, etc. is good or right insofar as it causes more good than ill to be produced. Some see the end as pleasure; Bentham saw it as utility. This last has a profound effect on economic theory, with frequent changes of alias. One of the major doctrines in ethics.

values A general term referring to those things which people regard as good, bad, right, wrong, desirable, justifiable, etc. We can speak of 'truth values' ('true' or 'false'), and of value judgments which are statements about what is valued, sound, deplorable, skilled, etc. It is useful to distinguish between technical, prudential and moral values. It is often (wrongly) assumed or asserted that value judgments ought not to be made in serious discussion, scientific discourse, etc.

weasel word A word used for the purpose of removing any real force from the expression containing it (*COD*). Many of the key expressions in ethical discourse can be, and often are, used as weasel words. The process is creative and sometimes difficult to pin down.

1 | ETHICS AND BUSINESS

International Perspectives

What business ethics is doing for business – and what it could do

Business is driven by values. In all cases, values determine what business people do and how others react. Values themselves can be chosen so that the driving force is harnessed to rational and agreed purposes, making the resulting business practices defensible and consistent. Often, however, they are not so connected and rational. In such cases, what happens in business can become irrational and inconsistent in every proper sense of the terms, wasting valuable resources as well as breaking moral and legal rules. What these rules are and how they are properly established and enforced, and by whom, are important ethical issues. Values and the rules for evaluating their application are issues that will recur throughout this collection of cases and materials, which is offered as a contribution towards their solution.

Values are potent sources of conflict as well as of cooperation, control and self-control. Through values, business can and does create value in the form of goods, services, employment and much else. Some values prevent this process from working properly, or at all.

In extreme cases, businesses and whole industries can cease to function because their continued existence is inconsistent with certain powerful values. These values may or may not be those of the competitive market-place. Some values are more defensible and constructive than others. There has been little systematic analysis of values in business. Such treatment has tended to be from the perspective of how they function in helping to generate business success, or, as Deal and Kennedy put it in *Corporate Cultures*:

Our goal in this book is to provide business leaders with a primer on cultural management. In showing how several excellent companies manage their cultures this book is meant to be suggestive only, not hard and fast, or prescriptive . . . . Along the way, we hope to instill in our readers a new law of business life: In culture there is strength. (Deal and Kennedy, 1988, p. 19)

1

This present collection of cases and materials represents attempts both to identify the values in European contexts that lead to the results indicated above, and to illustrate them with cases and other practical materials. It has a number of other practical and theoretical purposes. They are explained below, but first it will be useful to explain what values are, and what connection they have with 'business ethics'.

The account, or definition, of business ethics adopted here is *the systematic handling of values in business and industry.* Business and industry are themselves taken to include all the supporting institutions, voluntary and statutory, professional and trade bodies, trade unions and government departments, legislative and regulatory agencies and institutions. The institutions themselves include institutionalized concepts, such as 'the market' or 'market-place', bureaucracy, the Treaty of Rome, the closed shop and the European Social Charter. There are many other institutions, which appear both in the studies and in the discussions of them.

Values are of many kinds. They include the cultural norms that represent the expectations of business clients and customers, legislators, employees, suppliers and public. They also include those that set the standards of technical skills in business (how to run the processes competently) and those that establish how company managers should manage the resources entrusted to them. Values include, most importantly, the moral (i.e. ethical) imperatives that override all others. For example, the technical processes may be the most efficient in the world, the profit levels more than satisfactory, the danger of legal action against the company negligible, but if the production processes have harmful effects on the operators or users, and these are suppressed or lied about, or if the production processes are in breach of patent, or labour practices are in breach of human rights, the ethical standing of the company can be rated as low or zero. Frequently, this is sustainable, either when there are no consumer movements or when employee organizations or law enforcement are weak. There are many other circumstances (as will be seen from the cases) where such a state of affairs is sustainable.

Business ethics is mainly concerned with the more general and controlling values that are capable of judging the acceptability of the prudential and technical values. For instance, it can be ethically defensible to say that a business process is technically inefficient or even dangerous, and yet worth doing, or that it is efficient and safe but worthless. It can never follow from the fact that a process is efficient and safe that it is necessarily worth doing. Efficiency values, prudential values and ethical values do not imply and are not implied by each other. Ethical values can overrule the technical and prudential values, but the logic does not work the other way: a process can be efficient, prudent, illegal and immoral. Business ethics, as it has developed, deals with a wide range of practical matters. These include the principles according to which practices should be lawful or otherwise, the practical and acceptable mix between enforcement, persuasion and education, and the building of new structures and procedures for identifying and reconciling conflicting values. It cannot be taken for granted that those values that profitably unite the corporation and its employees in common purpose are therefore ethically sound. Equally, it cannot be taken for granted that because a corporation has been criticized, or has acted in its own interests, it is therefore 'unethical'. Nor can it be taken for granted that because a practice is declared desirable and lawful it will be observed in spirit or letter – or that if it is undesirable or unlawful that it will not happen, or that it will happen only rarely. In this area, almost anything can happen, but it often happens in the dark, and cannot be brought into the open because of the general embarrassment that is caused when discussing values, or when constructing effective frameworks in which they can be discussed.

Although not all values are moral (i.e. ethical) values, they almost always have ethical implications. For example, it is often held – and rightly so – to be a moral and legal duty to exercise due care and skill, i.e. prudential and technical values.

The European context has been chosen because much is happening, especially through the development of the European Community, that has a strong bearing on business ethics. A second reason is that few published case studies from a business ethics perspective and with European themes exist. Several excellent American collections have been published in recent years, and these will be drawn upon in the text. Ethics itself is one of the oldest disciplines or frameworks for thought and action, to which values and their analysis are central. Some philosophers even restrict ethics to the study of only a small number of values, namely those that deal with what is, or is thought to be, 'good', 'right' or obligatory. Such a restriction provides too narrow a perspective, which historically has led to esoteric and technical discussions which have provided little practical guidance.

Ethical issues in business have existed as long as business itself. There has been an encouraging growth of interest in business ethics in recent years, but it has not yet 'come of age' as a discipline. As will be seen, this may not in itself be a bad thing: institutionalized intellectual effort is not particularly innovative, and is not always a generator of constructive and rational values. Despite the considerable technical achievements, there is little cause for complacency about the operation of business, or about the contributions of the academic disciplines that support it or prepare students for it.

The aims in producing the collection are constructive. Although there is little room for complacency, it is a mistake to believe that business is either incapable of behaving ethically or that ethics is irrelevant to business. The cases predominantly describe and analyse constructive and defensible business practice and ideas. These are rarely found in a pure form. The best practices can and ought to be criticized continually, in the search for improvement. What 'improvement' means is capable of rational discussion. Even those practices which are the most often criticized can have justifying arguments, if only they can be put. That a business practice is unpopular or illegal does not make it unethical. That a practice is standard or universal does not make it defensible or right. Matters ranging from monopoly in the product market to compulsory union membership in the labour market, and even 'insider trading', have at one time or another been in more than one of these categories, according to some informed observers and participants.

Thus the business scandals (or to use a more polite expression, the *causes célèbres*) in this casebook do not predominate. They are outnumbered by two other kinds of material and case: those that represent *dilemmas*, in which one important moral imperative can only be acted upon at the cost of contravening another, and *constructive cases*, in which at least someone has identified an ethical issue, and has made serious attempts to resolve it on ethically defensible principles. No attempt is made to say which cases fall into which categories. The reader will no doubt decide that for themselves.

The cases are introduced first as illustrations of general points, then later as examples of the hugely varied forms in which ethical issues arise in business and are dealt with or ignored there, for better or for worse.

Before the cases are introduced, it will be useful to summarize the intentions and arguments of the book. It should be clear from this process what my own values are. All writing on business, as is the case with business itself, is driven by values. People can and do differ as to which values they prefer to have realized. What is a valued state or practice for one person can easily be detested by others. This does not mean that reconciliation is impossible, or that there can never be justification for enforcing compliance with a particular set of values. The point is that particular sets of values are continually being enforced in, by and upon business, and that only some of them are justifiable in terms of ethical principles and the evidence bearing on them. The (real or alleged) 'subjectivity' of values is an important topic in business ethics, and can never provide a rational ground for not discussing the issues at all. People must judge values and practices from where they stand, but it is possible to develop defensible ways of deciding what is or is not 'good practice'.

Because people do differ in their choice of values, the enforcement of one person's or one group's values on an individual is an ethical issue in its own right. It is possible, and even likely, that there is a good deal more commonality in the values that people hold in relation to business than is usually believed to be the case. Whether this is indeed so will only be discovered by applying a sound method for finding out. Without that, the propagation and enforcement of values can be no more than propaganda and manipulation.

I hope that it will become clear that there is much to gain from handling values systematically, rather than ignoring them but continuing to allow them to dominate. The latter appears to have been generally the case throughout the history of business and of business writing.

The contents and purposes of the book may be summarized as follows:

1 To help to meet the shortage of European case studies in business ethics. They are needed because modern developments are bringing together widely differing codes and practices. The proper analysis of these is within the province of business ethics.

2 To demonstrate that business ethics thinking can be constructive and supportive to business, providing positive examples, rather than catalogues of complaints. What have become traditional practices and standards are increasingly being challenged. Well-analysed cases can identify the strengths as well as the weaknesses of these practices and standards.

3 To provide material for the identification and continuing development of high ethical standards in industry, and to show that they are neither impractical nor rare, and have much to offer. This includes developing sound procedures for identifying what 'high standards' are, and what makes them so. This claim in turn should be viewed in the light of the further claim that 'short-term, hard-nosed, bottom-line' approaches to business have at best a patchy performance record in many key areas, such as economic growth, innovation, labour relations and inflation (NEDO, 1990).

4 To provide tools of analysis and materials on which to practise them. These will show that it is usually possible to be both profitable and ethical. Many businesses manage it. Where it is truly not possible, the tools of analysis will help to prove it, rather than using unanalysed difficulties as excuses for not really trying.

5 To contribute practical guidelines, based on experience, for forward-looking firms to try out.

6 To identify and help to overcome the genuine obstacles to the high-grade conduct of business and industry.

In analysing the cases it will become apparent that in many public discussions of business matters, values tend to become treated as 'facts', and vice versa. It should also become clear that what are usually taken to be the major obstacles to improved ethical standards in business, such as 'human greed', the 'hard realities of the market-place' and the 'corrupt nature of man', are easier to postulate and to use as explanations after the event than they are to prove. It is as likely that the major obstacles are easier to prove and move. They include pessimism and fatalism, naive scepticism (often disguised as hard-boiled cynicism), overconfidence in technique, and the use of what have been called 'factoids' and 'theoroids', without concepts. These can, and sometimes do, lead to ill thought-out general economic policies and company structures.

These obstacles are more serious because they are more widespread and influential. In short, when greedy and corrupt people (if that is what most people are), are up against market difficulties, they are often able to do better by facing up to what is really going on and devising means of dealing with it, than when they are being fatalistic or ensuring that prophecies of malpractice are fulfilled by assuming that they will be. Although ethics drives business, this driving force has rarely been systematically analysed or supported in its applications by much evidence.

The cases will help to show how and why the generally sound and defensible values that drive business sometimes become translated into the questionable practices and *causes célèbres* that can be seen described or criticized almost every day in the media, or become translated into occasional disasters, e.g. those at Seveso in Italy in 1976, at Chernobyl in 1986, at Zeebrugge in 1987 and at King's Cross in London in 1989.

The cases will help to show how, given the will, the gap between the impeccable aspirations and reality noted at the beginning of this chapter can be met effectively by using the concepts and frameworks provided by the various contributors to modern business ethics.

Driving forces in business: official and unofficial values – some cases

The values that drive business are of many kinds. Not all are moral (ethical) values in their own right, but all are ethically relevant. One important distinction is between the 'official' values of individual companies, and those which operate on them to produce the results in terms of actual standards and events. They provide the first cases in this study. One source of expression of them is easily found in the annual reports of companies, in the introductory remarks by their chairmen. The following extracts were chosen at random.

CASE 1 | A large European pharmaceuticals company

I am proud to be part of a company with such a fine reputation . . . . We developed a stronger management team . . . . We are eagerly and confidently pursuing these objectives . . . . I am impressed by the quality of [our] workforce, and its management includes many able and dedicated executives. [The company's objectives include using a superior competitive position in attractive markets, and developing a] . . . superior organisation committed to success by having the best people, training them, motivating them; establishing high standards and values as a company and as individuals. (Beecham plc, 1987)

CASE 2 | A communications company

Providing the quality of service expected of us is as important to shareholders as it is to customers. It is only by meeting our customers' individual requirements, and by offering good value for money that we will ensure continued growth and prosperity . . . . We will compensate customers should we fail to make repairs against published standards . . . . The board has decided to operate the employee profit-sharing scheme . . . . We value our close links with the many local communities we serve. We are proud to have contributed some £11 million on a wide range of activities in support of the community last year. (British Telecom plc, 1988)

CASE 3 | A broadcasting regulatory authority

The members of the [network] are public trustees for the standards of creative quality and of fairness and decency in the contents of broadcast programmes. It is their most important responsibility. It is a difficult and demanding task, since the standards of taste are necessarily subjective. [The authority publishes] Television Programme Guidelines . . . [intended] . . . principally for programme directors to maintain good practice, not only between the Authority and Companies, but also between the Companies and outside bodies and individuals . . . . They have established themselves as a valuable framework. (IBA, 1983–84)

CASE 4

A major financial services company

We are giving strong emphasis throughout the group to the development of close business relationships with our customers and potential customers, whether personal, corporate or in the public sector. Success in this relies entirely on the quality of the service we give; and we are making considerable efforts to improve our standards in all our operations across the world. The customer service programme . . . continues to receive high priority . . . . I am confident that we will improve our competitive edge by developing a specialised, highly professional service . . . . (Barclays plc, 1987)

These examples are remarkable only in that the values that they aspire to are so commonplace. Few reasonable people would deny that companies should aspire to being efficient, excellent, responsive to clients, competitive, appreciative of the talents of the workforce, and determined to see the management as a team, whose *esprit de corps* is a prized asset.

I am far from suggesting that these 'chairmen's statements' are empty rhetoric. The depth of commitment is well described by Goldsmith and Clutterbuck in *The Winning Streak*:

One of the surprises in our interviews at chief executive level and below was the passion with which our successful companies embraced integrity as an essential part of their culture. This was clearly not window-dressing. Each company was convinced that without absolute integrity the business simply could not operate. The reaction of these companies to any aspersions on their integrity is swift and vehement. Normally staid and placid chairmen's blood will boil at the suggestion that their company has been dishonest, sharp-practicing or deliberately negligent. (Goldsmith and Clutterbuck, 1984, p. 123)

In their later work, *The Winning Streak Checkbook*, the same authors develop this point:

In *The Winning Streak* we referred to this phenomenon as integrity. You might prefer to call it trust, or fair dealing. Whatever word you use, the moral is the same: companies that are successful in the long run establish relationships with all the people they deal with – customers, suppliers, employees and the public at large – based on absolute honesty and mutual respect. (Goldsmith and Clutterbuck, 1986, p. 178)

This is, in my view, true in the long run and on the average, but some of the cases in this collection demonstrate that included among the most highly respected, high-reputation companies and institutions are some which have been capable of breaking systematically the most elementary moral rules on the way, without redress for their victims. Companies and organizations exhibit the whole range of behaviour from acts, decisions and practices that are fully defensible in ethical terms, to following convention without thought, through to what can be reasonably described as 'moral poverty'. The extracts above show that integrity is by no means the only moral value which companies claim in their official pronouncements.

Despite the *causes célèbres* reported in the mass media, the problem is not typically the degree of commitment by company chairmen to 'sound values', but the ability of the cultures, structures and informal values that drive business to deliver these espoused values effectively, efficiently and acceptably.

Values – including ethical ones – drive business, but are rarely analysed. One of the many reasons for this can be stated at this stage: the word 'ethics' is radically ambiguous. In one standard sense it means 'those moral values that are generally accepted in a group, profession or state'. In this sense, 'ethical' means 'approved of by powerful people'. In the second sense, used by ethical theorists, it means 'pertaining to ethical reasoning' or 'capable of analysis or appraisal in ethical terms'. Business actions are sometimes 'ethical' and sometimes 'unethical' in the first sense. They are almost always 'ethically relevant' in the second sense.

It is not only company chairmen who hold or express ethical values in business. The cases will show many institutions, organizations, individuals, business texts, professional bodies and others who express them. The current rise in interest in business ethics covers a huge variety of concerns. The cases have been chosen to reflect them. Examples of the cases and the issues and values they exemplify include:

CASE 5	**An engine manufacturer**

A large manufacturer of engines for the road transport market is described as striving to be a leader in the corporate social responsibility movement. It is described as resolutely applying its code, even if it means losing business. The code includes participation in relevant matters with employees and a refusal to operate according to standards in the industry which fall below the company's code. The company claims that it rarely loses business, and has a very good record for survival, growth and profitability (for a discussion of this US example, see Williams, 1987).

Conclusion: maintaining standards is not an unaffordable luxury.

CASE 6 ▌ A large retail company

A company had the seemingly impossible task of raising output through a warehouse, apparently already at maximum capacity. Conflict over pay and low morale resulted in high levels of absenteeism and low productivity. The conflicts were resolved by establishing clear, agreed principles on which effort and reward should be based. The management technique, ethical standards and beliefs about the nature of the operation and the people in it had become entangled (for a full discussion, see Donaldson and Philby, 1985).

Conclusion: explicit ethical standards led to trust and the solution of problems that had seemed impossible.

CASE 7 ▌ A large, diversified multinational manufacturer

The company takes the view that it, like others, has a responsibility to deal with its own pollution and conservation problems, and to cooperate with governmental attempts to improve the environment. The company holds that, in the long run, it pays to have a positive policy of this kind, and it explicitly continues to carry out programmes which do not have a short-run positive return on cost. The company claims that overall, its policy is profitable, and has received wide praise for its activities (Donaldson and Davis, 1990).

Conclusion: setting and maintaining high standards can be an important investment for the future. Policies do not have to be 'pure loss' to be ethically defensible.

CASE 8 ▌ An engineering company

Faced with a widely fluctuating, but generally declining market, this company chose to conduct in-depth interviews with those employees who were willing to participate. Some of the interviews were held by arrangement with union representatives. Those employees who did not wish to use this formal system were entitled to join as individuals. The purpose was to understand the visibly declining state of morale. As a result of the programme, a variety of profitable means for improving productivity were realized.

These different means were likely to improve the realization of some values, and to compromise the realization of others. The company made the final decision, sometimes by agreement with, and sometimes against the preferences of, employees. Both the employees and the managers accepted these decisions, not necessarily because everyone considered them to be the best, but because everyone respected the way in which they were made (Donaldson and Davis, 1990).

Conclusion: operating to high ethical standards does not necessarily mean that all actions are beyond criticism. However, *how* something is done can be as important as *what* is done.

'When things go wrong'

Cases 1–8 were chosen to indicate the range of ethical values that are applied in business and industry. They also indicate that a business need not be a company of well-informed angels to be able to recognize values. There is sometimes a choice between profit and technical efficiency on the one hand, and operating 'high-level' values on the other. This trade-off is neither inevitable nor immutable, as cases 5–8 show. Cases 9–12 underline a different aspect: the ethical criticisms of business practices arising from litigation and from real or alleged harms done to users of products or services, employees and the general public.

CASE
9

The Zeebrugge car ferry

The sinking of the British-registered vessel *Herald of Free Enterprise* in 1987 and the consequent loss of 188 lives off the Belgian port of Zeebrugge led to a Court of Investigation. Colin Boyd (1990, p. 140) summarizes as follows:

The Report of the Court of Investigation concluded by naming ... three shipboard employees as contributing to the disaster, and while it also blamed the company in general it did not single out any other individuals within the company as having contributed to the disaster.

According to Boyd (1990, p. 145):

The central ethical issue of the disaster is the degree to which managers and directors should be defined as being responsible for the disaster. The report of the Court of Investigation revealed that the board of directors had failed to identify safety as a policy issue and had consequently failed to assign responsibility for safety. This absence of planning resulted in an astonishing degree of apathy, antagonism almost, toward safety across all levels of shore management.

He adds, 'This raises the question of the degree to which the law should play a role in the definition of ethical corporate behaviour . . .' (loc. cit). In the event, the company and several officials were prosecuted and charged with corporate manslaughter.

CASE 10   Seveso

In 1976, in the Italian town of Seveso, a chemical plant exploded releasing dangerous dioxin fumes. Many people died. Five company officials were eventually sentenced to terms of imprisonment. The nature of the risks arising from the plant had not been revealed to the eventual risk-bearers, i.e. the public. The assessment of the medical consequences itself became a disputed issue with strong ethical overtones. Upon this assessment depended whether or not compensation was payable to those affected. The town was effectively evacuated for several years (Margerison *et al.*, 1978).

CASE 11   Environment-friendly consumer products

Many consumer products are labelled in such a way as to suggest that they do little or no damage to 'the environment'. Some press reports express scepticism with regard to the claims. For example:

Amigo del Ozono, Melieu Vriendelyk, Environment Friendly, Amici del Ambiente, or just plain boloney? In the last 18 months a vast array of products on European supermarket shelves have [sic] sprouted green credentials. But how credible are these eco-labels that depict stylised birds and protective hands shielding the earth? Few have been awarded by independent testing bodies. Most have spurious credentials based on pseudo-scientific claims: the latest creation of newly verdant marketing departments eager to ride the rising tide of green consumerism . . . . (Davies-Gliezes, 1990)

The article proceeds to discuss the difficulties in authenticating claims, and the difficulties in establishing a European system that could replace the individual national systems, such as France's *Protége la couche d'ozone*.

CASE 12   Asbestos

Since the late 1930s, some forms of asbestos have been recognized as having highly dangerous properties. Substitute materials are available, and many uses of asbestos are forbidden by law and codes exist for its safe disposal. Many asbestos contracts that were placed in the 1980s in the USA were reinsured on the Lloyds of London reinsurance market. Some of the contracts became subject to litigation in the USA. Allegations of non-disclosure of risks and of cover-ups were made in the spring of 1990:

> The governing authorities in the £11 billion Lloyd's of London insurance market were yesterday effectively accused of a cover-up over the way disastrous asbestos contracts were placed in the early 1980s. The damaging allegations followed a decision by the ruling council of Lloyd's not to hold an enquiry into circumstances surrounding some asbestos reinsurance contracts where there had been accusations of insider trading and conspiracy. (Buckingham, 1990)

Between them, cases 1–12 present a range of ethical matters in business raised in official company aspirations, in independent reports of ethically defensible and constructive activities by companies, and in criticisms of company practices or claims. The 'official' values expressed represent only a very small proportion of the total network of values. These control or generate much that happens in industry and business, and prevent much that in rational, ethical terms *ought* to be put into practice. Cases 13–20 widen the range of issues and indicate that ethical matters are present in or implied by virtually everything that is done in business, by business, on behalf of business or in criticism of it. Some of them recur in much more detail in later sections of the book under various headings. The following categories express concerns that are currently on the 'agenda':

Environmental concerns

CASE
13   **The car and the environment**

Government, vehicle manufacturers and drivers – all have a role to play in reducing the impact of the car on the environment. Director General Simon Dyer says the AA will act responsibly to help to protect the environment *and* to effectively counter the 'unrealistic No-roads, No-cars lobby' . . . . He adds: 'The shameful lack of investment over the years in roads and public transport is a major cause of the congestion, and the accompanying pollution that bedevils the 1990s . . . .' Drivers themselves, he says, must remember that high speed equals high pollution. (Automobile Association, 1990)

CASE

14 | Environmental pressure and business attitudes

Pressure from environmentalists is resulting in a significant change in attitude among companies in the chemical, farming and paper industries . . . but the cost of protecting the environment is likely to be passed on to the customer. (Pinchcombe, 1990, quoting a survey reported by Colin Sharman, head of KPMG Peat Marwick McLintock Management Consultants)

CASE

15 | Toxic waste control

Another reason for slow progress is that national attitudes often reflect those of industry, so that legislation is based on beggar-my-neighbour principles or let's-keep-our-country-clean-and-never-mind-the-rest-of-the-world. We may go even further and observe that where environmental protection does exist, it exists mainly in the North – which has produced most of the present pollution – to the detriment of the South. (Wassermann, 1989)

The labour market

CASE

16 | International labour standards

The International Labour Organization, based in Geneva, consists of representatives from many governments, employers' organizations and trade unions. It has published business standards since 1919. The Unemployment Convention dates from 1919, and was reviewed in the 1960s, 1970s and 1980s. The values expressed in the various Conventions represent consensus, and owe much to the United Nations Declaration of Human Rights. This does not imply that there have been no debates, or that all statements are fully supported or are supported to the same degree by all participants. Still less does it imply that all members of participating organizations are in complete agreement. The conventions do demonstrate that a measure of agreement is possible between people with differing perceptions, backgrounds and interests, as well as political and religious affiliations.

The standards cover, for example, freedom of association and protection of the right to organize. This particular convention dates from 1948, and expressly aims at 'The right, freely exercised, of workers and employers, without distinction, to organize for furthering and defending their interests.' Other standards provide, for example, for collective bargaining (1949), prohibition of forced labour (1930), equality of opportunity and remuneration (e.g. 1951, 1958, 1981), 'full, productive and freely chosen employment' (1964) (International Labour Office, 1988).

Trading conditions

CASE
17

Government support for industry

The [British] Government has been given until August 17 to demand that British Aerospace return the £44.4 million illegal 'sweeteners' for the purchase of the Rover Group and explain whether the company has been given illegal tax concessions worth up to £411 million. (Hencke, 1990)

CASE
18

International telephone charges

The European Commission has launched a formal investigation into international telephone charges to determine whether they are set at artificially high levels by illegal cartels between companies. (Usborne, 1990)

CASE
19

The Guinness affair

In August 1990, a number of people in London were convicted on several charges arising from the takeover of Distillers by Guinness. On 16 August, the *Financial Times* commented:

After years of investigation, 107 days in court and many millions of pounds in costs, the question is whether the outcome of the Guinness trial is of anything more than historic interest. The answer is that the verdict is important, for a number of reasons. For one thing, any other outcome would have dealt a crippling blow to the Serious Fraud Office, which combines investigation and prosecution procedures under the same roof, and until yesterday had failed to win a big case . . . . A more difficult question is what the Guinness affair tells us about relative standards of business behaviour. Business morality, like business itself, is cyclical in nature: during periods of financial euphoria and strongly rising share prices, people cut corners and bend the rules: during the austere times which follow, the rule books are rewritten and everyone agrees that things will be different next time.

CASE
20

New teeth for a French watchdog

Last year the French authorities – rocked by a series of financial scandals – re-equipped their stock market watchdog, the Commission des Opérations de Bourse with a new set of powers to seize documents, interrogate suspects, suspend firms from trading and impose its own fines. (Dan Atkinson, 1990)

The provisions became operational in May 1990, and financiers were charged in June with insider trading. The European Community had long faced criticism from business that its merger control rules were unworkable. The rules had effectively been under discussion for seventeen years.

These twenty short cases raise matters across a substantial part of the spectrum of ethical issues raised in and by business and its related institutions. Some will be discussed in more detail in later chapters.

What is a 'case'?

In plain language, 'cases' are instances of things occurring. The purpose – or better the defensible uses – of cases can vary. In law, cases provide precedents and exemplify principles. In business analysis and education, a mystique has grown up around them, to the effect that if management students study enough cases, they will become adept at management without making the expensive mistakes exemplified in the texts, or through copying and, perhaps, adapting successful insights exemplified by astute managers.

Industrialists tend to value cases for a variety of reasons: these include the 'demonstration effect' to counter such objections as, 'It is all very well in theory, but I am a busy, practical person, and I need to see examples where it has really worked, rather than to hear a set of abstractions and possibilities'. A case can be a statement of facts, on which decisions may be made by impartial outsiders.

Cases can vary in structure and content. They can include, at one extreme *myths*, *fables* and *hypothetical cases* constructed to encourage a choice between principles in a way that is free from the distractions of detail and circumstance that surround actual cases. At the other extreme, we can observe *causes célèbres*, such as those that capture the media headlines from time to time, and continuing sagas, such as the fight against inflation and attempts by various means to control pay and restrictive trade and labour practices. In between these extremes, there are many events, states, processes, practices, structures, decisions, rules, attitudes, codes, institutions, relationships, beliefs, dogmas, assumptions and presumptions which can and do form 'the proper subjects' for investigation or pronouncement by some discipline or other. They all have at least one thing in common: they are all capable of description, analysis, appraisal and even prescription in ethical terms. The practice of doing so in relation to business theories and practice is relatively new.

The cases in this book, on the broad interpretation indicated above, are intended to sample the whole range. It is important to remember the old saying, 'there is nothing so practical as a good theory'. This can help to avoid the kind of pragmatism that is based on well-protected, and therefore unexamined, dogma. Immanuel Kant's reminder is also worth bearing in mind, that concepts without application are empty. My own view is that a constant dialogue between down-to-earth practical examples and the guiding principles of business, whether economic or philosophical, is essential if people wish seriously to see improvement. I do not take it for granted that most people in business do wish to see improvement, or for that matter that they do not. I think it more likely that some people have thought about it and concluded that no improvement is possible, however desirable, and that others have come to different conclusions. These include the notion that industry and business are essentially about individual maximization of satisfactions, at other people's expense if need be. This reduces business to a kind of politics, often in practice as well as theory.

Cases can demonstrate that more – and more rational – choices than these are available, and indeed are also more defensible. The practical purposes and uses of cases can usefully be summarized as demonstrating that values drive business and that:

1 'Positive' examples of conduct, structures, decisions, rules, practices, etc., are far from rare. They are examples in the sense that they indicate the existence of the kinds of thing claimed, and in the sense that others may adopt them if they wish. In these examples, people's actions and behaviour may not always be beyond criticism, but they may be rationally defended. It is always possible to hypothesize hidden, selfish motives, but rarely possible to prove them.

2 There are better alternatives to short-term expediencies and gimmicks. Thus, the 'hard-nosed, bottom line, short-term' approach to running a business, when examined with a little care, can often be seen to be ineffective, and even counter-productive.

3 How a decision is reached is as important as what it is. In older language, the end does not justify the means.

4 Even bureaucratic institutions and companies can be weaned away from many of the practices for which they have been justly criticized over the years.

5 Reasonable people may disagree on matters of fact, value and

interpretation. It does not follow from this that there are no values that transcend individual preferences, business cultures and politico-economic systems. Some powerful, though often vague, values have commanded the support of rational people across political, religious and philosophical divides for millennia. They are as near to universal truths as we are likely to get. Practical expressions of them have, it is true, provided fertile ground for debate and conflict. Commitment to truth, honesty and justice are not always empty phrases. They are powerful enough for people to fight wars over and to claim exclusive ownership. In its small way, business ethics might help to make these values available to people at large once again, and not just the private property of gurus, ideologues and manipulators.

Business *is* thus driven by values which may be systematically appraised in ethical terms. The case material will show examples of rationally defensible business values in operation. They will also show deviations from them.

In general, a defensible business operation requires that different voices be heard, and that their public expressions are authentic. This is not always possible. The obstacles are not mainly to do with innate greed, selfishness or malevolence, even though these do occur. They are more to do with the underdevelopment of ethical language and of concepts in business. They are also to do with structures and cultures more attuned to control by hierarchical authority than by rational, ethical values. Where rationality is claimed for such a technique-centred hierarchy, it has been of an unduly restrictive kind.

What the cases show: preliminary conclusions

Cases 1–20 have illustrated the values expressed in proud statements on behalf of companies, in criticisms and in proposals for change. By themselves, cases cannot prove or disprove any general beliefs about business or ethics. However, they *can* support or weaken arguments or beliefs; they can cast serious doubt on arguments or beliefs; they can encourage or discourage or help to persuade. People's beliefs about business and ethics are derived from a mixture of general philosophical beliefs (however much they deny it), habits and attitudes formed consciously or subconsciously, and experience.

In general, people's beliefs are well-protected from the violent swings that would occur if every apparently powerful piece of evidence or general point were to be accepted and acted upon. People do not 'follow the argument wherever it leads', as Socrates and Plato recommended. But standards and values do change, as can be seen from the history of mature, capitalist economies since the beginning of the industrial revolution (J. Donaldson, 1989, ch. 1). Standards and values sometimes change dramatically, as can be seen from the sudden abandonment of the centralized economic order in Eastern Europe.

The crisis of values in business, so well charted in the mass media and in the growing literature of business ethics, indicates the need for a systematic reappraisal of practice. Business ethics can help to ensure that defensible standards are identified and operated consistently, responsibly and responsively. Chapter 2 examines some attitudinal obstacles to this necessary reappraisal process.

2 | MAKING SENSE

Some Standpoints in Business and in Ethics

Reconciling diversity of views

Chapter 1 showed that values drive business, and that there is a gap (variable, but reducible) between aspirations and reality.

Chapter 2 follows the argument that businesses *do* articulate values and aspirations that are themselves difficult to criticize. It attempts to identify the sources and nature of the aspired-to standards, as well as the reasons for the gaps between these aspirations and actual practice. It can perhaps be taken for granted that because business is a human institution, and because human institutions can never be perfect, at least *some* gap between the ideal and reality is inevitable. If so, what needs to be explained is the variability of the gap between different firms, institutions, industries and perhaps, nations. I know of no disapproving criticisms, in matters of principle, of honesty, truth, integrity, or care for customers, for example, but there is no fully common ground on whether these aspirations are at the same time genuine, operable, well-intentioned or even relevant. It is true that the 'common interest' assumptions and the 'team' image of firms often promoted by companies have been criticized as unrealistic (see Fox, 1974, for example), but this is not a rejection of the principles as such, only of the possibility of their being made operable without some undesirable consequences.

Attitudes towards business and ethics range from those which see it as obvious that business is an ethical matter, to those which express outright hostility to business ethics on grounds of moral scepticism, apparently pro-business ideologies or anti-business ideologies, or in practice. An example of the last of these can be seen in Drucker's proposal that business ethics is a means, a Trojan Horse, for attacking business (Drucker, 1981). Authentic statements of ethical stances from the standpoints of the traditional business disciplines which present business and industrial management as discrete sets of techniques grouped around the functional disciplines of production, personnel, finance, and marketing are very rare. By implication, ethics, or the

20

systematic handling of values, is simply not seen as relevant. Although no serious dialogue is yet discernible, there are examples of attempts to integrate business ethics into these subject disciplines, at least in some of the business and management courses in America and Europe (Dunfee and Robertson, 1988; Mahoney, 1989).

Within the 'business ethics community' there is as yet little common ground in theoretical terms. What does appear to be shared is the belief that business ethics is possible, relevant and potentially useful to a wide variety of participants in business and industry.

European countries have differing and strong philosophical traditions. For example, the Anglo-Saxon tradition of 'analytical philosophy' is not widely accepted in parts of Europe, especially Southern Europe, where there is a strong Aristotelian tradition, arising in part from differing religious histories. Positivism, the belief that values (and metaphysical beliefs) cannot be discussed or analysed rationally exercises a strong influence in Northern Europe. Most forms of positivism deny the possibility of ethics (including business ethics) on theoretical grounds. Positivism is, of course, a metaphysical and ethical doctrine in its own right. Its supporters, as might be expected, are unwilling to acknowledge that this is so, but continue to maintain their values and metaphysical doctrines in place as powerful influences on business as well as on economic policy. There is a strong tradition, especially when connected with scientific and technical ideologies, of scepticism with regard to values of any kind. Most of these standpoints are discussed in detail in business ethics texts, and no formal exposition of them will be offered here. Interested readers may wish to consult, for example, De George (1988, third edition) *Business Ethics*, or John Donaldson (1989) *Key Issues in Business Ethics*, Tom Donaldson (1989) *The Ethics of Multinational Corporations*, or Beauchamp and Bowie (1988, fourth edition) *Ethical Theory and Business*. Short accounts of most of these outlooks are given in the glossary at the beginning of this book.

Despite these philosophical differences, there is a growing 'business ethics' movement across Europe. One expression of this is the expanding European Business Ethics Network (EBEN), whose members are to be found in most European countries. EBEN holds well-attended annual conferences, with contributors from business, professional business institutions, academics and consultants. Such developments indicate that matters of common concern have at least been identified, and that at least some attitudes, values and principles are held in common.

The problems of business ethics from European perspectives can be seen to be similar in form to many ancient and unresolved problems and dilemmas. These include:

- individual freedom versus the need for order;
- the relationships of individual states (or groups) to each other and to larger groupings, such as federations, the European Community;
- relationships of members of multinational enterprises to each other, to their nation states, and to supranational institutions;
- sovereignty and autonomy;
- whose interests and rules shall be taken into account, and how, and whose shall predominate;
- relationships between international law and state laws;
- which values shall predominate, and how the decision should be made.

These are problematic issues, because there are few, if any, generally accepted principles by which they can be resolved, and because any move in any direction tends to disturb some interest or value. This does not mean the attempt is not worthwhile, or that all values and interests have equal weight. Decisions can be and are taken and enforced on all of these matters. *How* things are done is as important as *what* is done.

Modern interest in business ethics can be interpreted as a recognition that standard business outlooks developed since the beginning of the Industrial Revolution, functional though they have been in terms of fostering industrial growth, have been incomplete. This incompleteness, or paucity of mainstream management thought in relation to ethical matters has permitted the rise and eventual explosion of ethical issues in business, and has been more visible as different cultures and traditions are brought face to face in the European Community (EC). Thus, the possibility arises that decisions could be better informed by use of the language and concepts of ethics in coming to terms with the fact that standards do vary. In some measure, the problem is less one of introducing new standards and concepts, or of exhorting business to adopt defensible standards, than of bringing some parts of industry up to the levels achieved by others.

It appears to be the case that the rise in interest in business ethics has not been inspired by dramatic new concepts, philosophical outlooks or scientific discoveries. The issues appear to be old problems in new forms, and the philosophical outlooks that have a bearing on them are equally ancient. It should come as no surprise that the attitudes, whether enthusiastic, hostile or sceptical, towards business ethics have their forerunners in ancient attitudes towards ethics in general.

If it is accepted that business standards do vary, then it is reasonable to search for explanations of the variations. Logically, the possibilities include:

Determinism The force of circumstances, economic necessity, behavioural imperatives (based, perhaps, in individual psychology), group norms and corporate structures and cultures.

Leadership The idea that the ethos of a corporation is determined by whomever happens to be at the head of the corporation.

Beliefs A naive but determined sceptic will find in any claimed high-grade activity grounds for believing that the activity was 'really' motivated by some base impulse, which will be uncovered if a diligent-enough search is undertaken. A 'market ideologist' can explain away what appears to others to be a lapse as an imperfection in the market, or as hard reality if there are none to be found. The same ideologist can explain impeccable business conduct in terms of the discipline of the market. A utilitarian can explain what happens in terms of the balance of 'good' events over 'bad' ones, and propose changes if it does not in fact happen. Any ethical theorist can explain the 'good' things that happen in terms of applying sound standards, and 'bad' things in terms of inadequate or low standards.

If this argument is correct, simple belief systems not only have an explanation (of sorts) for what occurs in business that is ethically relevant, but also help to determine what occurs. In this way, they can become self-fulfilling prophecies and self-justifying truths. This will explain the absence of dialogue between ethical theorists and mainstream management writers – at this level, no need is felt for complicated frameworks of thought when simple ones can apparently be made to explain so much, and indeed, to help to bring about that which the belief systems try to explain.

Myths As some philosophers have pointed out, people in groups seem unable to function without guiding myths, and most myths have some basis in truth. Socrates proposed that 'bad' or 'dysfunctional' myths (to use modern jargon) ought to be replaced by better ones. This has not been a popular view, as people by and large do not like to admit, at least in public, that their myths may not be the whole truth.

The rather abstract notions that many current issues are ancient in form, that stances towards them may be governed by

ideologies, myths, self-justifying truths and self-fulfilling prophecies can be made more concrete by using some further
examples. The examples will also bring out some of the
fundamental ethical matters underlying the EC, and will point up
some of the standard and ancient explanatory frameworks for
ethical action, i.e. some standard ethical theories.

Competition policy

Trade policy is central to the EC. The Single European Act
requires signatories to ensure four freedoms of movement: of
people, goods, services and capital. The stated object of the Act is
to improve standards of living.

As might be expected, the Treaty of Rome deals in some detail
with the rules and principles (Articles 85–94 of the Treaty).
Implementation is assisted by means of Directives which set out
specific means, and purpose-made institutions have been set up to
encourage compliance. The institutions include, for instance, the
Commission and the European Court of Justice. If there is a
conflict between the Community law and the law of member
states, the former prevails as a matter of principle, although the
European Court has no jurisdiction over national courts of law.

Case 21 draws attention to some practices and attitudes
towards them within the EC. Ethics includes among its many
aliases 'practical reason'. Using this perspective the study suggests
that some of the main barriers that can be anticipated to
harmonized and justified trade policy within the EC seem to be
remarkably unproblematic, while some of the more apparently
straightforward ones present major challenges. Specifically, the
'subjectivist' notion that the *mores* of one group or nation state
cannot logically be criticized in terms of those of another appears
to be a non-problem. The more intractable issues seem to turn on
lack of clarity between ends and means, the stubborn impene-
trability of many of the minor premises, and the entanglement of
facts and values, theory and evidence. The elaboration of these
points is delayed until the conclusion, after the practices and
attitudes have been identified.

Trading rules and commitments

In practice many issues have been raised in relation to the
enforcement of the rules. For instance, the successful suing of the
Commission in 1986 by Stanley Adams (in a long-running battle)
raised many issues of enforcement, and of conflict of rules. If
Community law conflicts with state law, as it did in the case of

the Swiss trade treaty, how is it to be enforced?

If the government of a member country condones practices against the rules, or drags its feet over enforcing compliance, how is that to be regarded? Should enforcement be even-handed, or is it permissible to enforce rules on those nations which cannot or prefer not to break them, leaving the defiant and powerful states to break them at will? If a country refuses to sign or agree to a provision, as is the case with Britain and the 'Social Charter', does it mean to say that Community law prevails?

One obvious answer is that the rules, as is the case with all laws, cannot be enforced without some measure of agreement. If the rules are respected by most parties, the occasional act of excepting oneself from them can be tolerable, if not ideal.

In ethical theory, a traditional debate has been on whether conflicting values or value-preferences can be reconciled. On one side of the traditional divide are the subjectivists (sometimes called relativists) who hold that ethics is wholly a matter of taste. If true, this seems to subjectivists to imply that if one country prefers a different set of rules from those of another, there is little to be said or done about it.

But this hardly seems to be an issue in the above examples. The rules are agreed to in the signing of the treaty. What is not agreed is the range of cases to which the rules apply. Also not agreed are the speed of implementation and the mode of enforcement.

At the other side of the traditional debate, objectivists hold that there are rules and principles that are valid for all time and for all circumstances. There are, according to this view, some moral truths that remain true even if everyone in the world rejects them.

At least one of these truths must be the logical requirement to follow an argument wherever it leads, even if that requires an uncomfortable change of practice.

But the issues discussed so far do not seem to present much of a problem here, either. The parties agree to the rules and the principles, but disagree on which of many rules and principles are the right ones to apply in a particular case. In fact, as will be seen, they offer arguments to show that the detailed circumstances, once properly understood, require that one rule be followed, rather than another.

Trading issues

The propositions are illustrated in a variety of examples, which include, as expressed in media headlines:

'EC launches inquiry into overseas telephone charges'

The headline refers to suspicions that telephone charges are set at artificially high levels by cartels. The clear principle that the cartels are in restraint of trade is mitigated by the fact that the members include operators in non-EC countries, on whom enforcement is impossible, although sanctions can in practice be applied. (*The Independent*, 11 May, 1990, p. 21)

'Shorts debts absorbed to ease sell-off'

The [British] government has smoothed the way for the privatisation of Short Brothers, the Belfast aerospace company, by absorbing £390 million of its bank debts.

The final absorption bill was expected to be in the region of £800 million. (*The Guardian*, 28 February, 1989)

'Renault face huge repayment to France'

The decision on whether car maker Renault must repay Ff12 billion ($1.3 billion) to the French government will be made next week by the EC. The Commission originally ordered the amount to be repaid last November but has subsequently been studying detailed explanations from the French government as to why the funding should not be considered an illegal subsidy under EC rules. (*The European*, May 11–13, 1990)

'Brittan deadline on "sweeteners" '

The government has been given until August 17 to demand that British Aerospace return the £44 million illegal 'sweeteners' for the purchase of the Rover group and explain whether the company has been given illegal tax concessions worth up to £411 million. (*The Guardian*, 21 July, 1990, p. 2)

'Customs "failed to block EC farm fiddles" '

The Common Market and the British Customs and Excise were condemned yesterday for failing to take action for nearly a decade to stop British and foreign companies fiddling claims from the Common Agricultural Policy's £14.8 billion a year budget. (*The Guardian*, 3 February, 1990, p. 3)

'Telecom giants named in Greek phones probe'

Telecommunications companies Ericsson and Siemens are at the centre of a major controversy over Greece's telecommunications agency OTE. The two companies which are updating Greece's outmoded telephone system, have been accused of overcharging on equipment and of failing to meet standards. The value of contracts awarded so far is 6.5 billion drachmas ($42 million).

The contract was partly funded by a major loan from the European Commission. N. Kotsokis. (*The European*, 10–12 August, 1990, p. 18)

Agreed ends

None of these examples suggests that the principles of free trade and the competitive market are rejected by the various parties concerned. If this is so, the argument between subjectivists and objectivists is irrelevant to them. Nor is it to be taken for granted that making the claims is the same thing as proving them. Many are as yet far from resolved. But what do the examples indicate?

Bertrand Russell once claimed that for the scientist, every observation is an instance. Without suggesting that business ethics is, can be or ought to be a science, it seems fair to say that Russell's proposition was a fruitful one. Should we say that the ethical principles of the EC are sound, but that, managers being only human, the high principles are difficult to maintain in the face of financial temptation? This would hardly do, because governments and enforcement agencies are not only closely connected in some cases, but offer detailed arguments in rejection of the charges or assumptions made by the critics.

It would not be satisfactory to generalize by claiming that the governments themselves are party to the breaking of the rules. This is not because they often deny that the rules have been broken, taking all relevant circumstances into account, but because, in some cases, governments do not have the power or jurisdiction. The Commission itself appears to be in such a position in relation to the claims referred to above concerning telecommunications equipment.

Having noted that the debate between the objectivists and subjectivists cannot shed much light on the examples, it is worth turning to some other ethical or ethics-related explanatory frameworks.

The free market ideal itself is not much analytical help in this context. For one reason, the ideal is officially aspired to in almost all cases, or at least it is not denounced as inappropriate by monopolists or cartel operators. The abstract models of economic theory do not offer advice on how anti-monopoly policy should or could be enforced. This is not because the theories are not able to yield ethical prescriptions.

They can yield them, and do so when it is argued that the 'free market is the embodiment of economic justice' (Hospers, 1978). Notions such as those of consumer sovereignty, and indeed of optima and maxima, are inescapably value concepts and are often ethical ones too. Market morality might well be often served when the theoretical conditions are fulfilled. The evidence provides reasons for thinking that the conditions are not fulfilled as often as might be expected, given the strength of commitment by business to the free market ideal, and from the resources allocated to the agencies that encourage it.

CASE
21
'Italy versus the Rest'

In October, 1990 the Italian government sought to dilute the powers of the European Commission to impose limitations on state subsidies where these were considered by the Commission to be in conflict with the EC's competition rules.

The official basis of the competition rules is to be found in the Treaty of Rome (1957). They relate to abuse of market power by companies holding it. The competition rules are basic to the EC, one of whose main purposes has been to eliminate obstacles to the free movement of goods, services, capital and labour between member countries. Prohibition in general of subsidies to industry by governments, control of mergers and of public monopolies, and general prohibition of abuse of market power by private companies are main elements.

The Italian government's view, as reported in the contemporary press, was that:

1 In relation to state-controlled industry, the Commission's powers are very wide, and are wide enough to permit inconsistent application of the rules as between members.
2 Individual countries were entitled to take account of the features of economic conditions domestically that made state industry a legitimate policy instrument.
3 Support was sometimes necessary in order to manage competition from outside the EC, in which the general rules could place member countries at a disadvantage.

In response, the Commissioner with responsibility for competition control, Sir Leon Brittan, argued in a widely-reported letter that:

It has been recognised from the very earliest days of the Community that state aid could be used positively to promote Community objectives, such as regional development, but also to frustrate them by unfairly altering the conditions under which companies compete in the internal market.

Other countries than Italy were (and are) affected by the issue. Attributed attitudes appear to vary. For example, official British attitudes reflect the strong move in the UK towards privatization of state-owned industry, implying a suspicion of state industry, and support for moves to restrain it or at least to monitor it carefully. Greek and Belgian attitudes towards state industry appear to be pragmatically more supportive, and hence were aligned with Italy on the issue. French attitudes were reported to be influenced in favour of more monitoring of private industry by a need to compete with a subsidy programme in Germany that could influence France's own industries.

An assessment

The matter is central to the concept of the European Community, and also to what can be called 'conditions of trade' ethics. In this area there have been long-running debates in which the ideal of free markets has been ranged against two 'opposites': private monopoly and public or state-owned industry. Free markets are often held to be the embodiment of, or sure generators of, economic justice. When the position of the state-controlled economies in Eastern Europe and the USSR came to be seen clearly as untenable at the end of the 1980s, this appeared to reinforce the need to support the free market ideal.

It so happens that the ethical arguments which support it depend upon acceptance of one of the main theoretical ethical outlooks, that of utilitarianism. The other main outlooks present serious difficulties in relation to the distribution of benefits, and the technical inability of any known economic system of itself to provide much protection for individual rights, or to meet objectives chosen on value grounds, rather than on technical economic grounds. Put simply, free markets can deliver, or create the conditions for the delivery of very many values, such as economic growth, some autonomy, technical innovation, flexibility and rising income. However, their ability to do all of these varies between countries, and within the same country over time. The most determinedly free markets are not necessarily the most innovative or the fastest growing. (On the general debate see: Mishan (1967); Buchanan (1985); Macpherson (1985); Sen (1981); and J. Donaldson (1989).)

Free markets are technical arrangements for production and distribution. They are never absolutely free, and attempts in economic textbooks to describe them as such have been so heavily qualified by 'simplifying assumptions' as to indicate what might have been suspected in the first place: they are myths (on this see J. Donaldson, 1989, ch. 2). They happen to be useful myths, but, as the examples indicate, the ethical issues cannot be resolved by basic statements of the usefulness of free markets in general: what are under discussion are the limits to the freedom, and the conditions in which these are to be applied or shifted. These are inescapably value issues, and it is not surprising if various parties to the discussions within Europe express their view in relation to the myth itself, or relate them to special conditions applying more to them than to others.

It appears that the justified harmonization of EC trading rules does not depend on reaching agreement on what might be called the 'official' free market moral rules or ends. These are securely agreed, the more so since the collapse of their only serious challenge, the central planning of the former Eastern bloc. It may be regarded as inevitable that there will be a gap between the high aspirations of the free market ideal and actual trade practices. The most intractable problems in reducing the gap to acceptable levels relate to factual claims and counter-claims, arguments from special circumstances and problems of enforcement. These are the traditional problems of ethics and law and policy.

What would be new would be research budgets, activities and methods aimed at the disentanglement of facts and values, and ends and means that are commensurate with the size of the problem. So long as the encouragement of compliance with the rules is treated merely as a technical matter, the problems and tensions are likely to remain. Reduction of the gap between aspirations and practice would also seem to depend on the development of effective checks and balances other than and in addition to the central bureaucracies at EC and state level.

The headline which serves as the title for this study may misdescribe the situation, but it does draw attention to it.

The importance of theory

The foregoing argument was intended to show that 'cases' and 'facts' really do not speak for themselves. They are filtered through people's perceptions and through biases created by the particular experiences that people have had, through ideological and many other kinds of assumptions, and through a multiplicity of influences arising from the time and place that people happen to be in. It does not follow from this that values are simply a matter of opinion. They *are* matters of opinion, or judgment, but so are 'facts' and evidence. The subjective element in judgments about values is not the most serious problem for anyone attempting the systematic handling of values. It is not even a particularly difficult one. It is discussed in Chapter 5. A more formidable problem is the sheer number and variety of values that enter into business and what people say and do within and about it.

An old name for ethics is 'practical philosophy'. Kant called it 'practical reason', and Aristotle reminded us that the conclusion of an ethical argument is an action. Much that is said and done in business involves identifying which (and whose) values to pursue, and which (and whose) values shall guide the pursuit. The values, myths, ideologies and persuasive methods used can be seen in the case studies presented so far. It should not be thought that myths, ideologies and persuasive methods are wrong in themselves. The point is that these are not yet generally treated systematically in business or by analysts of business. The claims are both that they ought to be so treated, and that it can be done. It ought to be done because, in my view, unwillingness to do so has generated ethical issues that are increasingly claiming attention. The assumption that there is a public wish to see them resolved is inferred from the fact that they *are* increasingly being discussed. That it can be done is the traditional claim of most ethical theories. In this context also it is worth making a passing reference to the positivist notion that value judgments are not the proper subject for analysis, and further, that they ought not to be made. The standard and conclusive answer to that assertion is that the assertion itself is a value judgment, and is self-contradictory. It does not help the positivist cause at this point to say that value judgements are not 'scientific', and may thus be safely ignored. There is no good reason to believe that 'scientific' value judgments are any better than any others, or that scientific judgments can replace value judgments. That was the dream of some scientific ideologues in the nineteenth century, but it remains an aspiration only. To my mind it is one that stands little chance of being realized.

The traditional way of reducing the volume and variety of values, whether ethical or not, is to attempt to seek general principles. The principles are designed to provide a pre-formed, pre-considered judgment about all those cases or instances that are held to exemplify the judgment. Like cases can be treated alike. Different cases can be treated in terms of whatever principle they fall under. This avoids arbitrary treatment of individuals, and makes for consistency in policies and judgments. All this is, of course, an idealized version of ethical reasoning that does not take into account the many sources of bias referred to above. The kinds of theories preferred in different cultures differ. Some traditions are more self-consciously 'analytical' than others. The theoretical options can best be illustrated by showing how they can treat the long list of values expressed in the cases. To show how this can be done it will be necessary first to list some of the values.

Varieties of values

The cases were selected to illustrate the range of values that drive business, guide it and limit its action. Some are expressed in legislation. Others are expressed in 'codes of practice', which themselves may or may not be enforced or 'taken into account' by courts and tribunals.

The list of values encountered so far includes:

Group 1
pride in the firm
'fine reputation'
'strong team'
confidence
quality of service
dedication
commitment to success
'the best people'
high standards/improved standards
quality of service expected
value for money
keeping to published standards
valued close links with the community
'public trustees'
'creating quality'
fairness and decency
responsibility
standards of taste
'good practice'
competitive edge
highly professional service

It is noteworthy that the official company statements from which this list was drawn did not include references to 'maximization of profits', 'harsh realities', or to any of the less admirable values so often referred to in the mass communications media. In interpreting this, it will not do to suppose that it is because companies only want to present the best image of their ethical worth, while at the same time being obliged by the nature of man or of competition to practice only the less admirable values described in the rather more exciting cases portrayed daily in the mass media.

The standard and conclusive answer to this line of thought is that the admirable values expressed are in fact aspired to, and in some measure often achieved. If the only values that companies were capable of operating by were the 'negative' ones, then there would be no experience of the positive ones, and hence any claim to them would be a complete waste of time. This is related to several of the traditional 'liar paradoxes' in logic and ethics: if all business statements were necessarily lies, then the concept of truth could not exist. As it happens, the standard forms of business activity include keeping promises (goods supplied to the quality promised, wages paid as agreed, effort put forth in return, and much else). That there are increasing problems in delivering these values proves, if anything, that they exist, rather than that they are universal mirages.

The other side of this particular coin contains the less admired values (why values are thought to be classifiable as 'admirable' or otherwise is a central topic for the ethical theories to be discussed). This list, again drawn largely from the cases presented so far, includes:

Group 2
  misuse of company resources at high levels, especially of
    financial resources (the financial services *causes célèbres*)
  organizational bullying
  nepotism
  misuse of appraisal methods
  office politicking
  evasion of risks (as opposed to prudent avoidance of them)
  tax evasion
  petty cliques
  autocratic rule
  cover-ups
  scapegoating
  misrepresentation of statistical data
  appeals against decisions heard by the body which made the
    initial decisions
  ignoring safety rules
  evasive responses to complaint
  groupthink
  sheltering behind bureaucratic rules
  'kangaroo courts'

Awareness of these possibilities has led to a variety of practices which make some values explicit and which seek to regulate them:

Group 3
  codes of practice
  representational systems (for employees or consumers)
  safety legislation and codes

consumer protection organizations
arbitration
contract law
appeals procedures
company rules, policy statements and handbooks

Clearly, any item in Group 1 might be little more than 'hot air', and any item in Group 3 can be abused, circumvented, evaded, ridden over roughshod, or ignored. But the widespread incidence of such abuse is not inevitable. The items in Group 2 which form part of the daily diet of much of the mass media, may well be very widespread, or endemic in particular institutions, corporations, or even sectors, but they are far from universal. Systematic thinking about values in business can help to reduce the incidence of abuse, given the will. That the will is sometimes lacking is because people in industry often inherit certain forms of language, concepts, structures and cultures. In the nature of things, it is not possible to estimate the level of incidence of the type of events listed in Group 2, but it is not necessary either. It is far more useful to offer ways to avoid the various practices, than to attempt reliable estimates of their frequency. In Wittgenstein's imagery (Wittgenstein, 1953), here is another bottle we can show the flies the way out of.

By itself, publication and description of codes tells us nothing of whether they are being operated to the letter or spirit. Some of the examples in this casebook will show the great lengths to which people sometimes go in order to subvert codes and rules, even those they themselves have promulgated. This raises very difficult issues of whether, by whom, and how codes and ethical rules may be enforced, and upon whom, and by whom. It raises issues of who is entitled to draw up, monitor and revise codes, and how (see also Chapter 3).

To return to a major topic of Chapter 1: the problems arising from the use of codes of practice (and of ethics) vary greatly in scope and seriousness. That there is an acknowledged gap in this area as well as in the area of official company aspirations is a problem to be faced, rather than a reason for dismissing codes as mere window-dressing. It could be that the difficulties of enforcing codes are due to a number of factors other than the honesty and drafting skills of their promulgators. There are what can be called 'intervening processes'. The case studies will help to identify them, but their identification needs to be referred back to the original aims of and justifications for ethical codes and reasoning. These are not always clear or agreed.

Implicit (and sometimes explicit) in most discussions of business ethics, and of business generally, are beliefs and assumptions that 'high standards' are unproblematic, that they can be known, and that, as a matter of fact, they are known. This is unproblematic until attempts are made to establish in general what the standards are, and the grounds on which support for them may properly be called upon.

One approach is to regard ethical behaviour as that which conforms to the established standards of the community in which one lives (for an example, see Griffin, 1987, second edition). The problem with this view is that it covers only a small part of what has traditionally been the subject of ethics: there is also the concept of ethics as a critical, i.e. analytical subject, in which the customs of time and place are examined for consistency and coherence. In this element of ethics it is possible to say that an action is lawful, and customary, but still wrong in that it does not meet more general principles. For instance, scapegoating may be practised, but still held to be unjust. A more general problem is that of deciding what are the authentic rules and practices of a time and place. They invariably differ between different groups within the same culture. Some hold to traditional values and practices, while others are in the act of substituting new ones. To decide which code is the authentic voice of, say, the nineteenth century, or of Victorian Britain, there is no escape from making value judgments, since Victorian Britain had a cacophony of voices, and a plethora of groups and sects, offering different visions of what the authentic voice of the age is.

It is possible to avoid these practical difficulties and at the same time offer a sounder theory. An example is provided by the American author Thomas Donaldson in his book *The Ethics of Multinational Corporations* (1989):

Yet beneath these shifting currents of opinion, almost lost from view, lies a connected set of normative and nonempirical issues surrounded by a remarkably durable collection of moral beliefs. As normative issues they cannot be reduced to questions of statistically interpretable facts or to the determination of maximally efficient strategies for reaching goals. Rather, they concern questions of rights, fairness and justice: they ask what goals should be adopted by economic actors, what rights multinational employees in developing countries should possess, and what obligations and rights corporations should recognize – other than merely legal ones – in their dealings with foreign governments.

Drawing attention to the neglect of these issues in economic and business research, he adds

A familiar assumption by such researchers is that they defy serious analysis because of the clash of cultural values.

That the assumption to which he refers is seriously problematic is, I believe, by now well-established. Detailed discussions of the issues of subjectivism, relativism, objectivism and related doctrines are readily available in the business ethics literature. They are summarized, with a critique in J. Donaldson (1989), *Key Issues in Business Ethics* (subsequently referred to as *Key Issues*). They are not treated in detail here.

Deciding what are 'good practice' and 'best practice' is thus not merely a matter of discovering what the companies who are thought of as the leaders are doing, or even of discovering what formal standards have been enacted. The decisions are unavoidably 'normative' decisions, and depend upon principles, whether consciously adopted or not.

Theories are, among other things, deliberate attempts to set out the relationships between decisions and the general grounds for making them.

One further step needs to be taken to establish the link between ethical theory and business practice: not all 'normative' judgments (value judgments) are ethical judgments, and not all judgments in ethical theory are normative. Some, for instance, are logical, and others are factual. Examples are provided in the issues surrounding safety standards. A legal formula in Britain is that safety procedures should aim at certain ends 'as far as is reasonably practicable'. This is not merely a 'weasel' expression to avoid specific legislation, but a recognition that circumstances can never be fully foreseen, and that specific expressions cannot be laid down in advance for all contingencies. What is 'reasonably practicable' can be determined by experience, using tested cases and precedents. These are related to the logical rule 'ought' implies 'can' – rules that cannot be enforced are no rules at all.

But the matter does not end here. Values may be *technical*, representing skilled performance of duties. The notion of 'duties' is unambiguously ethical. Duties can be contractual (drawing in many more ethical concepts), or imposed (drawing in many others). They may be *prudential* (duties of proper and careful use of resources, or of care for patients, of avoiding law-breaking, etc.), or they may be duties *in their own right*, such as treating people fairly, telling the truth, keeping promises, recognizing other people's rights as well as their duties.

This leads to some central issues in business ethics, to which the case material should be helpful: what can business ethics provide or do that skilled managers are not already doing? Is it simply a matter of finding out what the leaders of industry think is 'best practice', and then transferring it to others? Can and should 'ethical behaviour' be controlled by law and by more effective law enforcement? Should not the rules (or 'the right rules') be brought together in the form of codes of practice, applied to companies, whole industries and professions? Once the codes are known, and individuals trained in applying them, what more is needed, or possible?

The cases and ideas of Chapter 1 were used to show that values drive business. Those of Chapter 2 added that the diversity of values and of stances towards them, far from proving that no systematic analysis of values is possible, demonstrates that elaborate theoretical frameworks are in fact used. These involve assumptions about best practice, myths, and many other belief systems that support business. Business ethics can supply a more self-conscious and more appropriate framework of principles to support, and in some cases to supersede those already in place. The incompleteness of these can reasonably be inferred from the rise in business ethics *issues*, and from the piecemeal grafting of specific codes to old practices and structures.

Chapter 3 provides an analysis of the forms of argument used in business and in the management literature and of the practical expressions of them, in company policies, rules, codes and practices. An explanation is offered for the gap between official aspirations and practical outcomes. It should be apparent that we can learn as much, if not more, from all those normal business activities which are taken for granted and do not attract headlines in the mass media, as we can from the growing list of untypical, albeit exciting *causes célèbres*.

3 FORMS OF ARGUMENT IN BUSINESS AND IN ETHICS

Theories provide frameworks from which claims and statements, attitudes, questions and practices can be evaluated. They enable people to decide what is or is not relevant, true, promising, useful, constructive – and much else. Clearly a 'good' theory can save much duplication of effort and time. The other side of the coin is that 'bad' theory can lead to injustice, missing of opportunities, distortion of the truth, or ignoring of warnings and dangers. Theories and principles can be invoked to throw people off the track, as when, for example, agendas are set which exclude some topics.

CASE 22 Incomes policy

The history of 'incomes policies' provides an example of what happens when agendas are unduly restricted in public discussions. The crux of the matter has been the inability of policy-makers to acknowledge that the standard formula 'pay should rise in line with productivity growth' assumes that the distribution of income at a particular time is agreed and accepted. Attempts to acknowledge it have tended to look to 'special cases' (i.e. those with the strongest powers or with the most vigorous campaigns). Other 'anomalies' are from time to time recognized, but labelling them 'anomalies' reinforces the limited nature of theorizing in the area. 'Incomes policies' *sound* fairer than pay or price freezes, and tend to be presented as efficient (leading to quick achievement of policy objectives), equitable ('everyone makes the same sacrifice for the common good'), prudent (setting the conditions for smoother business operations in the future), and in everyone's interest (preventing job and company losses while maintaining international competitiveness). The issues involved are discussed in more detail in Chapter 9.

Cause and effect in economic and business policies are not easy to identify, and are 'theory-loaded'. In these areas, what happens is

38

often only describable in terms of particular theories. For example, inflation is an abstraction that has dominated economic thinking for many decades. Concepts such as 'excess demand' refer to theoretical constructions. They are not observable, and difficult if not impossible to measure objectively. Individual experiences of rising prices are not inflation, and cannot be turned into it by any amount of theorizing. Thus, inflation remains an abstraction, identified by how it is measured, and even the measurement is controversial and open to manipulation. This is not to say that people should not theorize about these matters, only that they should remain more open-minded in the face of such theoretical and practical uncertainty. The result is often oscillation in economic policy, such that ideas against the trend are simply officially inaudible. How to deal with them when equipped with inadequate theory is problematic. For instance, in my experience, eminent economists have dismissed fundamental criticisms of particular policies as 'nit-picking', thus avoiding having to face up to them. At other times, the same arguments have been dismissed by different commentators in discussions, as 'novel and idiosyncratic', according to one, and as 'nothing new' according to another. This possibility of experts taking opposite views of the same arguments or pieces of evidence (and of both being wrong) is characteristic of issues in which ethical and technical matters are interwoven. When this happens, ethical issues can be taken as technical, and vice versa. An example has been the search in economics for the optimum inflation/ unemployment equilibrium, or trade-off.

Theories and principles influence what people do. When union leaders call on workers to strike, or others oppose them, it is usually done on a principle of fairness (often expressed as a pay demand on one side and as a threat to jobs and competitiveness, causing inflation, on the other). Greed may be suspected or attributed by bystanders, but the rhetoric is a moral one. This is no accident. It will not do simply to say that people are being cynically manipulative. Sometimes they may be, but they could not be manipulative if people did not respond to high moral claims. This is quite general. Countries are called to war for causes – freedom, patriotism, ideology, rather than promises of quick profit. Indeed, war profiteers are usually disapproved of at the time, even if honoured later.

Theories and principles, then, are major motivators. In addition, they can provide excuses for action or inaction. They can address the issues of the day just as easily as they can ignore them, or for that matter cause them.

This chapter explores the kinds of theories used in addressing or avoiding the ethical issues of business, and offers a practical method for checking for the presence of sound and defensible procedures, and for generating and developing them, where appropriate. It offers a way of deciding whether they are appropriate, and why.

Some of the main questions to be addressed at this stage are: Is there such a thing as an 'ethical firm'? What does it mean for a firm to be 'ethical'? Can codes of practice (codes of ethics) help to improve business standards and prevent litigation or disasters? Does it pay to be ethical? Does and should 'ethics' begin 'at the top', i.e. is there a duty on the part of chairmen, chief executives, directors and major shareholders of businesses to set the tone by precept and example? Should that duty be enforced, and if so, how? Is there a case for major reform in company law, which is at present based on the joint stock principle, by which the shareholders own the company, and within the law, determine policy, directly, or through appointed managers? Is there a case for requiring companies to publish their ethical codes?

CASE
23

Company codes of ethics: a proposal

A recent proposal by David Huddy (published here for the first time) has suggested a way of incorporating further choice into dealings between companies and others. This was presented to the Society for Applied Philosophy in London in November 1990. The initial proposal is as follows:

Improvement in business ethics

The proposal: ethical performance is exposed to market forces.

The principle: in a progressive society, businesses known to have an unethical record will not prosper.

The method: a register is maintained where companies may voluntarily record their code of ethics either by including it in their memorandum or by filing a separate statement. Alleged breaches of ethical standards can be referred to the Registrar, who may take up the matter with the company concerned. Correspondence and the Registrar's comments are maintained on file for public reference.

The advantages
- It is simple and inexpensive.
- It is not uncommon legislative practice.
- It is well known to commerce and the public, for example in trade associations, in TV consumer protection programmes, and not least in the reference services for credit control.
- It will exert slow but effective pressure in the right direction.
- It will work.

Huddy has discussed the ideas in several contexts. Typical objections have been:

1 The 'registered statements' might become mere public relations exercises.
2 The 'good' companies will register and be subject to stronger pressure to improve than will the 'bad' ones.
3 Frivolous and unjustified allegations against companies will remain on public record.
4 Phoney justifications will sometimes be used, which cannot be checked within the company.
5 Employees will still be unable to 'blow the whistle' without the very real (and, in practice, almost inevitable) fear of being dismissed or blacklisted. Companies have enough to do without wasting time replying to cranks and uninformed critics.

In brief, Huddy's replies are:

1 They might. But (current or potential) shareholders, suppliers, customers and employees can find out by examining the record held by the Registrar. The absence of complaints or the correspondence with the Registrar will enable people to make their own mind up. If people give evasive replies, these can easily be recognized. Publication will still impose the obligation to meet the content of the statement, which can only be to the good.
2 The 'good' companies have already invited the pressure to improve by being 'good' companies: the 'bad' companies will be recognizable as such because they have not registered and should suffer as a consequence. Note that the proposal is that all companies must register, but a statement of 'No Declaration' would be permitted.
3 The Registrar will not be obliged to take up frivolous or mischievous criticisms, and there are other remedies for dealing with them. It will be the Registrar's discretion as to what is treated seriously and what correspondence is to be regarded as significant.
4 The complainant still has the right to argue the case. All will be on file for public judgment.
5 They will be in no worse a position than they are now. The proposal is not really designed to help employees in this situation. Also, I have slight worries about employees 'stabbing their employer in the back' in this way. They should consult the file before they join, and not work for companies they do not approve of. Of course, if they are wrongly treated, as appears to have been the case in some well-reported instances, then they can write to the Registrar, where the facts will be filed and stand as a warning to others.

Cases 22 and 23 between them provide examples of the way moral arguments run in business and industry. There are typically several and not just two sides to every argument. The arguments use general, even abstract, moral and behavioural principles, which are either explicit or implicit, but either way are clearly identifiable. The evidence upon which the arguments are based is partly an appeal to interpretations of historical experience, and partly a prediction of what reactions will be.

   If I am right in saying that people are powerfully driven by what they believe to be 'right', 'appropriate' and 'fair', this still leaves open the possibility that these powerful principles are typically and systematically used in business for manipulative purposes. The standard response in ethical argument is that the power of the arguments cannot be explained if business is typically run on amoral or immoral lines. If this were widely believed to be the case, then the principles would lose their power to persuade. It would then be normal for people to become motivated more by the expectation of gain than by standing by principles. There are arguments to the effect that this is indeed so, that business is in fact incapable of operating according to defensible moral principles. The problem is not so simple that it can be reduced to one of whether businesses operate on the principle of greed and manipulation, or on the principle of an honest profit for an honest product or service, honestly made. The myths, excuses, technical imperatives and hierarchical leadership processes discussed in Chapter 2 all play a part. The complicating factor is that they are so closely interwoven. A major service that business ethics as a discipline can provide is in disentangling these various strands, and recognizing their proper role. This suggests that we go back to some 'first principles'. One way to start is to address the questions set out above (see p. 40), beginning with the first one.

Can there be such a thing as an 'ethical firm'?

Behind the scepticism often expressed at the mention of business ethics, it is often possible to find an alternative viewpoint. Scepticism, both naive and informed, is discussed in detail in a later section, but some of the alternative viewpoints implied in or suppressed by sceptical arguments are worth noting. Among these is the notion that since the objective of business is to maximize profit, ethical considerations are irrelevant, even if they make sense in the first place. The short response is that profit maximization as the sole or principal objective of business, as seen in Chapter 2, is a myth. Like all myths, there is some truth in it, but the relevant truths are insufficient to make much impact on moral arguments in business. The first truth is that many firms, unless they are privileged to enjoy substantial monopoly advantages, do need to attain a certain degree of efficiency so as to get the product or service to the consumer at a price that is not too far out of line with those of other suppliers. That is, a firm, according to the rules of the market game, must make some profit if it is to survive. All attempts to identify a 'profit-maximizing firm' in practice have foundered on the rocks of 'counter-factual conditionals', i.e. what would have happened if the firm had pursued a different policy, employed a different chief executive, etc. These can only be handled by means of making assumptions, that the existing 'technical coefficients' – input/output relationships – are fixed, and not dependent upon perceptions, particular industrial relations policies, structural choices, marketing policies, etc. This opens a wide enough gap to recognize that company policies and plans determine the input/output relationships at least as much as do the technical possibilities of the plant. Case 6, Chapter 1, gives one among many examples of a company whose management in one key section had strong reasons for maintaining an output myth that set the maximum at a good deal less than half of what could be achieved by the then existing resources. The variations in output between firms with virtually identical technology can be very substantial. Further, the 'profit maximization' assumption relies upon some determinate time-scale, whereas long-term profits may often be secured at the expense of short-term ones. How long is the long term? This is a question of the same logical form as 'how long is a piece of string?' Further, there is a mass of evidence to suggest that firms have multiple and shifting 'goals', which depend for their prominence on the changing situation within the company and to some extent on the persons occupying key positions.

Thus, the idea that firms are capable only of maximizing profits, which themselves are determined by fixed technical coefficients, provides no proof of the impossibility of business ethics. It is a useful teaching device for newcomers to economic reasoning, but has little supporting evidence, and little of that is anything other than systematically ambiguous.

A second alternative viewpoint is provided by a view of atomized, individual motivation. On this view, individuals are capable only of maximizing, or at least of seeking, their own pleasures and avoiding pains and discomfort. Thus it is not an attitude peculiar to sceptics of business ethics. It applies to ethics generally. The standard, and in my view correct response, is that this atomized, hedonistic view of people is an assumption, and is neither provable nor refutable. It can explain everything after the event, but rarely beforehand. All evidence is interpreted to fit this assumption, including the not inconsiderable evidence that people are often unthinking or confused about what they do, and are often driven by mixed 'motives', i.e. they are able to recognize many different claims for action, and may not always act on the basis of what others would see to be their best interest. People are too complex to be mere pleasure/pain calculating machines, but even if we were, we would have no way of proving it. The idea is a theoretical assumption, not an incontrovertible fact.

Thus, whether there can or cannot be an 'ethical firm' is not a matter to be decided by making assumptions about the 'objective of the firm', or about individual psychology and motivation. They are both, as it happens, meta-ethical theories, not 'brute facts'.

The question is both a theoretical and practical one. At this stage, two further possibilities are worth mentioning. The first, widely discussed in American literature is that an 'ethical firm' cannot exist because ethical/moral attributes are applicable only to individuals. A firm or corporation cannot feel pride, guilt or remorse, and a firm or corporation cannot exercise responsibility or, for that matter, be put in prison. All these attributes are held, on this view, to be relevant and ascribable to individual human beings, but not to abstractions such as corporations.

This topic is discussed in detail by Larry May in *The Morality of Groups* (1987). The arguments against the idea corporations considered by May include the ideas that they are merely 'legal fictions', and that, as Watkins (1973) puts it,

Social processes and events should be explained by being deduced from (a) principles governing the behavior of participating individuals, and (b) descriptions of their situations. (Quoted in May, 1987, p. 14)

The notion of 'legal fictions' is a basic and practical concept in law. The notion that the nation state, or 'society' is no more than a logical construction of individuals is an old idea often attributed to Bertrand Russell. His purpose was to support the claims of individuals against claims to unthinking obedience made on behalf of grand abstractions such as the state. May (1987, p. 22) cites an opposing argument, by Peter French (1984), to the effect that the identity of a corporation persists through time, irrespective of the particular individuals who are members of the corporation. Silverman's (1970) similar idea that organizations and systems cannot successfully be treated as 'having' needs, rights or demands provoked a lively discussion on the theme of 'reification', according to which organizations and systems are abstractions, useful for analytical purposes. The details of these old debates need not detain us here, but it is useful to note that in plain language it is common, and correct, to speak of practices, statements, actions, codes, rules and decisions as being 'good', 'useful', 'improper' or even immoral. No one proposes to fine a rule, or put it in prison, or even, so far as I know, expresses anxieties about the logical propriety of ascribing moral predicates to these concepts. They seem to me to be at least at one remove, at an even higher level of abstraction than a corporation or nation state. The fact that a rule, practice or corporation cannot have moral perceptions and cannot be fined or imprisoned is no good reason for refusing to ascribe moral properties to it, or to criticize it on moral grounds. The alleged 'reification' of corporations does not form a barrier to describing and appraising them in moral terms. This is partly because corporations *are* 'things', and thus can be legitimately 'reified', and partly because being legal and not 'natural' persons provides no logical reasons why their practices, structures and rules should not be appraised in ethical terms. Slavery is not a natural person, merely an institution; lying is not a person, but a practice. Despite all this, it still makes sense to appraise them morally, as moral theorists and others have successfully done for centuries.

A final argument often put at this stage is the idea that even if all firms are not driven by selfish motives to maximize profit at all costs, standards tend to be set by the least scrupulous or boldest operators. This is, however, no more true for industries than it is for whole communities. Sometimes the operators with the lowest standards are caught and prevented from affecting the conduct of others. As the cases show, standards can and do vary. Those of the 'fly-by-night-sweatshop' industries *are* typically different from those of the liberal professions, of motor manufacture and of large retail chains. Variations in standards occur within the same industry. Some firms contribute to the setting of standards, others follow whatever become the 'standard conditions'. Standards vary, often over long periods. Some industries display long-term characteristics. From all this, it is clear that the determinants of standards have as much to do with circumstances and industrial structures as with the presence or absence of individuals with particular ethical characteristics. This can be seen from the case studies. Undoubtedly, the ability to generate funds that lift companies from the margin of existence permits higher moral standards than are possible in marginal industries, but it does not guarantee it, any more than poverty guarantees low standards. Richness of resources is one of the factors that make some 'ethical' practices cheaper to institute. It does not guarantee that they will be applied.

To summarize, the arguments for profit maximization, for individual hedonistic motivation, that firms are not individual human beings, and the argument for 'rogue operators' (sometimes known as Gresham's Law − bad currency drives out good currency) are all theoretical beliefs, and none is very convincing, either in theoretical or practical terms. The existence of rogue-operator, profit-seeking and hedonistic individuals, and the fact that corporations are not human beings, can all be accepted without accepting that they are universal, dominant or more than partial truths.

A slightly more plausible reason for thinking that the notion of an 'ethical' firm or industry could be a mirage is the possibility that the high standards claimed in official company statements are open to cynical manipulation. Claims that sound good but mean little *are* possible. But there is a difference between 'could be' and 'is'. The problem for supporters of the view that all business activity is ethically relevant and that much of it is highly defensible is one of dealing with systematic ambiguities in the notions of 'ethics'. Supporters of this view may limit themselves to the claim that business activity can be appraised in ethical terms. They may add that much business activity is justifiable in the light of more than one theory of ethics. But this will not impress the opponents of the idea of 'business ethics' if they can only conceive of ethics as some quixotic and idealistic notion that somehow people can be persuaded to behave as communities of saints against their true and baser nature. This last viewpoint is, indeed, a very common one, but its holders rarely admit to it in so many words and, in my experience, tend to mask it under a series of sceptical-sounding questions, such as 'but surely, company X would not have done that unless it expected a trading advantage' or 'how do you know that all these claims to "ethical" behaviour are not mere shams, to be dropped as soon as trading gets tough, or as soon as they are found out?', or 'give me an example of an ethical firm' or, finally, 'I have listened to what you say, and you have not convinced me that there are any "ethical" firms at all'.

This approach appears at first sight to be a 'hard-nosed realist' stance from someone who is determined not to be taken in by false claims. It is in fact a form of 'naive scepticism'. My own experience in meeting this kind of outlook is that its supporters have never, to my knowledge, provided an answer to the question, 'What would a firm have to do to convince you that it is pursuing policy X (e.g. a "green" policy, or an anti-bribery code) for reasons other than greed or cynical manipulation, etc.?' (i.e. for ethically defensible reasons). Given that companies usually do honour contracts, pay agreed salaries on the day due, compensate consumers for faulty products and services, report results honestly, etc., we need an explanation for their doing so, and we need to be able to make judgments on the level of acceptability in ethical terms of various actions, rules and intentions. For some naive sceptics, a single allegation of a lapse is sufficient to destroy the possibility of a company claiming an ethical basis for what it does. The general problem of what I have called 'naive scepticism' is discussed in *Key Issues in Business Ethics* (Donaldson, 1989), Chapter 10.

Far more fundamental and constructive questions for those who wish to discover whether it is possible to identify 'ethical firms' are:

1 Which standards, rules and values shall be regarded as 'required' for the 'ethical' label to be warranted?
2 Who is entitled to pronounce what these standards ought to be? The Church? Government? The Courts? Society as a whole? History? Contemporary *mores*?

So what *is* an 'ethical firm'?

The contemporary preferences model

One possibility is offered by Fritzche and Becker (1984). It can be labelled the 'contemporary preferences model':

Socially responsible behavior by managers is usually a matter of ethics. Ethical behavior is behavior that is consistent with prevailing social and cultural norms and mores.

This view does not allow for the possibility of evaluating the current rules on moral grounds, either affirming them or suggesting amendments to them, and it would make no sense to do so, other than as a mere act of will or an estimate of how current mores are changing. Yet a good deal of moral discourse and legislative activity is based on such critical judgment. Legislators can and do resist what is offered as new current *mores* on moral grounds. They could not do so if the only possible rational arguments about morals (ethics) related to what the current *mores* in fact were. But this creates a new problem: whose is the authentic voice of the 'new' *mores* and, for that matter, who is entitled to give authentic expression to established ones? Majority views by counting of votes? Legislators have persistently resisted, on rational ethical grounds, legislation by referendum. (A full discussion of the problems of relativism, raised by this viewpoint is given in Chapter 4.) Ethics, then, is more than a polling and listing of contemporary preferences.

The autonomous firm model

A very old approach is that firms are the kinds of things that can be and are *owned*. Firms are entitled to make their own rules. Within the law, a firm can do whatever its memorandum of association (or, in the case of other organizations, its formal constitution) permits. On this view, firms are autonomous and are able to make up their own minds as to what rules are to apply (or, at the very least, their spokespeople and chief representatives can do so). Merely obeying convention because it *is* convention is not ethical, nor necessarily immoral (= unethical). It is amoral on this view. The main problem here is that firms operate within a framework of law, and nation states and federations of states claim the right to set the terms in which firms operate.

The autonomy of firms and doctrines of private property rights did not prevent, for example, the enactment of laws governing some major activities within companies, from safety to accounting practices and hiring practices. The point is not that none of these laws is beyond criticism on moral grounds, but that they are made, discussed, criticized and often amended on moral grounds. There is a great deal to be said for the view expressed by the British industrialist Sir Adrian Cadbury: 'Ethical managers make their own rules' (Cadbury, 1987). One advantage is that autonomy means that people take full responsibility for their actions. When a decision is not prescribed by law, and competing moral claims are made on a company, someone must provide a basis on which competing claims are dealt with fairly. If, however, the autonomous firm is one in which a few managers make the rules on everyone else's behalf, and are judge and jury in their own cause, they are in danger of breaking some fundamental rules of natural justice in relation to others making the competing claims. To be autonomous and ethically defensible, companies must also recognize the claims made for autonomy in others. The extended cases in this book provide examples of companies and institutions which occupy different sides of the line in which shared autonomy is a limited autonomy, and an unshared autonomy, being autonomy for some, becomes traditional autocracy. Firms can still neglect their ethical duties. A good deal of law is uncertain, and no company can be sure that, in meeting only the minimum requirements, they are in fact meeting them. It is commonly believed, and correctly so, that any citizen (corporate or otherwise) who aims only to obey the minimum demands of the law will frequently brush with it. This applies equally to the moral law as it does to all other kinds.

The code of practice model

This account of ethical conduct of firms is increasingly popular. Firms can and do adopt codes of practice (or codes of ethics). These have several advantages. They lay down what the rules are, so that once the rules have been read, people know what they ought to do, according to the company. This is a major theme, and is the subject of Chapter 4. The general problem, from the point of view of answering the question 'Can there be such a thing as an ethical firm', is not whether 'ethical codes' are useful, but whether they are genuinely ethical. By determined sceptics, they might be seen as at best methods of defusing potential criticisms. From the point of view of the systematic handling of values (business ethics), the crucial factors are: Who draws up the code? Who validates, monitors and enforces it? Can its authors and promoters become sole arbitrators on whether it has been followed or not? How is it revised, and how are criticisms of it dealt with? Posing the questions offers a clue to the answer that is offered here: a code of practice/ethics is unavoidably ethically-relevant. Whether it is ethically defensible or not depends both on its content and on how it is used. Simply listing some general and widely respected values, whether or not they are enforced, is not sufficient.

The problem of 'the ethical firm': the procedural model

In my view, an 'ethical' firm cannot operate all of the above models. There are inconsistencies between choosing to operate according to what are considered to be 'best practices' and autonomy. A carefully-designed code can win the approval of all the persons consulted, but the range of persons consulted could be too narrow. There are many examples in which people are supplied with everything the administrators think they could possibly want, except the ability to articulate what they really do want. Agendas can be and are set, and codes drawn up, in ways that are in practice oppressive. Some examples are supplied in the longer case studies.

We have now arrived at the position where the common arguments to the effect that 'ethical' firms cannot exist are seriously flawed, and standard models of 'ethical practice' are incomplete and inconsistent. The knot can easily be cut. The problem arises from a systematic ambiguity in the notion of 'ethics', and can be solved by disentangling different conceptions of ethics.

In brief, what may be called 'ethics 1' means 'application of a given set of rules'. These can include, for example, participative systems, committees, quality standards, discipline procedures, anti-bribery stances, customers' guarantees, codes of practice and rules for their enforcement. It is this sense that attracts the accusations that firms can cynically manipulate the rules, and it is to this sense that the sceptical arguments are put, ranging from 'firms cannot be ethical because they are profit maximizers' to 'firms are driven by competition to operate the standards of the least scrupulous members'.

None of these sceptical and critical rejections of business ethics can touch the second meaning, what may be called 'ethics 2'. According to this meaning, ethics is the process of analysing the grounds on which any and all actions, practices, decisions, structures, rules and policies, procedures and methods of operating them are held to be correct, proper, justified, sound, etc. It is a critical activity.

Most public and private discussions on business and on business ethics do not recognize these two quite different meanings, and assume that there is only one meaning – what I have called 'ethics 1'.

The business ethics literature does sometimes discuss 'meta-ethical theory' ('ethics 2'), but more often leaves the specific theories to the preferences of the readers. It is possible to recognize both the main meanings of 'ethics', and still miss some key elements. The first, already alluded to, is that most meaning is 'subjective' in that the listener may not understand what the speaker intends to be understood. People can and often do differ as to what are desirable values. 'Ethics 2' can rule on what practices are sound, so long as people subscribe to the same theory of ethics. Arguments that will win the approval of a Utilitarian (i.e. arguments that point to the possibility that on balance the outcomes of an action are likely to be beneficial, may not command the support of a rights theorist, or even a rival utilitarian. Others seek to dismiss some claims to rights in favour of the 'common good'. Yet others can reject the 'common good' in favour of duties that are obligatory, even if everyone suffers. Examples are the alleged 'victimless crimes' related to some forms of 'insider trading' in company shares. Other examples include scapegoating and the use of 'fall guys'. This knot can be cut by offering a different rule and a different criterion for identifying 'the ethical firm'.

If it is accepted that business ethics is no more or less than the systematic handling of values in business and industry, then an ethical firm can be seen as one which has methods for identifying and meeting the legitimate aspirations of those who have to do with the firm.

Superficially, the approach could be criticized as including the expressions 'legitimate aspirations' and 'those who have to do with the firm'. These could be thought to be 'weasel' expressions, which supply an apparently strong idea with enough escape clauses to render it virtually meaningless. Any such criticism would be wide of the mark. The point of the account is to draw attention to the assumption implicit in many discussions of business values that there is a known set of values that all right-thinking people should aspire to, and that these are wholly known and agreed to by all. Thus a user of these assumptions can express indignation that the sacred role of business — to create wealth — can be forgotten by persons who propose a different way of doing business. Similarly, management's 'right to manage' tends to be taken to be a sacred trust, and any questioning of how the right is exercised, or suggestions that it may be being exceeded, are seen as somehow wicked, or at least muddled, and, even if inadvertently, putting the whole industrial system and ultimately the economy at risk.

Of course, proposing alternative strategies, policies, procedures and priorities may fall within these categories, but need not. The point of my account is to issue a constant (and in my view, much needed) reminder that deciding who has a legitimate aspiration in relation to a company's activities cannot be achieved by brandishing formulas and slogans. It can only follow from continuing dialogue in which the terms are not imposed by one party upon the others. The account given above allows for differences of view, which in turn can include criticism of the prevailing *mores*, which in this context are those that happen to be dominant. They can be, but are not necessarily, a far cry from those that are the most widely held, and can be an even further cry from those which are justifiable in ethical terms. A good deal of circumstantial evidence can be drawn from the case material that points to the general acceptability and general defensibility of most official current business *mores*. A good deal of the evidence suggests also that most firms and institutions go a long way towards putting them into practice. The problem is not that firms typically do not put into practice defensible and widely held values, but that these values can and do change, and the methods for recognizing the changes and incorporating them acceptably and properly are very poorly developed. This point is reinforced by an increasing number of apparent lapses in some sectors, and an apparent determination to enforce new, or at least newly popular, ones. The last include, for example, environmental concerns, customer and consumer care concerns, and the generalized popularity of codes of practice (codes of ethics).

The account that I have given recognizes that criteria for improvement are heavily dependent upon the adoption of a particular ethical theory, consciously or otherwise. For instance, a company code based on the 'greatest happiness of the greatest number' or upon the maximization of benefits (utilitarian outlooks), will not impress those who emphasize contractual obligations or, more generally, rights. Those who believe that the end justifies the means will be opposed by those who emphasize the need to reach agreement on both. Can the expectation of continued employment be legitimately broken on the grounds that it will be beneficial to someone else? Will the sacrifice be justified if the 'someone else' has a prior claim? On what basis can the priority be established? First in? Greater need? Higher value added to the company? How is it affected if the choice is made by one of the parties, rather than all of them? Can the free market system be justified to the losers on the grounds that the gainers are better off? Is the justification more that there must be losers, as in any game, and that the losers know and accept the rules? If they do not, then should we say that they ought to do so? Or that they must be deemed to have agreed to them? Or that it so happens that life is hard, and the existence of gainers and losers is really a law of nature? If this is true, is it not a major function of science and other forms of organized human endeavour to modify the outcomes of natural processes, for example by using one set of scientific or natural laws to mitigate the effects of others, as when people build shelters to avoid getting cold?

The questions can be multiplied without limit, and can only be answered by an appeal to general principles, including assumptions and theoretical outlooks. Thus the account I have given permits differing views to be aired as a matter of routine, rather than whim. This allows prevailing *mores* to be reviewed and criticized constructively, with a view to improving standards of behaviour and performance.

The account recognizes that everything that firms do has an ethical dimension, but not all values are ethical ones, and not all values have the same importance. To act ethically is seen as sometimes to do more than apply current 'best practice' and sometimes to do less. It recognizes that codes, for instance, are at a disadvantage when imposed 'top down', but may be enforced once agreed. They may sometimes be enforced even when not agreed by everyone, but only when a proper process of justification has been gone through. 'Proper' processes and 'phoney' ones are sometimes very difficult to distinguish, one from another, but the use of detailed case material interpreted in the light of informed theory can help.

In short, an 'ethical firm' is not one which simply obeys current conventions, but one which accepts or modifies them on principles that take into account authentic and informed expressions of the values of those who have to do with them. Sometimes this requires practical expression through users' committees, 'watchdog' organizations and codes, and sometimes these together are far from sufficient. Just as economic growth requires 'the will to economize' (Lewis, 1955), ethical growth requires the will and skill to handle values systematically. Ethical firms are able to defend themselves against mistaken criticisms without resorting to indefensible methods, evasion of issues, misinformation, etc. They do not need to be 'communities of angels', and do not rely upon bland or vague expressions of unexceptional principles.

Ethical firms do not dictate to customers, suppliers, employees or anyone else what values they ought to have, and do not have other people's values imposed upon them by pressure groups, governments, unions, business ethics writers or anyone else.

In their dealings, such firms and their representatives operate according to principles of natural justice in their relationships. Contracts are honoured; mistakes are admitted to and rectified. They do not need to be forced to behave ethically. Their appearances in courts, tribunals and the like are rare. They learn from their mistakes and listen to their constituents. They give rational responses to criticisms, and do not evade them.

All of these qualities tend to enhance the reputations of firms and, as is often claimed, can enhance the balance sheet at the same time. It is sometimes in the interests of firms which do not act in the ways described above to convince everyone else that they do so act. The detailed examples in this casebook show that many firms do operate to high ethical standards, as described above. The problem of distinguishing authentic examples from manipulative ones is a complex one, which the theoretical ideas in the business ethics literature and the detailed case studies are intended to solve. Clearly, claims cannot always be taken at face value. Their authentication, as argued above, requires the use of theories, but it also requires the identification of criteria and methods for improvement, as well as systematic methods for analysing cases and claims.

'Ethical firms' and the 'stakeholder' model

In the matter of claims by, for, from and against firms, a useful concept is that of 'stakeholders'. The expression appears to have been originated by Robert K. Merton in the 1950s, but it has enjoyed a vogue in recent years. The general idea of a 'stakeholder' is: 'A person or group that has a legitimate personal interest in the success of the organization' (O'Toole, 1985, quoted in Pierce and Newstrom, 1990).

The concept is a useful reminder that it cannot be taken for granted whom firms are to serve. The idea seems to be taken differently by different users. Norman Bowie (1990) puts the points:

Perhaps the interests of all stakeholders should be treated equally? This seems to be the view of Freeman and others. Since I wish to argue that the interests of employees often take priority over the interests of other stakeholders, I reject the view that treats all stakeholder interests as equal in all cases. Indeed, in some cases the interests of stockholders or suppliers might be given priority. Which stakeholder interests deserve priority in any case depends upon both economic and ethical considerations. Employee interests take priority far more often than is commonly thought. Hence I argue that the primary purpose of business is to provide meaningful work for employees and that if managers focus on this goal, business will produce quality goods and services for consumers and profits as beneficial by-products.

Bowie (1990, p. 108) refers to the hedonic paradox, that the more anyone seeks to maximize personal happiness, the less likely it is to be achieved, because happiness is achieved by the successful pursuit of other specific goals.

There are other limitations on the 'stakeholder' model. In my view, the main ones are that it cannot provide a rule or method for judging who is entitled to 'hold the stakes'. The stakeholder model implies a weighing-up of interests and, as Bowie points out, sometimes they may be weighted differently in different circumstances. Whether there is an implied equality or a variation in weighting, someone must in the end decide whose interests are to be realized. It is in the nature of ownership and control in industry that the adjudicators, the top managers, are stakeholders themselves, and thus forced into being 'judge and jury in their own cause', which is fundamentally at odds with basic notions of justice.

A further severe limitation on the stakeholder concept is that it is limited to interests, as opposed to principles. Bowie draws attention to this by proposing that an overriding principle should be the provision of meaningful work for employees. This can help to provide autonomy in which people are treated as 'ends' and not 'means', gaining responsibility for their actions. This is, when practised, a considerable advance on the traditional hierarchical structures in industry. The further implication of importance is that the principles are much more difficult to identify than interests, and can rarely be satisfied by trading economic or even psychological gains between established stakeholders. For one thing, the potential supply of new stakeholders is very large, as when industrial practices in parts of Europe generate acid rain elsewhere, or when the fishing practices of one nation deplete the resources and destroy employment for another. The problem is not that it is difficult to identify who might have a legitimate claim, but who is to decide its legitimacy and on what grounds. For example, in the acid rain case, an 'interest' model would imply identification of real damage to people's interests, which are presumably economic welfare, health, etc. If no real damage can be identified, the 'sufferers' could still argue for the right to an unspoilt environment on aesthetic grounds, or on behalf of future generations, or on the grounds that although specific costs have not been identified, it is only a matter of probability and time before some are. Not only is the list of potential stakeholders very long and variable, the list of potential grounds is limitless. Restriction to interests makes the process more manageable, but also more open to criticism on grounds of restricted application, and hence of relevance to ethical issues in industry. If some agreement can be reached on procedures for identifying the authentic stakeholders, the legitimate grounds on which they may make claims, and a defensible adjudication method, the concept has much potential. But all of these are highly problematic, and the concept is accordingly limited. Some of the later cases in the present collection illustrate that even the presence of clear codes and procedures raise major questions of justice and of ethical defensibility when the operation of the procedures is left to be operated by one of the parties, and that this is reinforced where there are major disparities in power or in resources available to the parties. Even invoking the law or tribunals can continue the disparities, and operate unfairly against one party as opposed to another. This is not merely to make the obvious point that perfection is unattainable, but to repeat the more problematic point that it is as important to see that the principles are identified and analysed by proper methods as it is to ensure that the proper principles are identified. In older and plainer language, the 'means' and the 'ends' are equally important, and are not likely to be adequately justified by grafting 'stakeholder' concepts on to existing structures for identifying and adjudicating between the huge number of values that drive business, and by which its activities can be understood and analysed. As Thomas Donaldson (1989, p. 45) puts it:

Despite its important insights, the stakeholder model has serious problems. The two most obvious are its inability to provide standards for assigning relative weights to the interests of the various constituencies, and its failure to contain within itself, or make reference to, a normative, justificatory foundation.

'Ethics pays'

The idea that companies can expect to incorporate explicit ethical thinking in a way that generates more in revenue than it does in costs, or, more generally, that 'ethics pays', is an attractive one, and one that is often justified. Goldsmith and Clutterbuck (1984, p. 130) quote Sir Kenneth Corfield of STC: 'We have one core value, mutual respect between all the people inside the company and between people inside and outside it'. They add:

'The integrity factor guides the thinking throughout the organisation, establishing high moral norms that provide automatic responses to ethical problems, and making top management intervention . . . rare.' The reverse side of the coin is that all of these audiences – especially employees and suppliers – tend to return the compliment, treating the company with the integrity it demands of them . . . . 'No professional manager can hold up his head if he keeps breaking promises', says Plessey's Parry Roberts . . . . *Up The Organisation* had a valid point when it advised, 'If all else fails, try honesty', says Bejam's Perry, 'But it's even more profitable to start with honesty in the first place.'

Possibilities for benefits through ethical behaviour are discussed, with many examples, by Carmichael and Drummond (1989, p. 70):

In the course of the next few chapters we will argue that business ethics are the key to business survival and business success. We will explain why this is so, and what business can do to gain what we call the *ethics edge*.

A cautionary note is sounded by De George and Pichler (1978, pp. 3–4):

[Business is] . . . basic to human society . . . [and] . . . it would be nice to show that moral action is always best for business. But this seems not to be true, especially in the short run: lying, fraud, deception and theft sometimes lead to greater profits than their opposites . . . [hence] moral judgments sometimes differ from business judgments.

Thus it is not always the case that companies 'do well by doing good', any more than it is the case that companies 'do good by doing well'. This leads to another important topic, touched upon earlier in the context of identifying what 'company objectives' are, that is, the nature of the moral basis for profit. In economic theory, in 'perfect' markets profit is a residual, available only to those companies which are more efficient than the 'marginal' firm, and only for as long as other firms are in the process of catching up with the more efficient firms. Of course, perfect markets do not exist in reality, but provide a powerful analytical concept for identifying 'ideal' cases, or, better, for identifying the logical limits to the concept of competition. In the real world, we are content to be more pragmatic. It is normally enough that there is *some* competition, not that it must be 'perfect'. This is not the place to analyse the nuances of economic theory, but it is useful to recognize that in the economic analysis, the idea that firms are profit maximizers is not intended to be a description of what firms do, but rather an assumption that allows a certain kind of analysis to take place. For present purposes, it is enough to point out that making a profit is not an 'end-value' in itself, but is a means to other values: from the point of view of the economy/society as a whole, profit is a necessary reward to enterprise. Without it, there will be no enterprise, and hence no production. That means no products, which are themselves means for satisfying the deeper-level ends (values) such as food, shelter, freedom, culture, etc. The notion that firms are profit maximizers is impossible to verify from observation or experience. Logically, what may be profitable in the short term can prevent even higher profits in the long term. However, no one knows how long the long term is.

We have now arrived at the point in which profit is a necessary means to highly valued moral (and non-moral) ends. Its moral basis lies in the extent to which the process of making profit does not itself break high-level moral values. The reasons given above for the growth of interest in business ethics seem to me to provide a strong case for the proposition that though the moral basis of profit is not in doubt, the moral basis for the way it is made is increasingly questioned, and that the questioning is at least sometimes well grounded in ethical terms. I have already pointed out that it is difficult (or perhaps impossible) to prove that a particular firm is a 'profit maximizer'. What remains to be said in this section is that it is not so very difficult to demonstrate that, at least in some cases, profit is only one major value among many, and is sometimes a very subordinate one at that.

In short, it can be seen that the link between ethics and profit is a very complex one. It is as wrong to believe that the legitimate ethical criticisms of business behaviour all arise as a result of the single-minded pursuit of profit as it is to believe that it is always profitable to be ethical. It is sometimes possible to raise ethical standards and profit together. These opportunities are more frequent than often seems to be believed, and they can often be created where they do not already exist, but it would be naive to believe that it is always so.

CASE
24   **A group of independent contractors**

This case, described by Velasquez (1988), illustrates the general point that at least in some cases, 'ethical' conduct, in any of the senses discussed so far, will not improve profit performance in the short term, or in the long term, as far as the latter can be determined. It concerns a group of defence contractors in the USA, but similar events are repeated elsewhere. The contractors provided equipment that was not available from suppliers outside the group (among whom there was no suggestion of collusion). Overpricing on government contracts, leading to excessive profit, was 'punished' by removal of the group from the government's list of contractors. However, the list was so small that removal for long was not practicable, since supplies of essential goods could easily dry up. There is no effective sanction against excessive profits. Arguments from enlightened self-interest, profit, greed or prudence can have no persuasive power in such circumstances.

Two more forms of argument which are common in the literature deserve at least a passing reference at this point. The first of these is in the category of '*noblesse oblige*'. People occupying positions at the top of firms often justify the income and power associated with their position in terms of their major responsibility. This is in the nature of a contractual obligation, falling under the general rule that contracts freely entered into ought morally to be honoured, as without this the justification falls. Additionally, not everyone is endowed with the ability to set up and run wealth-creating enterprises. There is an unspoken contract between entrepreneurs and top managers alike on the one hand and everyone else on the other, one of the terms of which is that due care for the legitimate aspirations of others is expected from those to whom power and privilege have been granted. The moral obligations of a private entrepreneur are no doubt different from those of, say, a public administrator or others in charge of public funds, but the differences are relatively minor compared with the similarities. This theme will recur later in the extended case studies. For the present, the argument is noted, rather than analysed. The lines on which analysis is suggested are explained in Chapters 4 and 5.

A final form of argument in relation to business ethics is what may be called a 'threat strategy', in which it is suggested to companies that damage will be done if business standards do not meet the rising expectations of the public. Thus, if a company permits conduct that leads to disasters such as have occurred in chemical plants, aviation, financial services, rail and sea transport, agriculture and nuclear installations, the result will be that legal punishments will become at once more severe and more certain. It will thus pay companies to engage in damage prevention activities.

By way of summarizing this chapter, the need to handle values in industry systematically is being increasingly seen as both important and urgent. Reasons for not doing so in the past have included claims that firms and individuals are somehow programmed not to take values into account on grounds of the nature of business goals or of individual motivation, or the alleged impossibility of making companies responsible for what happens as a result of their operations. All of these reasons (or excuses) rest on unsystematically analysed beliefs, and are dependent upon assumptions and theoretical outlooks, which in turn are only some among many which have at least as strong a *prima facie* claim as any of the 'excuse' theories. 'The ethical firm' is alleged by some not to exist, even to be an impossibility. This, however, can be seen to be a confusion, borne of the (usually unexamined) expectation that 'ethical firms' must be companies of 'well-informed angels', or arising from a lack of awareness that the term 'ethical' can and does also mean 'capable of analysis' in terms of ethical theories, and hence that all firms are ethical institutions. That they are ethical institutions does not mean that everything they do is justified, any more than it means that standards are typically low (which they are not).

Some, apparently promising notions, such as those of the 'stakeholder' model, and the idea that 'ethics pays', are useful, but cover only a part of the range of ethical issues in business. This applies equally to 'ethics as damage limitation' and to 'ethics as damage avoidance'. These all describe forms of argument frequently encountered in relation to business and the values that drive it. A final form is under the heading of '*noblesse oblige*'. This argument often takes on a social contract doctrine, but also looks back to the older, feudal arguments which ascribe lists of duties commensurate with office and status.

All of these arguments make their appearance in many cases and in many discussions on ethics and business. They go some way towards explaining and identifying, as well as solving, issues, but none provides a fully fledged ethical theory. These appear in summary form in Chapter 5, where an attempt is made to provide a compact framework for analysing case material, in an attempt to reduce the biases inherent in adopting a single set of assumptions into which all evidence must fit, and inherent in adopting one or more of the standard ethical theories, rather than using them primarily as sources of insights.

In the meantime, there are some matters that need prior attention. The ethical arguments in and about business take a variety of forms. Their practical expressions are increasingly appearing in the form of codes of practice. Chapter 4 assesses their uses and limitations.

4 | CODES OF ETHICS AND CODES OF PRACTICE

The growing popularity of codes

Key Issues drew attention to the increasing enthusiasm with which codes of ethics and codes of practice were being advocated and adopted by industry and in advice to industry from various bodies. The enthusiasm continues, and each day sees the publication or advocacy of a new code in one context or other. This chapter provides an expansion of the general argument of *Key Issues* about codes.

Codes are not universally adopted, and some company policy statements reject them on various grounds. My own view is that, on the whole, codes do provide a potentially helpful way forward in the matter of the systematic handling of values. The codes are usually, and reasonably, offered as ways of letting their audience know what is expected in terms of conduct and standards. When operated according to their express intent they introduce more predictability into what happens in industry. Mostly they express impeccable values, that is, values that are difficult to fault in terms of their being in tune with the prevailing views as to what constitutes 'best practice'. More problematic are the implied and omitted values, as will be seen from analysis of particular codes later.

Codes, codes of practice, codes of ethics, sets of working rules, model procedures and procedure agreements are all variants on the same theme. They are applied in various contexts, such as industrial relations, health and safety, and in general company policy statements. They are applied by governments as, for example, in highway and traffic codes. From time to time they are expressed as rules for the control of aggregate incomes (incomes policies), or of takeovers by one company of another. They are applied by trade associations and, most notably, by professional bodies. In so far as professional bodies for managers are concerned, such codes tend to be embryonic, but do appear to be taken more seriously, at least in the process of drafting, than they used to be. Codes can be very formal, as when statutes are set out systematically in an attempt to avoid inconsistencies. Sometimes codes are expressed attitudinally rather than formally, as in 'codes of honour', as something extra or even superior to the law, and often enforced more vigorously than the law itself, as was the case with duelling codes at one time. These informal and often unspoken codes are rarely replaced by the formal ones, whose fate often depends upon how well they correspond to the informal code. In effect, there is no important difference between a code of ethics and a code of practice, although is is arguable that there ought to be, from the point of view of the systematic handling of values.

An examination of specific codes is necessary, if only because of the wide range of attitudes towards them. A representative sample of attitudes would certainly include the idea that they are at best irrelevant to business, but more likely to be harmful, because they miss the 'main point' of business. On this view the 'purpose' or 'objective' of business is to make, or often to maximize profits, on the grounds that all persons should do what they are best at, and business is held to be best at making profits. The view has been presented and criticized often enough to make a detailed treatment, in addition to that offered in Chapter 3, unnecessary here. Helpful treatments can be found in Beauchamp and Bowie (1988), Velasquez (1988) and De George (1989).

The legitimacy of the idea that businesses have 'social responsibilities' is one of those old debates in which the holders of pro- and anti-attitudes often appear to have little or no intention of listening to each other. Supporters of one view (that businesses have no responsibilities other than to make profits and obey the law) point to what they take to be Adam Smith's authority, as expressed in his eighteenth-century masterpiece, *The Wealth of Nations*. Some authors, such as Sen (1987), see such a claim as a considerable distortion of Smith's views. Even if Smith had an uncompromising doctrine of 'the hidden hand', and could prove conclusively that if all businesses acted in the way indicated, economic welfare would be maximized, and even if all firms did act thus, the questions still remain open as to whether 'the public good' is merely an economic matter, whether economic outcomes are so easily specified, and whether 'the public good' is meaningful at all, rather than merely empty rhetoric, or a 'weasel' expression. Although much has been written on these matters, as witnessed by the huge list of references in Sen's book, there are no grounds for thinking that the matter has been settled within economic debate, or even that it could be.

The concept of profit maximizing is a highly metaphysical one, in which recognition of a profit maximizing situation is purely formal, with radical ambiguities as to the status of the general and the particular assumptions necessary to give a formal identification of a profit-maximizing situation. In particular the matter of short-run versus long-run considerations is radically insoluble, except as the arbitrary expression of value-preferences. Anything less than profit maximization appears to carry the implication that industry is wasteful of resources.

The problem becomes vastly more complicated when the notion is challenged that firms have single, clear 'goals', and that 'goals' are the kinds of things that firms can 'have'. Discussions of real firms reveal a multiplicity of goals or objectives that could be regarded as appropriately attributed to the firm. Each of these reveals further multiplicity of goals, expectations, objectives, claims, and much else, held by individuals and groups within firms. A problem is the identification of the authentic and legitimate goals. A second problem is pinning down the responsibilities. A third, and perhaps the most important, problem is on whose authority legitimate goals and actions can be identified.

Clearly, however technically-skilled the pseudo-Smith doctrine of profit maximization may be, the idea and its legitimacy are matters of value, and are open to debate on their own grounds. To paraphrase Hume, it is not contrary to reason to claim either that firms do or do not have responsibilities. If the claim is made that they do, then no particular set of responsibilities can be derived from any technical treatment of the behaviour, economic or other, of firms. The responsibilities of firms (or the absence of them) are, or ought to be, matters for grounded debate among those who are affected by the activities of companies. The technical and philosophical arguments are relevant to these potential debates, but cannot replace them. They are relevant, but could never be sufficient. As previously remarked, the goal of profit maximization is rarely explicitly claimed by companies, and rarely, if ever appears in formal company constitutions, memoranda, etc.

Our sample of attitudes towards codes would need to include the view that there is an implicit contract (as in the notion of a 'social contract') between business and the wider community. The terms of the contract need to be constantly revised in the light of circumstances. This view, or something close to it is discussed in Galbraith's *The New Industrial State* (1967), and in Beauchamp and Bowie (1988).

There seem to be some assumptions that are shared by opposing doctrines: that 'the public good' can be identified, and exists in the first place; that company objectives are unambiguous; that the matter can be settled by means of technical or philosophical argument without finding out what the participants want, and reconciling that with consistent, grounded, explicit moral/ethical princples. 'The public good' often functions as a 'weasel' expression that for analytical purposes is best omitted altogether: who is to identify it, and how, is as problematic as the notion of profit maximization.

If, therefore, it is not worthwhile to speak of codes in terms of whether they help firms to meet their (real or alleged) 'social responsibilities', and if it is merely dogmatic to assert that firms have no responsibility under the law other than to maximize profit, there is still the possibility of codes helping firms to ensure that they pursue legitimate activities in seeking profits, or in whatever else their directors are trying to do. Here, opinion is divided between, on the one side, drafters of government legislation that includes non-enforceable but legally-relevant codes, the executive councils of professional trade associations, and company boards who believe that codes can regulate extremely diverse behaviour; and on the other side, the critics who see the proliferation of codes as a kind of twilight legislation made and supported without due legal process or checks and balances. Studies of industrial relations codes have long shown a tendency for them to degenerate to become merely battlegrounds on which old conflicts are fought.

Whether the contents of codes of practice are truly ethical, or merely rules of skill and prudence remains to be discussed. Their prevalence in the major professions and their continued attraction to governments, companies and trade associations can safely be taken to indicate that they are often thought to have practical value by people with practical responsibilities.

The uses of codes of practice

Because codes of practice are normally offered as highly practical sets of rules and guidelines, they are not usually accompanied by detailed arguments as to their purposes and uses. They are typically expressed in a form that is well-protected from discussion, expressing aims in matter-of-fact language. Varieties of codes are so diverse that attempts to define them are particularly fraught with difficulties. On most accounts the Hippocratic Oath in medicine, the United Nations Declaration of Human Rights, the Geneva Convention, the American Penal Code, and the proverb, 'don't count your chickens before they are hatched' would be codes of practice. So would the agreement said to exist in criminal fraternities not to inform on each other. It is feasible to offer an account of their main features.

Codes tend to be expressions of mixtures of technical, prudential and moral imperatives

The inclusion of merely technical items alone would constitute part of the technique of a particular occupation. For instance, how to service a washing machine would be a technique. How the service engineer should behave towards customers would form part of an ethical code, but would be ethical only in that the code could be prudential, with ethical overtones. Such a code would be a technique from the point of view of a service training organization, which would have its own code in relation to what training contracts would be considered, and how the consultancy relationship between clients would be conducted. The principal use, ostensibly at least, of codes is to guide people, laying down rules to be followed. Their publication removes some doubt as to what is expected.

Codes vary in the extent and manner in which they can be supported or enforced

They range from, at one end of the scale, enforcement, with the sanction of obliging professionals to cease practice as a result of decisions by disciplinary committees, to expressions of disapproval from within or without a profession. The enforcement is sometimes weak in trade associations, for example when their expulsion of members who break the codes does not prevent the ex-members from practising the trade.

The single 'goal' of profit maximizing is neither admitted to nor aspired to

There is an ironical element in the contrast between this and so many academic and business disciplines which insist that companies do pursue maximum profit, ought to do so and would do well to use the academic techniques for that end, and that the advice is both value-free and worth having. It seems to me that companies and their representatives are more realistic than their academic advisers about what they are doing, its value content and its need for justification in terms of what are thought to be the legitimate interests of shareholders, customers, employees and the general public. Whether the attempts at justification typically succeed requires a great deal of research in depth comparable to the major studies of motivation, bureaucracy and restriction of output, such as those by Gouldner (1954), Roethlisberger and Dickson (1939a and b), Crozier (1964), Burns and Stalker (1961),

Lupton (1964) and Woodward (1965). Such studies are now unfashionable, and though it might be argued that they have had little direct effect on business behaviour, they have at least become part of the understanding of many educated managers.

Some companies have long used codes for setting standards of conduct across the company. Typically, codes incorporate a general statement of principles, such as:

Objectives: The objectives of the Group are to engage efficiently, responsibly and profitably. We seek a high standard of performance and aim to maintain a long-term position in each competitive environment . . . . Responsibilities are recognized to shareholders (to protect their investment and provide an acceptable return), to employees (to provide them with good and safe working conditions at competitive salaries, to promote the development of human talent, to encourage participation and responsibility), to customers (providing products of high value, using up-to-date skills), to society, as responsible corporate members of society, observing the laws that are applicable in the countries in which we operate.

CASE
25

A European multinational enterprise

An early example from a European multinational corporation is provided by Unilever in a pamphlet under the title *The Responsibilities of Unilever*:

The success or failure of a company – and Unilever is no exception – largely depends on its people, particularly its managers. Its reputation depends upon the way its managers behave. (Unilever, 1981, p. 2).

The statement adds some forthright moral commitments:

We never forget that our most important single responsibility is to keep Unilever profitable. Without profit we cannot discharge our obligations to shareholders, suppliers, customers and employees. Unilever's ability to create wealth in developed as well as developing countries increasingly depends on an understanding that our operations are beneficial to the countries concerned and that our behaviour is of the highest standard. (Unilever, op. cit., p. 10)

In the pamphlet, the company recognizes that the highest standards can be difficult to achieve, but express a commitment to the OECD and ILO guidelines for the behaviour of multinational enterprises, the United Nations Commission on Transnational Corporations, whose ground rules provide both for the conduct of international business, and for the conduct of governments towards business. The company expresses commitment to the free enterprise system and the market economy. It is committed to recruiting, where possible, employees with appropriate qualifications 'irrespective of differences in race, religion or nationality', and on page 6:

Though we do not take for granted a social structure which contravenes this objective, we cannot break the law or deviate offensively from local custom in pursuing the goal.

The pamphlet expresses a belief that employees have a right to be consulted on matters which 'directly affect their working environment' (p. 7), and a 'wish to be a good citizen . . . staying aloof from support for political parties' (p. 8), and operates an anti-bribery stance. It expresses a willingness to operate with legitimate groups such as trade associations.

In 1990 Unilever's employees numbered about three hundred thousand, operated in seventy-five countries, with a turnover of about fifty billion dollars. The multinational grew from a link between Margarine Unie, in the Netherlands, and the British firm, Lever Brothers. Its official values generate a devolved management style, 'which has grown up over the last 60 years' (*The Independent*, 3 May, 1990, p. 32, quoting Sir Michael Angus, joint chairman of Unilever).

Many codes include statements of responsibilities towards the environment, physical and social, of employees and of local communities. It can be seen from the statements that the values to which appeal is made include operating in a highly skilled way, managing the resources safely and responsibly, and prudently managing resources to promote safety, to avoid waste, and to apply the latest thinking on the environment, so that profit and responsibility can be achieved jointly. The possibility of conflicting values is rarely handled directly. Companies do not usually say that if no way can be found of avoiding environmental damage, or if they are not able to operate effective staff development programmes, they will consider closing down. The codes tend to hold that conflicting values can be dealt with even-handedly, and that such problems as do occur can be solved by applying more advanced methods. They imply that the company itself is the final arbiter on these matters, and rarely describe any methods by which independent sources may determine whether or not the powerful values to which the company subscribes are in fact put into practice. It is probable that they typically are, and that the aspirations are, on the whole, met. Reputations of companies have a bearing on this, and it is not likely that a company operating in a competitive environment can continue for long to permit major breaches, at least in cases where the disadvantaged parties have some ability to express their displeasure. Where this is not the case, the operation of the code is clearly highly dependent upon the presence of adequate determination and checks and balances within the firm. The frequent criticisms in some industries and contexts suggest that this is not always so. The fact that there is a variable gap between aspirations and reality does suggest, at the very least, that the publishing of a code is not by itself enough, and that enforcement procedures are necessary. The problem of who should draw up the code, which and whose values should be expressed in it, how they should be enforced, monitored and revised, is a recurring and far from resolved problem.

In Britain the promotion of corporate codes of practice is actively encouraged by the Institute of Business Ethics. From its own survey, the Institute has drawn up a model statement and code. It includes advice such as that the preface or introduction should be signed by the Chairman or Chief Executive Officer, or both, and that the areas covered should include the object of the business (including its role in society), commitment to share-holders, suppliers and employees, the wider community (for example, on environmental and safety standards, corporate giving to charities, and the ethical standards expected of employees) (Webley, 1988).

In introducing the model code, the Institute comments that the code should be the responsibility of the whole board, adding:

It is important that this is not left to an enthusiast on the board or delegated to the personnel manager but is seen as part of the responsibility of the whole board. Indeed those companies which value their statements and make use of them daily in business life have involved the most senior officers in drawing up and publishing such documents. In some cases, people throughout the company have been consulted. (Webley 1988, op. cit., p. 11)

In its model code, the Institute indicates that it ought to apply to all employees (rather than allowing only a few top managers to know of its existence and content, as appears often to be the case), and that '. . . any non-compliance will be considered a serious disciplinary matter' (Webley, 1988, op. cit., p. 12).

Reviewing the Institute's pamphlet, the *Industrial Relations Review and Report* (1988) notes:

While originating codes would appear to be a 'top down' exercise, the Institute of Business Ethics emphasises the need for wide consultation at the preparation stage. The IBE recommends that early consultation is needed with the heads of personnel and public relations, and with the company secretary or legal officer.

That company codes have both ethical content and intent seems clear enough from the examples used so far. What does remain problematic is the extent to which the published codes are truly 'ethical' codes as opposed, for example, to merely pragmatic, prudential or calculative ones. For example, if firms believe that they will 'do well by doing good', then ethics might be seen as another management technique:

'Integrity pays dividends.' 'But if it did not do so, would you abandon it?'

It would seem that there are few ways out once we are committed to the proposition that ethics pays. One way is to withhold recognition from evidence that indicates that this is not always the case. Another is to seek ways to force firms to apply integrity – 'It will go against you if you don't', through enforced codes.

An alternative solution, which I believe to be more realistic, is to say that it sometimes pays to be 'ethical', that sometimes it pays not to be, and sometimes it is possible to convert the latter type of case into an example of the former, but not always. These apply regardless of whether we define the term in either of the senses of the word used in the glossary and Chapter 1, of 'ethics 1', obeying a particular set of rules or *mores*, or ethics 2, applying systematic analysis to the values involved. The evidence from the cases seems to me to point to the conclusion that there are very major impediments that stand between company codes and the realization of the aspirations, and that these are by no means always within the control of the top managers. This is one indication of the need for external support for ethical codes and values. The existing *mores* that the company codes seek to incorporate (or, sometimes, to change) are themselves put in place and held there by many forces and institutions. These are the subjects of Chapters 5 and 6, and are thus not discussed in detail here. They include such matters as the codes of trade and professional associations. They include also a very large and increasing number of semi-official codes which in themselves do not have the force of law, but can be used as indications of wrong-doing if non-compliance is proved. Such codes include the Highway Code and the industrial relations codes of, to take a British example, the Advisory, Conciliation and Arbitration Service (ACAS). The European Court of Justice and the European Court of Human Rights also operate on this principle.

CASE
26

A professional institute

In Britain, the Institute of Personnel Management has published a professional code which covers a wide range of activities. The Institute's objectives are given as:

- To provide an association of professional standing for its members through which the widest possible exchange of views can take place.
- To develop a continuously evolving professional body of knowledge to assist its members to do their jobs more efectively in response to changing demands and conditions.
- To develop and maintain professional standards of competence.
- To encourage investigation and research in the field of personnel management and subjects related to it.
- To present a national viewpoint on personnel management and to establish and develop links with other bodies, both national and international, concerned with personnel. (Institute of Personnel Management (undated, about 1990), p. 3)

The booklet adds:

The Institute adopts a positive and initiating role, seeking to influence the occupational and social environments, legislation and management thinking – locally, nationally and internationally. It is the leading authority in the field of human resources and the guardian of high standards in the practice of personnel management. IPM members commit themselves to these objectives and to various codes of practice issued by the Institute. Members are concerned with the maintenance of good practice within the profession; they accept fully that their responsibility at work is to their employer and, within that commitment, to the organization's employees. (Loc. cit.)

The Institute expects its members to have attained a body of knowledge and to have attained a level of professional competence. Specific areas cover: resourcing, rewards and benefits, employee relations (including employee involvement and communications; morale and climate at work; employment law; representative structures, relationships with trade unions, and negotiation); training and development (including 'the continuous development of all employees') and the working environment, referring to health, safety and welfare, working conditions (internal and external to the organization).

The prescribed principles of behaviour are given as:

1 Confidentiality

Personnel practitioners will respect their employer's requirements for the confidentiality of information entrusted to them, including the safeguarding of information about current, past and prospective employees. They will insure the privacy and confidentiality of personal information to which they have access or for which they are responsible, subject to any legal rights of employees in respect of information relating to themselves.

2 Equal opportunities

Personnel practitioners will promote non-discriminatory employment practices in line with current legislation.

3 Fair dealing

Personnel practitioners will establish and maintain fair, reasonable and equitable standards of treatment of individuals by their employer.

4 Self development

Personnel practitioners will continuously update their skills and knowledge in respect of developments and legislation in the personnel field and the impact of technical, economic and social change on people at work.

5 Development of others

Personnel practitioners will seek to achieve the fullest possible development of the capabilities of individual employees to meet present and future requirements of the organization, and encourage others to develop themselves.

6 Accuracy of advice and guidance

Personnel practitioners will maintain high standards of accuracy in the advice and information given to the employer and employees in the fields for which they are responsible.

7 Counselling

Personnel practitioners will be prepared to act in a counselling role to individual employees, pensioners and dependents of deceased employees in fields where they have competence, and where appropriate refer to other professionals or helping agencies.

8 Integrity

Personnel practitioners will at all times act in accordance with this code of conduct and the duties that they owe to employers and employees. Where there is a conflict between these obligations, the practitioner will make a personal decision after considering the options, of which resignation may be one.

9 Legality

Personnel practitioners will not act in any way which would knowingly countenance, encourage or assist unlawful conduct either by employer or employees.

10 Professional conduct

Personnel practitioners will at all times endeavour to enhance the standing and good name of the profession. Adherence to the principles of the Institute's codes of practice is a prerequisite of this aim. (Loc. cit., p. 4)

It is clear that in drafting the code, the Institute has taken into account the major pressures that can produce, or have produced in the past, ethical issues between corporations and personnel. The values that practitioners are expected to adhere to are clear, and the Institute recognizes that there may be circumstances in which the practitioners can no longer reconcile adherence to the code with continuation in their present employment. The values include respect for the rule of law, equality of opportunity, the principles of natural justice, principles based on rights, even-handedness, and confidentiality.

All this clearly represents an advance in terms of what I earlier called the 'good' values as generally included in the various national and international codes. These are the 'ethics 1' values that have emerged as being capable of satisfying parties with different interests and aspirations, and if generating orderly and relatively peaceful operation of business in the product, resource and labour markets.

The development should be seen in the light of the preceding situation up to the early 1980s when few formal, self-consciously ethical codes existed. They can in part be seen as a natural development, as the limitations of management and business as an unconnected set of value-free techniques have become plainer, and partly from awareness of the growing number of ethical issues that reached the courts and the headlines throughout the 1980s. These have often but by no means exclusively been associated with behaviour at what used to be called 'the commanding heights of industry', or more generally, 'the top'. In the late 1980s a series of enquiries, investigations, frauds and collapses had appeared in many countries, in manufacturing industries and in services, particularly the financial sector. They have ranged from individual frauds to collapses of major banks, massive overcharging on defence contracts, major bribery accusations, and prevention of professional 'watchdogs' such as auditors from performing their duties. Anxieties that professional bodies are often unable to support individuals such as senior managers when faced with knowledge of malpractices are raised from time to time (for example see Kenny, 1976; Velasquez, 1988; Irvine, 1988).

What many of the examples used by these authors tend to show is that the ability to encourage or enforce the widely-accepted values incorporated in the codes is limited by the extent to which the code-generating institution has control of entry into or exit from the profession, and the ability of members of the societies or institutes to draw upon support from their professional bodies in case of conflicts with employers. In some cases, as things stand, the conflict must be resolved entirely by the individual concerned, and the problem then arises as to how far individuals should be expected to go in support of codes that can offer no effective reciprocal support. Corporate whistleblowers are rarely popular, and indeed, may be rejected most emphatically by thos/ the whistleblowing is intended to help. In this context, distinguishes between 'internal' (within the firm) whistleblowing, and 'external' whistleblowing. He notes:

The latter generally harms the firm while the former has the potential for benefiting the firm through reduction of liability and reputation costs and through better relationships with employees. In spite of this important difference between the two forms of whistleblowing, firms have traditionally discouraged both. Concerns about inside whistle-blowing include its impact on confidentiality, the possibility of improper motives on the part of those making disclosures, and the potential negative impact of an environment supporting internal whistleblowing on the operations and reputation of the firm.

The standard objections to encouragement of internal whistleblowing either don't cancel out the value to be gained from such activity or can be controlled by proper design and administration. Confidentiality, which means that one may disclose anonymously, is essential to the operation of an effective system. (Tom Dunfee, in G. Enderle, B. Almond and A. Argandoña (eds), 1990, p. 137)

The operation of professional codes can thus place individuals at odds with their employers. Some professional institutions have seriously considered, and supplied, legal advice 'hotlines', and have considered supplying some forms of professional indemnity insurance. It is far from unknown for whistleblowers who act in accordance with the professional standards expected of them to find serious impediments in the way of securing a new job after the almost inevitable severance from the original employer. One reason among many for this is that loyalty is a value that is very highly prized by companies, including prospective employers, and whistleblowing can be seen as an indication of a propensity to disloyalty. Another is that whistleblowing can put those who did not blow the whistle in an embarrassing position. If there *was* something wrong and they did nothing about it, their own complicity can be called into question. The whistleblower then appears, through the informal, unwritten, and very powerful codes, to have 'let the side down'. Their loyalty (or at least, their non-threat) to the employer must then be demonstrated by distancing themselves from the boat-rocking whistleblower.

The problems do not end there. In some cases, individuals believe that they have cause to complain not so much against their employer, but against their bureaucratic superiors, and sometimes against the management services professionals (inclu-ding personnel professionals) who support these bureaucratic superiors. Some detailed cases in this area are presented in later chapters, but for present purposes, the problem can be seen as one in which agents for the corporation, for whatever reason (usually connected with internal politics and the career structure), conceal or distort evidence as it passes up the chain of authority. Thus, the people at the top of the organization may find themselves defending indefensible decisions, initially through ignorance, and subsequently through what might be called a 'will to win'. There seems to have been an element of this in many of the financial services lawsuits in recent years, including what became known as 'the Guinness affair', in which the will to win becomes a dominant value, replacing those of established codes, and even of concepts of natural justice, or responsibility. These effects are seen in industrial relations cases in which a few companies appear to adopt a 'money is no object' stance, pursuing cases through the tribunals, and, in some cases, the European Court of Human Rights, in order not to be seen as weakly reversing a decision once it has been made.

Where the individuals concerned are not members of a professional body, the codes do not apply, but where they are members, a different set of problems emerges. One professional institute consulted in this study reported that the officials and committees were aware of development work that needed to be done. A representative gave the following considered view:

What we lack at this stage is the defined procedure which should be followed by anyone who feels that [our] codes have not been adhered to. This is currently the subject of intensive discussions, and will shortly be subject to widespread consultation [within the professional body]. At the moment, complaints are handled by the Secretary [of the professional body], and dealt with on an individual basis. We receive one or two such complaints a year at present but we feel that we need the defined procedure in order to ensure for consistency . . . . The legal implications of introducing this new procedure are also in the process of being explored.

Another institution made the point that applying sanctions to professional members found to be in breach of the codes could open the doors to a great deal of litigation, which could be damaging and very expensive; further, making general ethical statements in the wake of legislation or litigation affecting their members or category of professionals, whether members or not, could damage the credibility of the professional body, giving the impression of high-sounding expressions of principle, but too little action. The other horn of the dilemma could involve a dramatic fall in membership if such action were taken, and the organization came to be perceived as punitive towards, rather than supportive of members. One possible action could be to seek the kind of status for the ethical codes of professional bodies that has been granted to those of, say, the European Charter of Human Rights, industrial relations codes of practice, incomes policy codes, and those of financial services bodies in some countries. In this way, breaking or ignoring the code would not be an offence in itself, but would weigh heavily in any legal or disciplinary actions.

If the codes themselves require that the actions of people subject to them should be judged as to whether natural justice was applied, the same criterion, at least, should be applied in any complaints or disciplinary procedures, to all sides of the issue. But all of this presupposes that the codes have themselves been drawn up, monitored and revised according to sound and agreed ethical principles. To my knowledge, none of the codes seen so far contain explicit reference to this. Specifically, are codes to be primarily protective of the profession, punitive, encouraging and supportive, utilitarian in that they seek to maximize some gain (such as 'social welfare'), based on duties (e.g. to uphold the codes, even if it means that they impact unfairly in particular cases), or based on rights, so that rights can be established even at the expense of sacrifices in other rights? This is a serious matter for discussion in the context of the European Social Charter (printed in full in Chapter 9) in which objections have been made that the fine principle of establishing equal employment rights to part-time workers could damage overall employment prospects, implying a conflict among important values that can only be settled by deciding that some values (for example, growth) should have priority over equality of treatment at work for employees with differentially-based claims.

So far we have considered company codes, multinational corporation codes, pay and traffic codes, those of professional bodies and those of supranational bodies such as the EC. They differ in a number of ways, in the range of 'stakeholders' and other affected parties consulted in the drawing up of the codes, and in who is privileged to know of the codes' existence, and of their contents. They differ in terms of degree and manner of enforcement and of the extent to which affected parties can withhold commitment to all or part of the code. Clearly, the relative powers of the parties is a relevant factor in the explanation of these differences, but the sources of this relative power need to be explained. One explanation which has been hinted at, in the context of whistleblowers and of general explanations of the gap between aspirations and achievements in putting values into practice in business, is to do with informal codes. Another is money. If professional institutes can be concerned at the potential costs of litigation, then so can individuals. Unfairly-dismissed employees not only have to find money for representation, but also to secure the means of subsistence. At least in some countries, the resources available through the state are limited, and difficult to secure, often proceeding through a quasi-judicial process in which the cash-supplying agency is also the arbiter of merit. As with whistle-blowers, unfairly-dismissed employees can be regarded (however innocent they may be) as 'troublemakers', carrying problems of uncertainty as to the fairness of references needed from the employer who was guilty of the unfair dismissal.

The potency of money is recognized, of course, in the sustained attention afforded to financial services by governments and the mass media, and the codes, rules, skills, and, frequently, lawsuits that occur in that sector. Some contemporary discussions of codes in operation in financial services industries in Europe can be noted here, pending a fuller discussion in Chapters 12 and 13.

The European carried a useful review of one aspect of financial services that has attracted much attention from governments, the mass media and learned journals alike: insider dealing. According to Tim Castle, under the heading, 'All EC countries must outlaw the unacceptable face of capitalism by June 1991':

Insider dealing is the unacceptable face of capitalism. It sums up all the aspects of anti-social behaviour that regulators try to keep out of the stock market. Until France brought in laws in 1970 it was legal throughout Europe to buy and sell company shares on the basis of privileged, or 'insider' information. Since then the regulations have become tougher and now western European countries without some sort of statutory prohibitions against the practice are the exception. Only Luxemburg, Italy and West Germany have no legal penalties. However, West German stock exchanges have had a strict code of conduct on irregular dealing since 1970 and Italy has included insider dealing provisions in the large banking act now sitting before parliament.

Writing before the outcome of the 'Guinness affair' in a British Crown Court, in which four defendants were given prison sentences in August, 1990, he added:

European jailers are still waiting for their first insider-dealing guests. In the US – where the origins of the insider dealing laws go back to the Thirties, the Securities and Exchange Commission has recorded some spectacular successes. Its most notable victory came in 1986 when it began its case against Ivan Boesky, who was fined $100 million, barred from working in the securities industry and subsequently jailed for three years. (*The European*, June 15–17, 1990, p. 21)

The essential argument against insider dealing is that people often have privileged information, for instance that a merger is to be announced that will alter the value of shares in a particular company, or that there is to be a larger or smaller than expected dividend, or that a major government contract is to be announced. The objections to insider dealing are based on the idea that the rules of the investment game should be the same for all investors. If insiders can gain from privileged knowledge, and even influence share values, they are profiting unfairly from their privileges. There are counter-arguments, for example that insider dealing is a 'victimless crime', and that in any case, the actions can only be reduced, not eliminated and that many opportunities still exist for some to continue the practice with impunity, but these have been overruled.

The essence of the codes, whether voluntary or statutory, is an attempt to define insider dealing, usually in terms of when knowledge is received, requiring isolation of different dealers within the same organization so that information cannot be passed on, prohibition of dealing by others likely to trade, and seeking to avoid the possibility of trading in shares using the privileged knowledge by members of the family of the holder of the privileged knowledge. There has been much discussion on whether the codes should be voluntary, by 'industry self-regulation' or statutory, but even those countries which opt for voluntary codes and self-regulation also retain statutory powers, and have been more inclined to use them recently. Again, the principles are constantly set against the likelihood of their becoming operational. This problem shades into the related topic of enforcement policy: should a large supply of 'watchdogs' (whether internal, in the form of 'compliance officers', or external, in the form of control agencies) be established to raise the likelihood of detection, or should offenders face exemplary sentences 'pour encourager les autres', making people less likely to risk the offence for fear of the severity of punishment? It will be suggested that for both enforcement and encouragement of compliance, in these areas, as in the areas of industrial relations, professional practice, company and multinational corporation codes, the sincerity of the promoters can be taken for granted, but that the causes of the gaps between aspiration and achievement have much to do with a large variety of 'intervening processes', both formal and informal.

Summary and conclusions

Codes are increasingly popular. They incorporate and attempt to put into practice, usually, a mixture of technical, prudential and moral rules and principles. If they do not have this mixture, they are usually called something else, such as 'instructions', 'philosophies', or 'safety instructions', 'precautions', etc. They are *ethical* codes when the values they include (formally or by implication) refer to *prima facie* duties – what Kant called 'categorical imperatives'. These duties typically include promotion of 'good', or 'benefits', 'welfare', 'rights', 'obligations', 'duties', or prohibit practices and actions held generally to be destructive of these.

These different kinds of values – skill, prudential and moral – are analytically distinct, for the reasons shown by R.M. Hare (1963) in *Freedom and Reason*, but in practice they are interconnected. For instance it is rightly regarded to be a *duty* to act prudently, and with appropriate skill. Failure to do so can rightly be seen as negligence, and often culpable. I would argue that there is a stronger duty to know our ethical (moral) obligations than there is to know our technical obligations. The latter are, and have long been, typically codified to the extent that the strong impression from business and management literature is that the technical norms are the only ones that matter. In extreme positivist arguments it is often held, without recognizing the irony, that moral values cannot be treated systematically, but there is a duty to operate technical values at a high level of skill. These arguments are discussed in detail in *Key Issues*, and are not repeated here.

The most likely reasons for the increasing popularity of codes are:

1 The illusion that business can be reduced to a set of techniques can no longer be sustained, as a result of the rise of consumer pressures that reject the values encapsulated in some products and processes, including the technical ones. 'Environmentally friendly' products are now increasingly demanded, with added requirements that they should not involve testing on animals, that the conditions of work, and even the countries with whom trade is conducted, should be acceptable to consumers.
2 Scandals and litigation, heavily concentrated in some groups of industries.
3 Juxtaposition of different value-sets originating from different countries within the EC. Normally, in the past, differing value-sets between groups and countries could, with some plausibility, be written down as 'subjective', or the proper concern only of the country concerned. The bringing together of differing value-sets is not sufficient by itself to raise demands for codes and the like. A more potent cause is the fact that the holders of the different sets are in a position to enforce their values,

possibly generating win-lose situations that could lead to conflict. Throughout history there have been many examples of opposing codes, but where there is a major disparity in power, the codes of the weak have rarely been seen at the same time as the prevailing values, even if they have later become so, as with the rise of the great religions.

It is possible that some modest influence can be attributed to writers on business ethics, but it is more likely, in my view, that such writing is typically ignored until concerns have arisen from more powerful causes. There is not, as yet, a free market in ideas. They tend to be filtered through a mass of institutional pressures and norms. This can no doubt help to generate stability in the dominant values, but is also a potent source for missed opportunities, as demonstrated by many of the cases in this collection which involve innovation, technical or otherwise.

Codes can be useful in that:

1 they inform people of what is expected of them;
2 they give guidance as to how it can be done;
3 they express values that many participants aspire to, or claim to do so;
4 they can and often do raise standards.

Their limitations are:

1 Their expression of values can be vague, general and bland.
2 The ethical content can be minimal. Although it would be difficult to argue that ethical codes are or ought to be designed for purging people or for providing opportunities for displaying their moral worth, if people only do 'the right thing' because they are sheltered by a code, or by the backing of some powerful body, their actions are not likely to be done with much conviction, and may even be perfunctory. This provides one reason why so many people are sceptical as to their worth. To paraphrase G.B. Shaw: 'professional codes exist to protect the professionals from lawsuits, not to protect the clients from sub-standard professional behaviour.' Even in this context, the morally strongest persons can easily have higher standards than those of the code (and especially of informal codes), and may thus find themselves at odds ethically, with their profession. Claiming higher loyalties is a common form of ethical argument, and there is much evidence from the cases of conflict between personal and professional codes. Despite all this it is clear that managerial groups are beginning to aspire to the standards in the liberal professions, even when their members

are already members of various professional bodies.

3 When codes are voluntary they apply only to some of the relevant persons. This can put them at a disadvantage, and let the promoters of the codes 'off the hook'. There is some evidence that the rise of consumerism is having the effect of allowing those who operate according to published codes to gain trading advantages from doing so – but (also those who claim to do so, but in fact do not practice what they claim).

4 Enforcement of morals to some extent denatures them. There is an inescapable voluntary element in ethical behaviour. We have already seen that merely following the crowd and doing what is fashionable has no moral content, except to the extent that it can be appraised in ethical terms. The enforcement of morals, without agreement, is the enforcement of one person's, or one group's values on another.

5 If codes are not enforced, their effectiveness can be reduced, sometimes to zero. This is another version of the 'freedom and reason' argument. Most arguments, from compulsory union membership to professional standards, state or imply that there is a moral obligation to comply, and that this is based on explicit or implied terms in their choice of occupation. Rarely is compliance demanded, officially at least, on grounds of pure power or force. Even the use of force to gain compliance is usually justified, however, or at least explained in moral-sounding terms suggesting that if people really understood the situation, they would readily comply.

6 Non-enforced codes can easily be evaded, even when pretending to operate them. Examples of cases taken to industrial tribunals in Britain demonstrate that 'unfair dismissal' decisions are often given by tribunals against companies who claim to be applying the code published by the Advisory, Conciliation and Arbitration Service (Whincup, 1990; Lord Wedderburn, 1986). The ease or difficulty of access to the tribunals, and the speed with which they are allowed to operate, as well as the possibility of a determined company spending large sums of money, can all provide a major difficulty in enforcement of labour codes. This is reinforced when dismissed employees cannot afford to seek redress, and cannot obtain work on the grounds that they might be 'troublemakers', even when a tribunal finds in their favour.

We need to be able to explain why these serious weaknesses in codes persist, and to suggest ways in which they may be overcome. One constructive proposal from David Huddy for using a register of values, codes and philosophies, linked to a quasi-market procedure, was discussed in Chapter 3. This, to my mind plausible, proposal needs to be taken seriously.

An additional area in which voluntarism and the discipline generated by openness would repay investigation is the matter of identifying, and working with, rather than against the informal, usually unpublished and unspoken codes that can intervene between the high aspirations expressed by companies, and the realities of business life. Such analysis will, I believe, show that the excuses for doing nothing that are provided by 'naive scepticism' and by cynically-expressed rejections of business ethics are far from sound. Additional possibilities are thus opened up, in which codes can play a significant part, even though by themselves, they are likely to achieve relatively little in terms of consistent improvements in business standards. This is the subject of Chapter 5.

5 ETHICAL STRUCTURES FOR INDUSTRY

Standards of conduct vary between industries. Methods of enforcement of standards also vary, ranging from statutes to semi-official codes, formally-published, voluntary codes, with varying sanctions, and processes which are discussed in the various literatures under such headings as 'corporate cultures', 'groupthink', 'group dynamics', 'informal systems', 'sub-cultures', and 'infrastructures'. Standards vary between industries, over time, and between countries, tribes, sects and many other groupings.

The problems arising from international standards are little different, logically, from those that occur within national boundaries, and between industries and groupings over time. It is no more difficult, ethically, to establish a common set of ground-rules for the operation of multinationals (see Tom Donaldson, 1989; and Case 25, Chapter 4) and for the operation of industries across national boundaries in the EC, for example, than it is to identify standards for operation within one country. The simple matter is that values within countries and within many groupings in countries are varied enough to raise all the important ethical issues. Claims that different countries cannot be compared because they have different histories and cultures, or that their codes and practices cannot be evaluated ethically, are implausible – it is sufficient to note the deep variations which can be found within national boundaries in ethical standards, with the implication that differences in national standards, and in industry standards within one country, are all due to other factors. Chief among these is the degree of willingness to confront the structural and attitudinal factors that encourage, but do not determine the variations. Conflicts of interest do occur across national boundaries, of course, as was seen in the conflicts between some French and some British farmers in the 1980s. Similar conflicts occur within national boundaries also.

CASE
27 **Britain and the 'Social Charter'**

The wide adoption of the principles of the UN Declaration of Human Rights, and the near unanimous adoption throughout the EC (the exception being the United Kingdom) of the European Social Charter at the end of 1989 demonstrates that a common set of values can be reached by agreement. Even the United Kingdom's refusal to adopt the European Social Charter has been explained as not due to a disagreement in principle, but to a claim that job creation is an agreed priority, and that some of the provisions of the Charter would, for what are held to be technical reasons arising from the operation of labour markets, lead to the opposite effects to those intended. Thus the provisions in the Charter have been argued to be likely to reduce employment:

Some of these general principles and priorities are reflected in proposals that the Commission is bringing forward under its *social action programme* of measures. The programme comprises around 50 separate measures to make good the declaration of intent embodied in the *Social Charter* which was agreed by 11 member states in Madrid last year (the UK did not sign the *Social Charter*). In so far as proposals are compatible with the general principles on jobs and subsidiarity, the UK supports them. On the information available so far, the Government is expecting to be able fully to support around a third of the total number of measures, subject to negotiation over detail. There is a further third where further clarification is needed before a position can be taken. However, the remaining third of the proposals are, in the view of the Government, incompatible with the priority of jobs and the principle of subsidiarity. These include two directives to regulate part-time work. The Government does not accept that EC legislation is practical or desirable in this area. A recent survey showed that a great majority of part-time workers worked part-time because they preferred to do so; and that only 7% worked part-time because they could not find full time jobs. This indicates that employers and employees alike benefit from the flexibility provided by part-time and temporary employment. The directives would have the effect in the UK of both increasing the cost of employing part-time and temporary workers, and of increasing the amount of regulation governing such workers . . . . In the Government's view, a likely consequence of such regulation would be to *increase* unemployment as employers sought to contain costs by cutting back on staff. (UK, Department of Trade and Industry, Autumn 1990, *Single Market News*, p. 11)

The principles to which reference was made at the beginning of the quotation were:

• freedom to move around the Community for work;
• freedom of establishment for business purposes in another Community country;
• equal opportunities for men and women at work;
• the importance of training;

- access to information on opportunities for employment;
- high standards of health and safety protection at work.

Given that the priority agreed to be highest is the creation of jobs, the British Government invoked the principle of subsidiarity, that action should not be taken at Community level unless it could only be achieved by action at that level.

It is clear from the quotation that the dissent from the Social Charter by the British Government was explained in terms of consistency with agreed aims and priorities, and in terms of consequences that were believed to be incompatible with the principles enunciated. At this point I do not attempt to assess the truth of the factual claims. It is enough to point out that it is possible for representatives of countries with different histories, cultures, traditions and much else to agree to a very wide range of ethical principles.

In the general literature of ethics, this problem area is usually discussed in terms of objectivity versus subjectivity. Subjectivists hold that all moral attitudes are merely a matter of taste. Objectivists hold that some moral matters are obligatory whatever anyone or everyone thinks. In extreme forms of subjectivism, there are, and can be no moral obligations, because morality (ethics) is held to be beyond rational debate. In extreme forms of objectivism, revealed or otherwise claimed truths are seen as true beyond question. Consideration of any actual moral discussion will demonstrate arguments drawing attention to agreed principles, attempts to show that particular proposed actions do or do not fit the principles, and that the facts of the matter do or do not support the stance taken by opposing sides. It is possible to accept that there is a germ of truth in both sides of this great divide, but to reject the basis on which the debate is traditionally conducted. Thus, Hare remarks:

Moral philosophers of the present time, with a few honourable exceptions, all seem to think that they have to take sides on the question of whether 'objectivism' or 'subjectivism' is the correct account of the status of moral judgments. Most of them have the ambition to establish their objectivity, that being the more respectable side to be on; but quite a number are attracted by subjectivism (sometimes without any clear distinction of meaning called 'relativism') as being more go-ahead and freethinking. Hardly any of them give any clear idea of how they are using the terms 'objective' and 'subjective'; and, almost none realises that, in the most natural senses of the words, moral judgments are neither objective nor subjective, and that belief that they have to be one or the other is the result of a fundamental error (viz. descriptivism) which both objectivists and subjectivists, in one of the senses of those words, commit . . . . (Hare, 1981, p. 206)

It has been noted for a long time that almost any rule that is adopted as a moral requirement in one group at one time can be, or has been rejected or replaced by its contrary in some other group or at some other time. It has likewise been noted that what seem to uninformed outsiders to be morally reprehensible customs among some remote groups or remote times can be explained not in terms of arbitrary choice of values, but in terms of factual beliefs about what is the case, and what are the causes and consequences of actions. It perhaps ought to be recognized more often that the traditional practices in some cultures are in fact objected to by some members, and this has long been so — long enough to indicate that the grounds of equity on which some outsiders may object to (or approve of) practices within other groups or within other countries are often those appealed to by dissident insiders. In short, the existence of huge variations in the dominant values in different times and places does not prove that 'anything goes'. If it proves anything, it is that dominant groups can display great variety in their peculiarities.

This reduces the problem of subjectivity to manageable proportions: different cultures, nations, groups, individuals are entitled to adopt different values and customs. Ethics provides no methods of proving that one set of values is inherently superior to another. It provides no grounds for imposing one set upon another, apart from the logical one discussed by Hare (1963) that even if people are free to prescribe whatever values they like, such prescriptions of values can be incoherent or inconsistent, and thus logically have no more claim to be taken seriously than do inconsistent statements about matters of fact. Ethical arguments, unlike the major ethical theories (and perhaps some less well-known ones) can be, and often are refuted conclusively.

A second reason why an ethical claim can be overruled is that it breaks *prima facie* obligations, e.g. to tell the truth, obey the rules of natural justice, etc. A third reason is consent. If people are free to prescribe what values they like (subject to consistency) then it applies equally to the recipients of a practice as it does to the actors or instigators. Therefore the adoption of one set of values in preference to another also requires consent for legitimacy. Where consent is withheld on rational grounds, there are practical problems about whose values shall prevail. The strength of democratic solutions is that, at least in principle, they rely on agreement on procedures: a 'wrong' decision, properly made becomes acceptable, whereas a 'right' decision, improperly made is problematic. 'Wrong' decisions, improperly made can cause major and virtually insoluble ethical issues, but, as can be seen from some of the case studies, can often be accepted without question. Why this is so is a major problem in business ethics in its own right.

To sum up the theoretical points: ethical rules *can* be established, for instance, on the grounds of consistency and coherence, natural justice (i.e. the *prima facie* duties), and consent. It is thus possible to find practices such as suttee (immolation of widow on husband's funeral pyre) in some countries, slavery in others, and all 'unfair industrial practices' as ethically unsound according to these principles. By the same token, it is possible to recommend some sets of values, as is done in the codes, including, for example, the European Social Charter. It is also possible to criticize them, on grounds as discussed above. Such criticism can be constructive and supportive as well as disapproving. Any individual has a right to do so. Whether individuals have a right to be taken seriously is determined only by their obeying the same rules by which they make the criticisms of the current codes, norms, etc. As we have seen, one of the most serious flaws in most codes is the lack of provision within the individual systems in which they operate for constructive debate between the originators and the other relevant parties, both on the content and the operation. This explains why so many cases appear before courts and tribunals, even though covered by elaborate internal (and often external) codes of practice. It explains, in part, the difficulties faced by 'whistleblowers' who wish to draw attention to hidden breaches of rules and codes.

Most moral argument as it happens is addressed to an assumed common set of beliefs and values. The British refusal to sign the European Social Charter does not reject the values enshrined therein. Instead, it says, in effect, that there are priorities within the values expressed in the Charter, but that there are factual doubts as to the efficiency of some of the measures to which all are agreed, despite agreement in principle to the measures. This is typical of moral arguments.

This leads to a set of propositions, explaining why the values expressed in codes, chairmen's speeches and public relations statements are so free from obvious flaws – they are based on what appear to be agreed ends. The codes, etc., state the ethical principles (usually in somewhat vague terms), and are addressed principally to the means. In doing so, they often entangle ethical and factual matters, but that is a different problem. The truth about the means usually requires a great deal of detailed technical and factual knowledge, and it is the control of this factual knowledge that most ethical arguments turn on. In terms of the traditional formal logic, the major premises are taken to be agreed, but the factual premises are problematic. The 'ends' themselves are frequently more problematic than they seem, in that they often assume an agreed philosophical outlook. They often contain incompatible prescriptions and rules, with little guidance as to their resolution. In business codes the outlook of utilitarianism usually dominates, in uneasy alliance with principles of rights and duties. It is normally difficult for insiders and outsiders alike to raise fundamental issues in relation to such codes, which are protected in many ways.

Several of the cases in this book show examples of skilful setting of the agenda so that some matters, held to be important by certain 'stakeholders', cannot be effectively raised. It will be seen that this is not necessarily deliberate, and does not imply that the eventual decisions are unacceptable, or fail all of the many 'ethics' tests, such as those discussed so far in this chapter, of consistency, coherence, natural justice (*prima facie* duties) and consent. (Other criteria are considered in Chapter 7.) Examples are provided by the changing arguments for and against the use of nuclear power, from emphasis on cheapness (denied by opponents) to the prudential argument that other forms of energy will (or will not) be sufficient for future needs, to the cleanness and greenness of the method of generation and of waste disposal. Another example, from agriculture, is the old argument that large fields are necessary for efficient, low-cost farm produce (appeals to utilitarianism, to the prudential threat of food shortages, and rights of agriculture to at least its current share of the national income). Similar arguments are used to justify public financial support for replacement of hedges, including soil erosion, for example. Pouring raw sewage into the sea continues, its justification changing from a claim that the sea is an inexhaustible natural cleanser, to the utilitarian and prudential argument that a change of practice would be too expensive. Thus are the relevant facts adapted to meet the need to support pre-existing preferences, routines, mutual obligations, career structures and much else. Anti-military attitudes common among some unions wither away among members whose livelihoods depend on continued military spending.

We are now in a position to explain the gap first noted in Chapter 1, between aspirations and actual outcomes. The primary causes are not 'human greed' or the amoral imperatives of the market. People develop commitments to ways of doing things, and to ways of life that require huge efforts of will to change. It is easier to change the justifications for what is done than it is to change practice. In this way, many defensive processes are set up. They explain why the 'green' movement has been slow to develop, even against mounting evidence, and why some 'green' claims appear to be phoney. It explains why attempts to raise innovation levels are so disappointing.

CASE
28 **Supporting innovation**

The next example has been provided by Mr Frank Edwards, inventor and principal of Twentyfirst Century Actuators and Sensors, of Cardiff. The correspondence is with some companies and some major suppliers of funds for technical innovation. The funding bodies have as a major objective the encouragement of technology-based innovations, and support in bringing them to market. The invention is an advanced prosthetic arm that is lightly engineered, touch-sensitive, and inexpensive, with fully-articulated fingers, its welfare prospects providing for only one out of a huge range of applications.

From a development agency, March, 1990:

Dear Frank,
    I write to confirm my telephone statement that [we have] decided on the basis of [our] investigations not to make an offer of finance to TCAS.
    I regret to say that whilst prospects may be good in the animation area, I have been unable to substantiate the optimism [of a market research agency] across a broad range of applications as projected in the business plan. This was particularly disappointing when following up individuals named in your supporting documentation. As I have indicated in the past, a proposed wealth of applications was the basis for our interest.
    I believe you would be best advised to take note of the response we have received and to focus on specific animation-related applications where, albeit of insufficient potential to interest [us], the reception to your product does appear more positive than in other sectors.
    I wish you well with your deliberation.
                                    [Yours sincerely]

From a funding agency:

Dear Mr Edwards
Prosthetic Arm Invention
    The [professional body] have referred the above invention to us.
    We have examined the details with interest but feel that any patent granted will not contain sufficient depth of cover to provide a successful licence that would warrant [agency] support.
    On that basis we regret we will be unable to offer the support you require. I am sorry that we cannot be more helpful but would thank you for showing it to us.
                                    [Yours sincerely]

To the funding agency:

14th Nov 1990
re. Bionic Arm Project.

Following your conversation with [representative of business research company] of [the business research company] he has asked me to contact you to expand on the investment figure included in our paper.

In essence there are five main sections to the operation with the following estimated costs:

  (i)   DEVELOPMENT/Product testing;
 (ii)   COMPONENT MANUFACTURE;
(iii)   ASSEMBLY;
 (iv)   WHOLESALE MARKETING;
  (v)   EXPORT.

The total figure in the document we sent to you included an estimate of the sums needed to set up a manufacturing facility. Operations (ii)–(iv) can be contracted out. This would naturally adjust the level of investment required.

One option is to have the entire manufacturing done under license. In this latter case the investment to prototype stage would be about 250k.

We estimate the market to be very large, and the cost of this more advanced product will be much lower than that of competing products.

As the possible variations of structure and finance are extensive it would be mutually beneficial if we met to discuss the options in greater detail.

I would like to take this opportunity to thank you for taking the time to review our project.

[Yours sincerely]
Frank Edwards

From the funding agency, a week later:

Dear Mr Edwards
Re: Bionic Arm Project

We were surprised to receive your letter dated 14th November, addressed to Mr X [member of the funding body staff].

We think there has been some misunderstanding. When [we] received your proposal it was reviewed by several of my colleagues and it was decided that this was not a situation in which [we] could help.

In these circumstances, if we could put the proposer in contact with someone who might be interested we would do so, in this case we could not.

In our view it is very unlikely that you would be able to raise the funds you require from the commercial sector and your only chance would be to interest some grant giving organisation. A number of Universities have experience in developing prostheses and these know what organisations support research. Again, we think it is very unlikely that the level of funds you have requested to develop your idea could be found, even if you involve a University.

[Yours sincerely]
[Official]

To the funding agency:

15th December, 1990

Dear [Official],

[Bionic Arm Project]

Mr Edwards has asked me to respond to your letter of 23rd November. [The research company] is a not-for-profit company specialising in business research and publication in service activities generally, and in business ethics. We are helping [the inventor and his colleagues] to develop some of their many inventions and applications.

As you say, there do appear to have been some misunderstandings, and I believe that it should nct be too difficult to clear them up, hence this letter. Our original approach to [the funding agency] was through [a professional institution] whose ... services we are using. Our particular interest in the prosthetic arm can be summed up as arising from: (1) its potential benefits from a welfare point of view; (2) the considerable advances in design and capabilities; (3) the huge potential market; and (4) the expected large price advantages over other existing products.

Your letter of 8th November appeared to indicate that you had reasons for doubting the security of the patents. I telephoned your office and spoke to Mr X. He was very helpful, indicating that there appeared to be no serious doubts as to the patents, but that the figures given in our document suggested that the investment required might be too high to attract industry as things stand. One of the figures in our early documents was of £2½ million for the setting up of a complete new facility. With the use of bought-in parts and other options an investment to production stage could be as little as one tenth of that figure, at £200,000 to £250,000. [Your colleague], on the telephone, helpfully suggested that if we had further ideas, it could do no harm to get in touch again. That was the purpose of the letter from Mr Edwards of 14th November.

The prosthesis is only one of very many applications of the basic ideas. Others include film animation and animatronics, robotics, automotive products, tasks required in hazardous situations, ... disposal situations, and many more. Some [major institutions] have shown an early interest, and we have had support in testing, [and on the same day as your letter], a proposal for joint ventures from Universities.

We had originally hoped that [your agency] would be willing to meet us briefly to discuss the possibilities of this large range of innovations and applications [without commitment, of course], and we still think it would be surprising if it turns out not to be the case.

We thought that it would be helpful to provide you with this background, and it would be appreciated if you would let us know whether, after taking it into account you still believe that [the agency] could have no interest.

The possibility that you found some weaknesses in the patent position is a matter for concern, and we would naturally be appreciative if you would let us know what they are.

I look forward to hearing from you in the light of this further clarification, especially on the matters of the many potential applications, the specific matters relating to the patents, the large markets and the relatively small investments required for most of the applications individually.

[Yours sincerely]

From [University],
received on the same day as the letter from the funding agency:

Dear Mr Edwards,

Following our recent telephone conversation please find enclosed a draft proposal for a test centre to be set up at [University]. Should you have any further questions or comments on this I would be very pleased to hear from you.

It may be possible for the [University Department] to assist with your particular . . . requirements, or to advise on matters relating to performance testing . . . to standards. The facilities and expertise in the [University Department] are available to manufacturers and users . . . on a collaboration basis. I have included further information on these services. Should they be of interest please contact me at the above address.

It was interesting to discuss with you your [inventions]. Should you have [further] information on this work I would be interested to see it. I feel that we may be able to assist you on [a technical matter] and would welcome any further discussion. I have enclosed some details of the work we have already undertaken in this field.

We would welcome a visit to the University so that we may show you the full range of our expertise and facilities.

[Yours sincerely]
[Officer]

Two months later, having received no reply from the agency, the inventor and his representatives abandoned the expectations of further discussions with the funding agency, having entered further discussions with the University Department.

A contrasting style to that of the funding acency was provided by a manufacturing company:

Dear Mr Edwards,

I apologise for not responding to you earlier. I have now had the chance to study the information provided . . . about your TCAS actuators. I have concluded that [the company] would not be able to make the kind of contribution for the further development of your projects that you are seeking.

The main reason is that we only very rarely get involved in the funding of technology and product development outside the framework of our existing operations. While your inventions have some common features with the kinds of thing we do in some of our divisions, I believe that the commonalities are in the less important dimensions.

[Yours sincerely]

The correspondence clearly exhibits a variety of factors. The ethical requirements seem to be clearer to some of the writers than others. In particular, no applicant for funds for business development can reasonably expect support for an invention or product that is not viable. Nor can support be regarded as a matter of right, as opposed to a mutually beneficial exchange. Funding agencies do have competing calls on scarce resources. Managers are employed to make informed and proper judgements. At the same time, there is a proper expectation that the facts of any such matter should be properly investigated, and that decisions should be made on sound reasons, which should be competently conveyed to others entitled to hear them. This is particularly so when the decision-makers are in a position of trust as agents for companies or for the public. These matters are part of the set of values assumed to operate in business. They often are, but the case shows, to my mind, that the recognition and practice of this is, to say the least, patchy.

It is unlikely that the matter is simply an indication that people can, legitimately, differ in their judgements. Quite clearly, in some cases proper investigation is made, and reasons carefully given, while in others, the main points are systematically avoided, or even evaded. Where this is so, it is unlikely to be the result of the mere fact that individuals differ in their judgements. The low rate of take-up of innovation in some countries is systematic. This rate of take-up is not by itself an important ethical matter, nor necessarily an ethical matter at all: that depends on the nature of the product and the reasons for the level of take-up. There are sufficient clues in the correspondence, which after all relates to a product whose welfare benefits are very substantial, to suggest that there are problems in the ethical climate, which lead to some decisions being made without due investigation. Again, an 'unfavourable' decision, properly made is not an ethical issue. If it is not properly made or explained, it becomes one.

In general, the fact that it is so much easier to change the justification for what is done than to change practice explains also why disappointment has been expressed at the outcomes of institutionalized research, and the defences of them by the research institutions. The response by the university department in Case 28 is common, but by no means invariable. As one (anonymous) academic explained it,

business research itself has made little impact on business practice, and currently appears to concentrate on picking winners from the insights of industrialists. Such insights themselves seem to owe little to business research – rather the opposite. Can you identify ten major, performance transforming concepts from business research in the last twenty years or so?

If this academic is right, the process of transfer of even technical ideas is fraught with difficulties, and the less tangible ideas incorporated in official codes and company statements are even more difficult to convey, especially by managers whose assessment by their superiors is concentrated on the attainment of easily measured, technical achievements within a framework provided by previous innovations, not current ones.

There are then, important processes that intervene when the impeccable aspirations of public statements by company spokesmen and code-writers reach the various implementation stages.

Intervening processes

Structures provide frameworks within which rules are made. Initial choices of some structural dimensions, such as centralization, decentralization, number and role of departments and 'functions', such as marketing, production, personnel, and finance are traditionally made by 'top management'. They are in part provided for in the Memorandum and Articles of Association, i.e in the official legal structures of companies and institutions. Substantial variations exist between formal structures. Few students of business would deny that structures influence conduct, standards and explanations. This is no doubt one reason why establishment of standards of conduct in codes of practice is sought through the formal structure. It is generally recognized that the simple publication of codes is not sufficient to standardize behaviour in conformity with the codes. For this reason, it is common to support the formal requirements with methods for individual development, such as attendance at seminars, courses and conferences. There is a tendency for these two dimensions – formal structures and individual development to form a polarized method of seeking improvement: the need to reinforce the operation of formal rules, codes or techniques leads to attempts to overcome it by offering individual development. A succession of individual development policies (suggesting a degree of uncertainty as to their operation and value) leads to promulgation of new formal policies, abandonment of promising methods (from T-groups and group dynamics, to participative management, to quality circles). It is not suggested here that these methods are always disappointing, or that their abandonment always indicates their failure. Abandonment can be due to a very large number of reasons. What is suggested is that the polarity between formal structures, rules and codes, on the one hand, and individual development on the other, can be a sterile one. The gap between the expectations generated by the formal methods and the practical outcomes noted in some of the cases and in so many reports in the mass media on the conduct of business requires explanation. The inability of revised formal structures and individual development to come up to expectations suggests that there must be, to use scientific jargon, at least one 'missing variable'. There are, in my view, many 'missing variables', but some of them can be usefully grouped under the heading of 'intervening processes'.

The diagram below is taken from a paper to the European Business Ethics Network in Milan, in October 1990. In the diagram, the boxes labelled 'structures' and 'individuals' are intended to represent the poles along which attempts are made to influence business conduct, including conduct in compliance with ethical norms. Although these are powerful influences, the influence is often diverted from ethical ideals; the polarity is often sterile. This sterility results from a set of intervening (and usually informal and often unacknowledged) processes. The processes have made their appearance in the social science and behavioural literature, but have been described and analysed in terms of 'group norms' and 'group processes'. Enforcement of norms against 'deviants' is acknowledged, but only in the context of providing 'scientific', predictive models of behaviour. These processes are equally matters for ethical analysis. They are represented in the diagram as intervening between aspirations and outcomes in business.

There have been many studies of rule-adaptation and rule-evolving conduct in industry. Various labels have been invented from time to time: 'the informal system', 'the living system', 'buropathology', 'group dynamics', and many others, usually within the discipline of social psychology. The studies show remarkable similarities in different countries. They include, for example: Gouldner (1954), Burns and Stalker (1961), Cartwright and Zander (1962), Crozier (1964), Bennis (1972), Argyris (1974), and many others which have clearly demonstrated the power of these informal processes. Deviations from group norms are not tolerated. The consequences of attempts to impose rules on groups who have some power to resist are varied, and difficult to predict. In Gouldner's study, *Wildcat Strike* (1954), the strike was known to have been likely for at least a year. It was known that it would happen. No one knew when.

It is not, in my view, a proper role for business ethics to attempt to persuade business that applying any particular set of

Performance and standards: a model of deviation

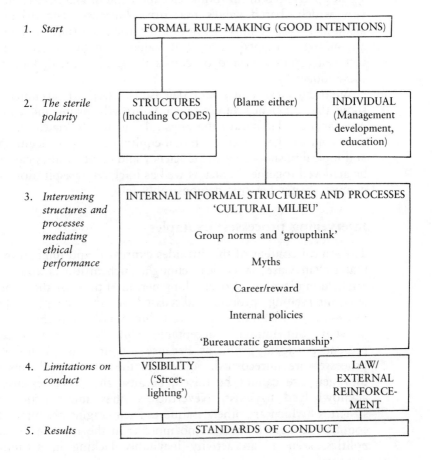

1. *Start* FORMAL RULE-MAKING (GOOD INTENTIONS)

2. *The sterile polarity* STRUCTURES (Including CODES) — (Blame either) — INDIVIDUAL (Management development, education)

3. *Intervening structures and processes mediating ethical performance* INTERNAL INFORMAL STRUCTURES AND PROCESSES 'CULTURAL MILIEU'
Group norms and 'groupthink'
Myths
Career/reward
Internal policies
'Bureaucratic gamesmanship'

4. *Limitations on conduct* VISIBILITY ('Street-lighting') LAW/ EXTERNAL REINFORCE-MENT

5. *Results* STANDARDS OF CONDUCT

Source: Peter Davis and John Donaldson (1990) 'Ethical Structures for Large Organisations: Review, Prospects and Proposals' (Paper to European Business Ethics Network Conference, Milan, October, 1990).

first-order ethical principles or rules will necessarily improve economic performance, without specifying what that performance entails. Nor is it a proper role for business ethics to claim that it will help in the fashionable drive for 'excellence'. My own view is that, so far as standards of conduct are concerned, improvement in the achievement of their own official standards is possible in most firms, desirable in many, and imperative in some. To say this, of course, is to make value judgements, and raises again the central issue of business ethics: whose values should be promoted, and how? It is at least arguable from the evidence in the case studies presented in this book that there are in fact defensible and very widely-shared values that drive business. The driving is, again as the cases show, somewhat erratic from time to time, but anyone who accepts the 'official' values, and that there is a gap between aspirations and outcomes is logically entitled to make these judgements.

What business ethics can defensibly offer are arguments to show that efficiency values (such as growth, profit and control) can generate damage to the physical and psychological environment and to internal and external equity. It can also, legitimately and logically, show that the efficiency and equity values can often be achieved together in fact as well as in claim or aspiration. That it must always be so is demonstrably false.

Intervening processes: examples

The ethical content of the attitudes expressed and implied by the material in Case 28 is clear enough. Such attitudes and values are held in place, often over a long period of time, by the informal and intervening processes discussed in this chapter. These processes are by no means typically 'unsound' from ethical points of view, but mutually acceptable control of these processes presents particular problems. Because of their nature, many of the processes are unrecorded. Sometimes the ethical problems that they generate cannot be raised, because the processes are not acknowledged to exist. Nevertheless, they inject action into structures which are otherwise inert. Their origins are many. It is common to regard them as no more than the result of internal politics, seen as an activity inevitably lacking in scrupulous conduct.

The informal processes are generated by unacknowledged, often unexamined value-assumptions. They provide essential space, giving latitude in interpreting and applying formal missions, rules and structures. They inevitably provide scope for misinterpretation and misapplication. They are at once unacknowledged and lacking in an adequate vocabulary with which to recognize, describe and evaluate them. Their outcomes are difficult to predict. Their operation and their opposition to formal structures are not necessarily indefensible according to ethical criteria. Sometimes they provide a 'coping' method, by which people can get on and fulfil their tasks despite the formal rules and structures. It seems to me that it is an important task for business ethics to recognize, describe accurately, and to evaluate these processes.

A few examples can show this. Reviewing an account of the nuclear disaster at Chernobyl, and how it was allowed to happen, one author summarizes:

[the answer] . . . lies in institutional deceit sanctioned by many strands of workers, 'independent' safety officers, government officials, and scientists. The deceit was protected from the public by an impregnable wall of collective secrecy with punitive recriminations for anyone tempted to blow the whistle . . . where technology creates an inbred and unchallengeable mindset reinforced by corrupting management regimes that breed a mixture of unthinking complacency and fear of being the odd one out. (O'Riordan, 1990)

Although I am not in a position to verify the evidence on which this conclusion is based, it fits well with the processes described by the authors cited above. The processes are clearly features of bureaucracy *per se*, and are no respecters of ideology or of political systems.

CASE 29 | A multi-product manufacturing company

The managers of a multi-product manufacturing company identified a slowing down in the pace of work (cf. Case 8, Chapter 1). A solution was to introduce a new, computerized control system that identified, as each job was worked on, the exact state of progress. If work on a particular contract or item was stopped for any reason, the reason was to be recorded on a document, so that remedial action could be taken. It was not feasible to send a supervisor immediately to every job. In the event, the control system failed because the information identifying the stoppage was typically providing one of three reasons: shortage of materials, shortage of tools, or 'any other reason'. This was not a case of sabotage. The employees were required to work from drawings that originated from the sales department, and were sometimes not up to date with the materials available. Urgent jobs, near to completion, were allowed for the sake of expediency to divert materials and tools from less urgent jobs. Employees with special skills and pressure to 'make the bonus' would raid the stores to secure the materials needed. Uncompleted jobs would be formally booked out for the same reason, or in order to satisfy the day's production expectations. Every department blamed every other department, but at the same time had reasons that could not be gainsaid for its own inability to meet the needs of the other departments. Morale and output fell together. The company solved the problems in various ways and, over fifteen years, continued to grow in both revenue and profit, with no indications that it would not continue to do so indefinitely.

The ethical matters raised range from manipulation of the bonus scheme (so that it did not represent work done) and breaking of official rules by employees, connivance by harassed supervisors in order to maintain output, an atmosphere of extreme anxiety in the drawing office, as employees were required to produce two sets of drawings for each job, but not allowed to admit it. (The reason was that the actual details of specialized jobs and the specifications drawn up for sales purposes diverged. Accurate drawings were necessary as the job was passed from one section to another.) On the part of managers, the continuous changes in demands made on employees in order to complete production orders gave the impression that there were no rules at all, or if there were, that they were capricious, operating only for the purpose of passing the blame elsewhere.

The central ethical problem, as I see it in cases such as this (which are by no means rare in some industries), is that each identifiable group sets its own rules, based on its own values. These do not take account of the values of other groups, only their manifestations in pressures applied. Top management's interest in control values to the exclusion of equity values can lead directly to the loss of both. To the extent that equity values are claimed, but the values of others are not ascertained, there is room for endless activity at cross-purposes, and for ethical short-cuts for the purpose of achieving what are seen to be legitimate ends, which are neither recognized nor understood by others.

The informal processes and values that rarely make their appearance in formal statements of official company values or in official reports generally, but which intervene between official aspirations and actual outcomes also include taboos. I know of one major manufacturing company, often criticized for having a lacklustre performance, in which the word 'problem' was taboo. In some academic institutions, the taboo is upon 'shop talk', as it is in certain military messrooms. But even there, the main business is discussed sometimes, at least in operational contexts. In some academic institutions, however, the taboo applies at all times, not only during off-duty spells, reducing research output. Of course, many of these taboos can, in the social science tradition, be provided with explanations showing that they are 'functional'. But what is 'functional' for the quiet operation of a research institution or funding agency may be far from functional from the point of view of their constituents, including those who actually pay for the service.

A final example of informal intervening processes at work is taken from financial services. It is common, in some countries at least, for institutions providing finance to individuals to seek to repeat financial arrangements with 'reliable' clients. It is far from uncommon for the client to receive in the same post an invitation from one department to apply for a loan 'as a valued client', and a threat of legal action if the 'outstanding balance' (whose payment triggered the offer of a loan) is not paid. Again, anyone can make mistakes, but the process described is too common to be merely the product of a mistake, or of the bureaucratic left hand not knowing what the right hand is doing. Some banks have been criticized for imposition of non-agreed, obscure and high charges to individual clients.

In Britain, a new banking code of practice has been drafted to deal with such matters. The ethical problems are not ones of mere politeness and sensitivity to prudential gains to be made from the cultivation of clients. They are ones of abuse of power, given the vast differential in power between large organizations and individuals. The persistence of the 'intervening processes' over time demonstrates that the problem does not arise because 'top management' is unaware of the symptoms of the gap between aspirations and outcomes, but is symptomatic of the under-development of both concepts and language to deal with them. This generates the oscillation between the poles of 'formal structure' and 'individual development' to which attention was drawn above (p. 94).

The methods by which the informal, intervening processes are held in place are discussed in Chapter 7, which summarizes the theoretical and practical points raised by the cases and the discussion so far. It offers a framework for analysing cases in business ethics, with a view to proceeding from accurate recognition of issues, via analysis, to development of procedures for improvement.

6 | BUSINESS ETHICS
The Institutional Framework

No business is an island. Businesses operate in a cultural milieu in which the overall level of business activity is determined to a substantial extent by many factors. These include governmental policies towards inflation and interest rates, international trading policies, monopolies and the rules of competition. Policies in these areas raise their own major ethical issues concerning the design and implementation of policies and of distributive justice. In addition, the formation of technical standards implies moral as well as technical values. These become incorporated into company law, environmental planning and legislation and accounting standards. Pressure from consumer groups, changes in technical and trading conditions, pressure from unions and from investor institutions, including those for 'ethical investment', all contribute to this milieu.

The allegiance of employees to companies is tempered by their allegiance to professional bodies or trade unions. The separation of home and work life is a stronger tradition in some countries and occupations than others. The values that individuals bring to work are influenced by many value-setting institutions. Some of these, such as the Churches, have, for many reasons, profound influences upon the cultural milieu, and even upon individuals who have no formal commitment to them. No doubt these value-setting institutions would prefer to have more influence than they do, but they too are constrained by values that have become dominant. Churches have been criticized for staying aloof in the face of major moral dilemmas, and have been accused of interfering when they do not remain aloof. This is not different in principle from attitudes to most sources of new ideas: they are safer confined to 'the ivory tower'. Their originators are thought of as impractical people, whether or not they allow themselves to be confined. All this makes for stability, because new ideas can be painful to absorb. It also makes the cultural milieu relatively impervious to innovation, whether technical or ethical, as is seen in the case studies concerning innovation and investment in new ideas.

100

Firms are also targets for advice from academics, ephemeral 'quick-fix cookbooks' and many other claimants to possession of insights. This last remark is not intended to denigrate these sources of advice, but rather to make the point that for firms, the targets of the advice and the offers of new ideas and inventions, a serious problem arises of sorting the wheat from the chaff, the genuinely innovative and helpful ideas from the phoney or from the rehashing of old ones. The solutions themselves can raise major ethical issues.

The point is often made that new institutions and new behavioural discoveries can shed light on these matters of innovation, but the rate of take up of this research is itself problematic. In choosing how to respond to the various pressures and uncertainties, firms do need rules, insights and guidelines. These are typically presented as technical management matters, such as the search for the 'right system', practice or cadre of top executives. How they respond raises its own set of ethical issues. These are illustrated in this chapter.

The idea that company owners and managers ought to be free to do what they will with their property, the company, is both old and unambiguously ethical. It belongs to the period of the early industrial revolution in Europe. The abuses, pollution and disasters that followed are part of history. The idea that people did not know better in those far-off days, and that therefore we ought not to judge the nineteenth century by twentieth century moral standards, even if true, is irrelevant. In introducing factories legislation, such as the 'ten hours bill' at the height of the industrial revolution, Lord Shaftesbury produced evidence from mill owners to show that quality suffered towards the end of the day, and that reductions in hours could and did result in a rise, not a fall in productivity (Bready, 1926, p. 204). This was by no means his principal argument, however, which was a refutation of the factual claims made at the time that any relaxation of harsh business regimes would lead to economic disaster that would cause the most suffering to those whom the bill was intended to help. Echoes of this argument persist. The claim that proposals for reform tend to damage the intended beneficiaries is rarely supported with much evidence, but continues to be applied in the context of trade and development policies, in connection with proposed boycotts, and in criticism of the European Social Charter. This does not imply that the targets of the untested argument to which I refer are in themselves necessarily justified, only that if proposals for reform are to be rejected, it should be on rational grounds, backed by evidence, rather than by enquiry-closing assertions. Shaftesbury's arguments were designed to refute the old argument that since 'ought' implies 'can' – and that, since improvement cannot in fact be achieved, it therefore ought not to be attempted. Even at the height of the industrial revolution, there were successful companies that deliberately strove to operate to what can clearly be seen as higher standards in these respects. Then as now, managers imported their own values into a business milieu rich in values but poor in opportunities for criticism, however constructive. The claim that business has the sole duty of maximizing profit is a hangover from the days in which firms claimed, and generally won, the right to be 'little island kingdoms'. Business takes its values and the rules by which it prospers from the values of its cultural milieu, and adds to those values. Much of the argument about codes and self-regulation, or monopoly and privatization, for example, are predicated on the problem of adjusting acceptably between 'company sovereignty' and the values and freedoms of the people affected by it.

A topic which needs to be tackled is the basis upon which the various institutions are entitled or have a duty to support or offer advice to business on how to conduct its activities. This is an ethical matter in its own right. That the institutions, religious, governmental, legal, professional and trade and academic, have offered advice on values and how to achieve them is a matter of historical and contemporary record. The causal relationships between the advice offered by the institutions to business, and the advice that business has offered to them are major fields of study in their own right. These processes of giving and receiving advice, to adapt a phrase from the social science literature, can be grouped under the heading of 'value-sending'. The early history of business ethics has been summarized by McHugh (1988, p. 3):

A feature of all attempts to apply ethical principles to the reality of business life has been the tension between the ideals of fairness in human transactions and the imperatives of competition and profit-making. As regards the ethical ideals which govern business, they are not very different in contemporary society from what they were in ancient Greece . . . . In their theoretical ethics, the Greek and Roman writers of antiquity may have allowed for debates on morals in business, but their actual attitude to business was hostile on the grounds, firstly, that commerce seemed always tied to avarice and fraud; and, secondly that it was a potential source of moral corruption by reason of the necessity of dealing with barbarian merchants, whose *mores* and manners could be presumed not to reach the high standards fixed by those ancient civilisations. This suspicion of business and trade, however, was not shared by all the early guardians of moral rectitude. The Jewish religion, for example, regarded wealth as a gift of God; and the religious leaders of Judaism (as of Buddhism and Chinese religions) regarded success in business as a sign of God's approval.

McHugh adds that the medieval prohibition of usury was a continuation of the Aristotelian tradition. The practical effects included vigorous action against usurious lending. The removal of the prohibition was associated with the rise of Protestantism. The process has been intensively studied, for example by Weber (1920), and Tawney (1926).

Value-sending by law has thus not developed in isolation from the prevailing religious outlooks and, as has often been pointed out, the separation of Church and State, and the rise of secularism, even at their most thoroughgoing, have not produced institutions which have removed all traces of the major values 'sent' by religion and the Churches. Again, the fact that the influences have occurred and still exist is a different matter from that of the legitimacy of the influences, and, more particularly, of the forms which they take. Reference was made earlier to that ambivalence towards direct religious influence in some contexts. Recent evidence, at least, suggests that in politics and in business, the power of values to move people is well-recognized; and attitudes towards intervention by religious organizations seem to be profoundly influenced by whether they are judged to be supportive or not to commentators' preferences.

So far as attitudes towards value-sending among teachers in academic institutions in Continental Europe are concerned, there is survey evidence that also suggests ambivalence: in his survey on *The teaching of business ethics in the UK, Europe and the USA*, Mahoney (1990) summarizes:

Asked whether the teaching in their institution included any consideration of what might broadly be regarded as the moral or 'values' or social aspects of business, eight of the thirty-three institutions which replied said that it figured a lot, fourteen that it figured a little, seven that the subject figured very little, and four replied that it did not figure at all in their institution. (Mahoney, 1990, pp. 110–11)

On the question of whether the world religions ought to be drawn upon, the Mahoney survey indicates:

Again, the comments were illuminating from various points of view. One who saw no place for such consideration explained: 'Business ethics has been too much related to religions. It may be the basis, but not necessarily'. (Op. cit., pp. 145–6)

I think one should not start from religious principles but one can note the manner in which they agree or not with the principles of ethics. (Loc. cit.)

Value-sending by the law is more direct, although it must be borne in mind that the law itself is influenced by the dominant values and by less dominant but influential ones held by lawmakers, and by public opinion (which itself is far from being uninfluenced by the various institutions). Value-setting by law includes not only statutes but enforcement policies and methods.

The case studies demonstrate the variety of ways in which institutions engage in value-sending to influence conduct and encourage or enforce values. These include:

1 **Laws** – usually made with consultation and lobbying.
2 **Codes** – often set by professional bodies, and agreed to by some stakeholders, though not by all: often linked to legislation.
3 **Regulations by voluntary/self control.**
4 **Whistleblowers**, who serve to remind institutions of the gap between aspirations and outcomes.
5 **Professional practice.** The role of professional bodies often includes establishment of standards, provision of justifying theories (often relying upon higher education bodies to provide suitable materials) and (often indirect) support in the process of regulation of entry by qualification of candidates for membership.
6 **Support institutions** – e.g. universities, capital provision, financial services.

All of these, including the religious organizations, provide the formal structures whose interplay produces the 'resultant' values alongside and sometimes inconsistent with the official ones.

As indicated, these values and their applications often go through lengthy validation processes, through discussion papers, meetings, debates, and opinion-soundings. This provides a strong clue as to the long delay in the arrival of formal disciplines in relation to business ethics. The various institutions appear, on the whole to have been able to provide business with a *rationale* in which values (technical, prudential and moral) have been imported indirectly. The emphasis for day-to-day operation has been on the technical and prudential values, leaving the expression of 'high-level' values to chairmen's speeches and official publications, often written by skilled public relations specialists. The 'high-level' values are, as has also been seen, usually impeccable and genuine. The problem then arises as to why it has been recently concluded that formal treatments of ethics in business are needed. As one respondent remarked in Mahoney's survey, the university system and tradition are 'adverse to these non-quantitative and hard-to-verify topics' (Mahoney, 1990, p. 112).

The respondent was presumably referring particularly to the teaching of business, management, and professional and technical disciplines, as more speculative and literary subjects appear to have been somewhat less overtaken by 'quantitative' methods. This raises the matter of *positivism*. The doctrine has been very influential, especially since the 1960s. Though its influence appears now to be waning, its legacy is identifiable. We now turn to that topic.

The legacy of positivism

positivism The philosophical system of Auguste Comte, recognizing only positive facts and observable phenomena, and rejecting metaphysics and theism (*COD*). The doctrine predates Comte. Despite its rejection of metaphysics, positivism is a metaphysical doctrine.

Positivists make a sharp distinction between 'normative' judgments, that is, those that relate to values, and 'positive' judgments, that can be tested by formulating (usually in mathematical form) testable hypotheses (usually in statistical form), so that predictions can be compared with actual outcomes. There is much to be said for this approach. Logically, the distinction between 'facts' and 'values' is a sound one, originally expressed in the eighteenth century by the Scottish philosopher David Hume in his *Treatise On Human Nature* (1739). The achievements in the business context of this outlook include a whole range of useful techniques and ways of thinking, such as statistical and econometric analysis and prediction, the concept of *system* in management, the analysis of group formation in organisations, and of group behaviour, the description of syndromes such as those of frustration behaviour, stress, and the dynamics of conflict. These strengths and achievements need to be set against the limitations, ambiguities, points of incoherence, gaps between aspiration and achievement, and omissions. Their weaknesses are the other side of the coin faced by their strengths. It is important to note that positivism, unlike most other metaphysical doctrines, is often claimed not to be one. It is not a single, clear set of theorems, but a 'family' of related ideas and aspirations.

A central problem for the doctrine is that in holding that values cannot be handled systematically and decisively, positivism offers a very strong set of values, of accuracy, of 'true' method, of clear, cool objectivity, and of denying responsibility for the results of its enquiries: the value of freedom to design and test 'scientific' hypotheses without let or hindrance tends to be very highly prized by positivists, who are logically unable to recognize it as a value, but prefer to see it as the obviously 'scientific' way to the truth. Science is above all a value-system, as is commitment to truth. 'Truth' is a complex set of values and concepts. They are both inescapably ethical matters.

Secondly, the claim that enquiry 'ought' to be free is itself an expression of value. If values are beyond rational discourse, then so are the merits or otherwise of positivism. But of course, values are not beyond the reach of rational discourse.

The third flaw in the positivist outlook is that its dominance in intellectual circles, and its complacency with regard to values, has contributed to the growth of ethical issues in business, by omission at the least. Some critics would say that its overconfidence has also led to a massive investment in techniques whose yield and acceptability to business is quite low.

Returning to the role of institutions, several matters are salient: firstly, they influence the cultural mileu, which in turn influences them; secondly, they are subject to regulation which is in many ways similar to that of business itself. This includes accounting procedures, voting rules, concepts of natural justice, criminal and civil law, and many more. Thirdly, the institutions tend to share many bureaucratic and hierarchical features in common with business, and fourthly, the institutions are no more immune to the operation of the intervening processes described and analysed in Chapter 5. Case 30 illustrates these points.

Formal aspirations and intervening processes: some examples from universities

The sources of information for this case are varied, and include discussions over several years with academics and students, press reports and official publications (including prospectuses) from several universities and university departments, as well as other documents collected at various times. The special nature of universities requires that for this study, information should be drawn from a single country, Britain. An inter-European comparison is not attempted here. That would merit a volume on its own.

Universities are part of the institutional framework through which business values are transmitted and, to some extent, formed. Universities are at the junction of many systems – economic, political, ethical, kinship, class, knowledge and influence. In total they exert a significant influence on the transmission of values. The ways in which they do so are complex. For instance, there is no direct way of measuring the influence of university moral philosophy within universities themselves or on behaviour in the wider contexts of business and industry. This is partly a result of the tradition of self-government in which, for example, specialists are not consulted when the university has a problem within their area of expertise. Thus, industrial relations academics are rarely consulted when an industrial relations problem occurs. At least one university has an ethics committee, whose brief is limited to rules governing experiments on animals. The content is easily enough explained, but the omissions are more problematic. No evidence has been forthcoming in this case of consultation of moral philosophers in relation to the scope of the committee. It may be suspected that the influence of specialist philosophers is small, partly for the reasons suggested above, partly as a result of a general preference to keep them in the celebrated 'ivory towers', and partly as a result of preferences among many philosophers to stay there.

It cannot even be reliably claimed that the appointment of a 'live-wire' or a 'dud' as the head of a university or university department makes any noticeable impact on the performance of industry or the economy as a whole, or on standards of conduct in public life. It may be suspected that it can make some difference to the morale in the university or department, and can help to stabilize any turbulence within the 'micro-system' of the university or department. The continuation of characteristic styles and cultures in particular institutions suggests but does not prove that the values tend to be self-perpetuating. A strong research tradition tends to be self-reinforcing, and reliance on expansion of student numbers for making up shortfalls in income can also be self-perpetuating.

The 'official' values that universities are widely regarded as serving include mainly the increase of knowledge through original thought and research, and the extension of this knowledge to the community as a whole through the teaching of students.

Apart from the very difficult, if not impossible task of assessing the impact of universities on the economy as a whole (or on the body politic), particular issues include: the basis for judging standards of research, teaching and administration and allocation of funds; the proper relationships of universities with industry and government; selection criteria for staff and students; the proper operation of procedures and committees; stewardship of public resources; the position of trust that is a concomitant of the autonomy granted to universities (particularly important in the selection and examination of students); links with learned societies; issues of academic freedom, its expression, meaning and limits; pay levels, motivation and morale; research and teaching standards and their assessment, i.e. who is justifiably entitled to assess them, and how? Should the standards be consumer-driven, and who is the consumer, anyway?

The questions are of current concern, and are interrelated. Objectivity in judgment is considerably hampered by universities' vulnerability to the political expectations of the government of the day, which controls much of their funding. A legitimate concern of the government, as the public's representative, is how far the autonomy granted to universities can be used to mask the size of the gap between official statement of the values of universities and their achievement.

Examples of the gulf between different assessments of the current situation can be drawn from contemporary press reports:

As the Association of University Teachers lobbied MPs at Westminster, Mr Clarke [the Secretary of State for Education] issued to MPs details of the Government's record on higher education, saying that since 1979 maximum pay for university lecturers had risen by 14.5 per cent in real terms and public spending on higher education had never been greater. (*The Independent*, 12 December, 1990)

Diana Warwick, the AUT General Secretary, said that academics' pay had risen by only 1 per cent in real terms in the past 20 years and that the higher education system was in danger of collapse, with worsening staff-student ratios, uncompetitive pay levels and plummeting morale. (Loc. cit.)

Interchanges of this kind have been frequent in public debate, with both sides selecting evidence to support their case, rather than looking for agreed evidence from which to draw conclusions in the light of stated and analysed values. This mode of debate is by no means confined to discussions between ministers and employees' representatives.

A headline in *The Independent* illustrates the point: 'Universities reject MPs' allegations of poor mismanagement' (Crequer and Macleod, *The Independent*, 7 September, 1990, p. 2).

The article referred to a draft report by Members of Parliament, alleging 'shortcomings in realistic and effective management'. University representatives were reported as dismissing the allegations as 'nonsense', and one thought them to be 'crass and idiotic' (loc. cit.). The Chief Executive of the Universities' Funding Council was reported as commenting that, 'We cannot stop universities spending their money as they choose, taking on staff when patently they cannot afford to' (loc. cit.).

Staff costs are particularly relevant in this context, because they amount to well over ninety per cent of university costs. Reductions in funding, and demands that universities raise more of their own income, have been associated with rising deficits in a number of universities. This led to one major *cause célèbre* in a decision by a university to make a tenured member of staff redundant, as part of a policy to 'resolve the overstaffing situation'. In the event, the appeal against the decision was officially rejected in 1989. Tenure was, and is, held to be important because it is thought to protect free enquiry and its results from improper pressure when the results are unpopular, or uncongenial to particular individuals or groups. It should be noted that tenure applies only to teaching staff, as opposed, for example, to research staff. In some cases, even some teaching appointments have been on fixed-term appointments. There can be no doubt that the universities are under some financial pressure to reduce costs, and several methods of persuading tenured staff to leave, or rewarding those who do so, have been devised.

We have noted the special place occupied by universities, at the junction of many value-driven systems, and in providing and testing ideas. The difficulties in identifying both the influence and in terms of whether the public gets value for its money and the size of the inevitable gap between aspirations and practice have also been noted. This is a quite general problem in relation to large-scale systems. It is also an example of the traditional historian's conundrum known as the 'Cleopatra's nose problem'. Logicians know it as the problem of counterfactual conditionals. Would the history of the world have been different if Cleopatra's nose had been longer, and because of it Anthony had shown no interest? Did Keynes's economic theories of the 1930s (Keynes, 1936) save the world from repeating after the Second World War the mistakes that produced the depression after the First World War? Or did Keynes merely crystallize ideas that were already present? Did 'monetarism' in Britain really bring the country's economy on to the same growth path as that of other Western European countries? The possibility of addressing, let alone answering any of these questions objectively is remote, partly because they are moral matters, and partly because the technical means available, though sophisticated, are limited to answering questions set within the assumptions of particular value-frameworks. If the frameworks are faulty, the technical results will probably be, too. If the frameworks are sound, the technical results may or may not be, depending on the quality of the data available and the methods of analysis.

All this is part also of another set of general problems of interpretation which lead back to the assessment of the gap between the aspirations held for companies and institutions (in the present case, the universities) and their achievements.

Some of these topics are difficult issues in historical method. They have many similarities with notions of cause and effect in policy decisions in institutions and in government. These problems relate to the resources available to tackle the issues discussed above. There is, of course, no reason why other institutions than universities and research establishments linked to higher education should not undertake research in these areas, apart from the high cost involved in establishing libraries and the other necessary facilities. In the event, the universities (along with other institutions of higher learning) have become the main sources of expertise on the general economic and industrial problems referred to above. Despite occasional differences between university experts and government ministers, they share the same framework of thought. This has been clearly influenced historically by positivism, which seeks to explain events in a way that is centred on technique, and which self-consciously avoids the systematic handling of values. If values drive industry and the economy, and if values may not be systematically analysed in an applied way in or to universities, outside the few moral philosophy departments then it is not surprising that the research has produced so few compelling answers to the evaluative questions.

A final general puzzle on the topic: if universities are underfunded, as the AUT claims, then this fact would partly explain the reported low morale, and the uncertainties involved with the issues discussed above. More resources would presumably generate more research, which in turn, it might be hoped, would generate more and better answers to the puzzles. If the universities are not underfunded, as the minister appeared to be claiming, then both the low morale and the lack of compelling answers would both be very puzzling, and perhaps disturbing also. If, as I suspect is the case, the universities are overfunded in some areas and activities and underfunded in others, and that the low morale is not only a matter of funding, but also a matter of their operative (i.e. dominant) value systems and cultures, the problem will be at once less puzzling and less tractable.

The operating procedures that have elsewhere been called the 'informal systems' or the 'intervening processes' are often hidden and protected from sight. They exist in all institutions, and universities are no exception. If the overall effect of universities cannot be convincingly assessed, and the causes of low morale are subject for debate, at least some light can be shed on the detailed operation of some of the 'intervening processes', and their links with the formal ones.

Thus the universities can be examined as moral institutions, using the more modest method of 'illustrative incidents'. These modest illustrations of processes are sometimes dismissed as 'mere anecdotes', but experienced investigators are aware of their value in revealing what normally remains hidden. Readers can decide for themselves what the incidents are examples of. A suggested general framework is given in Chapter 7.

The illustrative incidents chosen for this case are reported from different universities. Some intervening processes help to narrow the gap between aspiration and practice. Others maintain and increase it. Most, though not all, of the descriptions are of the latter kind.

A discussion of examination results

It would probably be widely if not universally accepted that when students become clients of universities and prepare for examinations, there can be no guarantee that their efforts will be judged to be successful by the university. Some failures are inevitable, and their existence seems to indicate that standards are being maintained, and that degrees, which tend to enhance the earning powers of their holders, must be paid for, but ought not to be bought. That is, they certify that an education process has been undergone, and that the holder has competence in the subject, but this is not achieved without cost. The education process is an investment, for which someone must pay, but degrees should not be awarded unless the investment has taken place properly.

The task of judging whether the investment has been properly made in terms of students' efforts and results is left to the universities, whose standards are monitored, in the British higher education system, by external examiners, who, as the title suggests, are not current members of the examining universities. In all this, the level of trust is generally high. Occasionally, students consider that their results do not do them justice, or that the judgment that they have 'not satisfied the examiners' needs to be appealed against, on the basis, for example, that the student was ill when the examination was attempted. Examination boards provide rules for appeals. In some cases the appeals are held by some other body than the board that made the initial decision. Sometimes the appeal is made only to the board that did make the initial decision. It is arguable that the boards in the latter position are under a stronger obligation to operate the strictest rules of fairness, because the checks and balances on their decisions are weak. It is also arguable that board members are fully aware of this, and make conscientious efforts to take all circumstances into account. It can be pointed out, on the other hand, that where appeals to a body other than the board that made the original decision, there may be a reluctance on the part of the examination boards to make 'fail' decisions, because appeals will be automatic, and appeals boards may tend to be over-generous to students, regularly overturning the decisions of examination boards. It can equally be argued that appeal boards can be insensitive and over-harsh, leading to examination boards being correspondingly reluctant to make 'hard' decisions. Either way, the standards might be thought to tend to fall. This would be testable if the standards themselves were capable of assessment according to agreed and defensible criteria. Typically, they involve an amalgam of judgments made by individual teachers, and expressed on a common scale, in percentages, or in alphabetic notation. External examiners are expected to make reports on standards to the universities, and are able to offer advice, and sometimes to act as arbitrators. Confidence in the system is generally high. The following sequence of events and correspondence illustrates the operation of informal values and rules, and is presented without comment. It is not suggested that the sequence is typical, or even that it has ever been repeated. The identity of the university and the individuals concerned are excluded, as they are not relevant to the general point, which is an illustration of informal systems and values in operation. Comment is restricted only to notes explanatory of the sequence.

Summer examinations for a post-graduate degree were mostly scheduled over several consecutive days. One of the students had been admitted to hospital on the day before the first examination, but anxious to attend, had discharged herself from hospital, arriving late for the examination, which she was advised not to take. Later in the day she approached her personal tutor to ask for advice on whether she should continue with the examination. Her tutor was unsure of the precise rules, and approached the very experienced member of staff responsible for administering the degree course. His advice (which was followed) was to sit the rest of the examinations, and send in a medical certificate explaining the absence from the first examination. The rules allowed a student, with the agreement of the university, to sit the missed examination in such cases, without having to take all of the examinations again. For this to happen, the examining board concerned was required to submit a case for such action to the university within a specified time period, counted from the date of the missed examination.

In the event, the student was judged to have failed the examination, discussion by the examiners being cut short on the grounds that:

1 only part of the examination had been attempted;
2 in the absence of a medical certificate, there were no mitigating circumstances to take into account; and
3 even if the 'missing' examination had been taken, the student would have been unlikely to score enough marks in it to enable her to pass.

As will be seen, the student had in fact supplied a medical certificate some weeks before the examination board was due to take place, and had received an acknowledgement from the officer in charge of the course during the period in which the examinations were held. The acknowledgement stated that the medical certificate would be brought to the attention of the examiners. That officer was present, and, unaccountably, had lost the certificate, and, as it happened, did not remember having received it. The absence of the medical certificate meant that the possibility of asking the university to permit a separate examination in the subject 'missed' in the original examinations was not considered.

As a general policy of that particular board, two doctrines were held simultaneously:

1 That the examiners can decide anew each time on the rules or criteria that candidates must satisfy in order to 'pass'. These rules were never divulged to the students, who, strictly, did not know what they needed to achieve in order to pass the examination, and after the event, students were not allowed to know what their marks had been. As it happened, students were often able to obtain a good idea of how they performed from some markers, though not from others.

2 That the decision has always been made by allowing a candidate only one, 'marginal' failure per examination, and that the examiners had never used their powers to order a second paper to be set for a candidate, and had never asked the university to allow it.

In other words, the official (but unrecorded) statement at the beginning of examiners' meetings was that arguments from precedent are inadmissible, but earlier practice, though not binding, is sacrosanct.

The following correspondence is reproduced, omitting the names of the persons, department, and university.

20th May
From University Medical Officer to Course Director:
Re: [Student]
Miss — was admitted to — Hospital on 21st April for observation. She asked to be discharged the next day despite medical advice to the contrary as she was concerned about her exams. She sat all but one of her exams and felt extremely unwell during them. I hope that this will be taken into account when assessing her exam results.
[Yours sincerely]

22nd May
From the Course Director to the Medical Officer:
Thank you very much for your letter dated 20th May concerning Miss —. Your letter will be brought to the attention of the examiners at their [next] meeting.
[Yours sincerely]

21st June
From Tutor to Course Director:
Miss — has approached me, as her tutor, to ask about the position regarding her examinations. She was unable to attend the first examination, and has a medical certificate to show that she was not fit to attend on that day. She did attend all the other examinations, and the last time we spoke I told her that there were no precedents, and that the examiners would be empowered to decide, and if they chose, to make a recommendation to the university which would normally be accepted.

I assume that that is still the position, but if any other possible interpretations of the position have come to light, I would be grateful if you would let me know.
[Thanks]

25th June
From Course Director to Tutor:
[The Tutor was also an Examiner]:

   Further to your note dated 21st June, it is important that the student present a medical certificate for the Board of Examiners to see. It would also be helpful if she could append to the certificate a short statement regarding her absence from the [first] examination. If this is not possible in time for the examiners' meeting, I will raise your note at the time of the meeting and will expect confirmation by way of the medical certificate to be presented by [Miss — as soon as possible].

   I cannot tell you at the moment what the examiners will decide in her case but suggest that the student should contact me as soon after the examiners' meeting as possible.

   [The Examiners' Meeting was held a few days later, and the student was 'failed']

2nd July
From Tutor to Student:

   I am now in a position to offer you some advice on conducting your proposed appeal, having studied the regulations. The regulations are quite complex, but I do believe that your circumstances need to be set out fully, so that all possible avenues can be explored. As I said last time we met, the next decision point is likely to be in November, but an early appeal is desirable.

   I am not in a position to estimate what the prospects are for each course of action, but I can suggest what seem to me to be the most useful lines.

   I will be in [the University] on Wednesday and Thursday afternoons. Perhaps you would phone me to arrange a specific time – otherwise just call in.

7th July
From Tutor to Chairman of Examiners and to Course Director:

   I understand that Miss — will be making an appeal to the Board of Examiners. I am not fully conversant with the grounds on which she will make the appeal, but there are some features of the decision at the examiners' meeting which I find disturbing. My present purposes in writing to you are to seek your advice on the regulations governing examinations, to draw your attention to some matters that did not come to light at the examiners' meeting and to express my view that there is a need for a more detailed consideration of Miss —'s case than we had at the examiners' meeting. The student approached me as her first-term tutor. I had, you will perhaps recall, advised her [on advice] on the first day of the examinations that having missed the first examination due to medical reasons, it was still possible that if she did the rest of the papers, the examiners would be able to take due account.

   In brief, the matters which I believe point to the need for a reconsideration are:

1 The discussion in the examiners' meeting of Miss—'s situation was brief, and some pertinent matters were not considered by the examiners. In particular there was a medical certificate [from the University's Medical Officer], covering the examination period, contrary to what the examiners were told.
2 According to my reading of the rules, more options were available than were,

in fact, considered.

3 Her illness was genuine and was compounded by severe financial pressures on her family.* The outcome of these latter is still uncertain. These factors must, in combination, have adversely affected her performance in the examinations.

4 There are precedents in which illness or injury has been considered to be an extenuating circumstance, and the candidate has been allowed to pass. Mr — springs to mind. He was injured and unable to take part of the course, but was allowed to pass. I do not believe that the marks, on the comparable papers he took were much, if at all, better than those of Miss —.

5 Miss —'s performance in the papers that she took [details of the particular papers taken have been omitted for this case study] was no worse than that of other students in the past, who have been allowed to pass, though not having extenuating circumstances, as in the present case (I am preparing a list of precedents to support this point).

Thus my arguments relate to what might be termed lapses in the 'due process' (mostly due to a combination of unforseeable circumstances), extenuating circumstances and precedent.

On the first item: The brevity of the discussion in the meeting seems to have been due to the information that there was no medical certificate other than the (yellow) certificate from the hospital stating that the student had been an in-patient for a period up to and including the [date] morning of the first examination. The information was mistaken. There was in fact a medical certificate from the [University Medical Officer] dated 20th May, certifying that Miss — was ill during the examination period, and expressing the hope that the examiners would take it into account. [The Course Director] replied on 22nd May to the effect that the certificate would be brought before the examiners. This is, I believe, sufficient reason for a re-examination. Presumably, the May correspondence was somehow misplaced in the file. I believe that the board might well have considered other options if the information had been available. As the medical certificate was sent [to the University] a month before the examiners' meeting, it is clear that the certificate was no afterthought. I gather that the consultation [between the student and the University Medical Officer] was during the period of the examinations, and the delay in sending it to the University was due to the Doctor's going on holiday before the medical certificate (for technical reasons) could be forwarded. None of these events could in any way be the fault of the student.

As I read the regulations, the options available to the examiners include the following:

(a) setting a special paper in the subject missed [reference given to specific rule], or a special assignment.
(b) allowing her to complete the examination on the next occasion [rule reference].

---

* The student came from a country undergoing internal upheavals, and which was far from the height of popularity in Britain at the time.

(c) regarding her as not having completed the examination, her attempt being the result of a genuinely mistaken interpretation of the examination rules, on advice from an examiner (me, also on advice from the Course Director). The problem about the examination rules at this point is that option (b) above only seems operational if the Board of Examiners forwards a medical certificate to the authorities within seven days of the examination. I do not know whether by this is meant the first examination, or whether the November date is a suitable one for these purposes. My guess is that it means the last written paper. If this is the case, then the technical inability of the university to supply the medical certificate [within seven days] is another unfortunate coincidence from which the student seems to have lost another avenue for consideration, again, not her fault.

As it seems to me, the principle here is that her illness, which could have depressed the results provides grounds for a sympathetic consideration of her case. It seems an inappropriate burden for her to suffer from the coincidences that made a sympathetic hearing seem undesirable to the examiners.

This brings me to the second point ((b) above). The options, according to the regulations appear to include: a special paper in the subject missed; to take the examination next year as though it were for the first time (thus the 'fail' decision could be revoked; or reversal of the 'fail' decision, and allow her to pass the examination). The grounds for this latter decision would be *precedent* (the precedents that occur to me at present are listed separately) and *due process*. This is the equity ground that the candidate should not be made to suffer from even inadvertent mistakes on the part of the authorities (in this case the Examiners' Board). This, as I see it would include the old adage about 'justice being seen to be done', i.e. the omitted considerations taken into account.

The third point ((c) above) is perhaps the most straightforward: she was ill, and under family financial stress, and may not be able to take the examination a second time. This point becomes relevant when all the circumstances are taken into account, but would be part of the known risks in normal circumstances.

Finally, taking all the points together, I think that the decision was harsh, and, *prima facie* could be held to be unsound, if only on the grounds of 'due process'.

I would appreciate a meeting to discuss some of these points, especially the interpretations of the regulations. Perhaps you could then advise me whether I ought to send a formal letter to the examiners, or whether this note is sufficient for the purpose.

9th July
From the Chairman of the Examiners to the Tutor:

Thank you for your note about [Miss —]. She has appealed and her case will be considered at the next examiners' meeting in November.

For the record, I have not seen her medical certificate and if [initials of the Course Director] has it then he will no doubt enlighten the board. It is the responsibility of the student to ensure that the certificate is delivered to the office in good time.

17th July
From the Tutor to the Chairman of the Examiners:

Thank you for your note to say that Miss — has formally appealed. I understand that she will send a detailed statement of the circumstances.

In the meantime, I have obtained from her a copy of the letter from [University Medical Officer], dated 20th May and the reply [from the Course Director], dated 22nd May. These are the letters I referred to in my earlier note. They confirm that she did indeed meet her responsibility, and that the certificate was delivered to the office in good time – over a month before the examiners' meeting.

At the next examiners' meeting, the matter was raised and discussed. The tutor and chairman are reported as raising point and objections over a lengthy interchange, in which one member of the board had been moved to suggest that the tutor be allowed to express the occasional phrase without constant interruptions. It was decided that the student was in any case allowed to resit the examinations the following spring, although the tutor's proposals were not formally rejected, the first sitting of the examination was to be regarded as not having taken place. The matters of the medical certificate, and the points raised by the tutor were not formally put to the vote. An examiner subsequently asked the university authorities what the provisions were for monitoring the procedures used at Examiners' Boards, and was informed, by telephone, that any complaint to the university would be sent back to the Examiners' Board that then made the decision for re-examination. The possibility remained open that there were more formal procedures available, but the process of finding out seemed to be laborious, as well as a closed loop. The matter was allowed to lapse at that stage.

25th November
From Tutor to Chairman of Examiners:

Thank you for the minutes. I note that [the Course Director] is listed as present, but was in fact absent. Could we have a corrected copy circulated?
[Thank you]

26th November
From Tutor to Course Director:

I note that in the circulated minutes of the examiners' meeting of 20th November, your name has been inadvertently added to the list of examiners present. Although it will be a straightforward matter to have the minutes corrected at the next meeting, in my experience of meetings, confusions can arise if the record is not corrected immediately. I foresee no difficulties in this case, but in the interests of accuracy, I would be obliged if you would confirm that you were not present at the meeting. Perhaps it is a little pedantic of me, but I think that the Examiners' Board needs to stick to the rules.
[Thanks]

27th November
From Course Director to Tutor:
   In reply to your note dated 26th November, I confirm that I did not attend either the staff meeting or the formal Board of Examiners' meeting last week because of lecturing commitments elsewhere.

[The next letter follows a discussion in the corridor between the Chairman of the Examiners and the Tutor, in which the Chairman is reported as insisting that the minutes could not be altered once circulated, and that in any case, if he claimed that the Course Director was present, and the Tutor claimed that he was not, then the Chairman's authority was more likely to be believed.]

29th November
From Tutor to Chairman of Examiners:
   As promised I have checked in the various sources on the procedures for correcting minutes. Precirculation of minutes is seen as a matter of convenience only. Amendment is possible at any time until they have been formally adopted.
   It is only after that stage that corrections may not be made, although subsequent meetings can correct the record.
   According to Renton: 'If it is possible to circulate copies of the minutes, this should be done to save time. The form of the motion is then "that the minutes as circulated be taken as read and confirmed", or if necessary, "That the minutes as circulated and as amended be taken as read and confirmed".' Thus the authorities seem to regard the matter as one of convenience, not of principle. Members should be able to tell easily which copies are the correct ones at the meeting at which the minutes are adopted.
   I hope this helps.

The student took the examination again in the spring following the November examiners' meeting, in the event, scoring a mark in the subject in which the chairman was examiner well below that (informally) normally regarded as a pass mark. Considerable discussion followed, in which the tutor and one other examiner advocated a full discussion of the case. Few other examiners are reported as participating in the discussion. The two external examiners were invited to comment. One did so, focusing on the exact marks awarded in the 'second sitting that was regarded as the first one', and supporting the traditional informal rules that were nevertheless not to be regarded as precedents.
   It is reported that other students that year, whose marks were better in some subjects and worse in other than those of Miss — were allowed to pass. The matter of whether a 'fail' decision should be recorded, taking into account the history of the case, was put to the vote. It was decided by a majority vote that the 'fail' should stand, with some members abstaining and others (including ones who had taken no part in the discussion, as was their right) supporting the majority decision.

The matter appears to have ended at that point, but as a footnote, the practice was to inform students who 'fail' by inviting them to meet the course director, who informed them personally, rather than pinning a list on a notice board. By coincidence another female student (who had passed the examination) visited the course director on a different matter. She was mistaken for Miss — and informed of her failure. By coincidence the student was due to visit the tutor who had taken up the case of Miss —, and had been able to have the error corrected immediately.

Readers will no doubt decide for themselves what ethical issues or principles are involved in the case. It is sufficient to note that the 'intervening processes' are visible in the case, though their operation appears to require a mixture of ambiguity and of discretion allowed to managers of procedures. This discretion is of uncertain extent, and the means for checking it appear to rely upon initiatives from higher up the hierarchy. By itself, this is a commonplace enough conclusion, but it adds detail to the well-discussed lack of juridical processes in bureaucratic organizations. In this particular case the consequences for the student of what might be seen as lapses in the application of natural justice might not be considered as very serious — failure in a post-graduate examination. It might be asked whether the processes described as following this are so very different from those described in the cases of some disasters, such as those at Chernobyl, Seveso and Zeebrugge. Do the highest authorities in companies and institutions have a duty to inform themselves of the processes which protect them from discovering and correcting the processes that can lead to minor or very major moral failures? If we answer that they do, then it is far from clear whether any sufficiently sound procedures have yet been developed for their use. Some of the disadvantages of codes of practice have become clear, along with some of their advantages. Relying on education of individuals in ethical principles, including those of elementary justice, risks putting them back into a morally-constraining situation. Can the commitment (or is it crankiness, malice or jealousy?) of whistleblowers be relied upon to do what might be thought of as the duty of others others not prepared to act?

A few short examples will perhaps be appropriate. By their nature, it is difficult to authenticate them, as none of the participants would wish to be identified, and the purpose of this collection is not to lampoon the author's favourite targets, but to provide evidence that might help in the development of procedures for improvement:

- A headteacher of a state primary school has difficulties with discipline and control. His solution is to prevent parents from coming into school without his permission and without a prior appointment. He stations himself as if under seige, so that he can see all who come into or leave the premises (helpful for security reasons). Teachers in different parts of the school are not allowed to fraternize during school hours. In an attempt to regain control, large numbers of children are designated as 'educationally subnormal', and dispatched to special schools. Staff turnover is high, but it is also high in other schools which do not have the same discipline problems. Articulate parents are able to defend the children and move them. The local authorities are reluctant to act because of difficulty of proof, and because a scandal is feared.
- High-level managers in a particular large institution use the company equipment for private purposes, sometimes contrary to the formal rules. Lower-level employees are fired, or prosecuted on the allegation of doing the same thing.
- In another institution, inaccurate minutes of meetings are circulated to justify decisions already taken in the light of selective evidence, reporting the remarks and contributions of favoured members of the group, and ignoring those of others. The disadvantaged members ascribe this to admirable cunning on the part of the manipulators.
- In yet another institution, promotion games are played in which the rules are changed to suit the preferred candidate, or waived for some candidates and enforced, or even reinterpreted unfavourably, for others.

In most of these cases, not only are the moves in the game well-protected from official action, though widely known, but they are as likely to be supported and protected by the 'victims' as by the beneficiaries. This no doubt goes some way towards explaining the unpopularity of whistleblowers.

It should be emphasized that the events described in this chapter are selected to show how the gap between impeccable aspirations and actual outcomes can arise in institutions. It is not suggested that they are the norm, because I do not believe that they are. If procedures for improvement are to be developed systematically, the depressing influence of informal intervening processes needs to be recognized. On the other hand, the 'intervening processes' can be harnessed to justifiable common purpose. Hypotheses as to how they work are also difficult to validate. The business literature is replete with uplifting tales of how they work for individuals, or for individual companies at particular points in time, but they tend to be filtered through the eyes of individual commentators or management writers.

The research challenge, as it seems to me, is one that can be addressed to the managers of companies and institutions and to researchers. Much is known about the operation of companies and institutions. This knowledge can be gained through examination of corporate histories, particular incidents, biographies of leading protagonists, and the operation of particular management systems. Little of it has been established through the use of 'research paradigms' (methods) that are informed by ethical theory. Historical studies of companies produce historical explanations. Scientific studies (for example in economics, sociology, social psychology or organizational behaviour) provide scientific explanations. What seems to me to be needed is a joint willingness on the part of companies and researchers to pursue constructive research designs, informed by ethical theories, aimed unashamedly at improvement, and showing 'warts and all'. It may even be discovered that what is sometimes had at present through the dubious medium of manipulative practices may often already be available and provided through more ethically defensible means. Although it is rarely true that the end justifies the means, the converse may well be true more often than not. Business ethics can allow for research and negotiation on how 'means' and 'ends' may be properly combined, using acceptable criteria for decisions and for monitoring, guiding, and, where appropriate, changing them. This process is not necessarily one of concealment, internal politicking or cynical public relations.

Conclusions

I conclude that:

1 Business is driven by values.
2 These values are always either directly moral or ethically-relevant.
3 The values are initiated, preserved or transmitted by many supportive institutions, and because of this, the actions of the institutions themselves are not immune to ethical evaluation.
4 It is possible to speak of 'duties' in connection with the activities of companies and institutions. Such duties include obeying the law, subject only to the duty to make objections on grounds of conscience to laws that cannot be changed by due process. The duties include all those *prima facie* duties to

which Ross referred, long ago, and are connected with the concepts of 'natural justice'. They involve keeping promises, telling the truth, developing an effective juridical process within firms in relation to hiring and promotion, discipline and dismissal, treatment of suppliers and customers, accurate advertising and reporting and many others.

5 Most of these are supplied as a matter of routine by very many, if not most firms.

6 The primitive nature of many internal juridical processes is a cause for concern.

7 Many institutions, as can be seen from the case studies, are tackling these matters, but the continuing problem of 'whistle-blowers', and the rising tide of codes and litigation and media attention to ethical matters indicate that there is still a long way to go.

8 Some of the institutions which lay claim in their constitution or charter to a leading role in moral/ethical standards have as far, and perhaps in some cases, further to go in this respect than many who make no such claim.

All of these claims can logically be made without any need to identify what are held to be 'good' values to be encouraged, or 'bad' values to be avoided. The argument of the book so far has been addressed to how values can be systematically handled in business, and how they are, in practice, handled by firms and supporting institutions. The case studies have varied in length from a paragraph to pamphlet-length. I claim that they illustrate the pervasiveness of values, and the wide variations of standards adopted, the wide variations in which the standards are enforced or taken seriously, and the lengths to which some institutions will go to preserve their values, or, sometimes to lay spurious claim to them.

None of the arguments and cases deployed so far is capable of listing the values and practices that are held to be 'good' or 'bad', justified or otherwise, except by appeal to some more general principles. These have included the notions of duty, benefits, interests, gains, improvements, skill, prudence, natural justice, and to other concepts. Several criteria for judgment have been applied, including consistency, consent, and the extent to which practices or decisions are grounded in recognizable ethical principles. The arguments have been centred upon an account of business ethics as 'the systematic handling of values in business and industry'.

In Chapter 7 an attempt is made to deal with the recurring problems of demands for definitions of 'ethics', and demands to answer questions of the form 'Yes, but why *should* I or anyone be "ethical"?' An attempt is also made to bring together several different procedures for analysing the cases, in terms of some standard, and partly rival, alternative ethical theories. It is these theories, rather than individual whims and preferences, that enable judgments to be made consistently as to the content of ethical rules or codes. Some of the later cases are presented descriptively, so that they can be used as 'raw material' on which to try to use the various perspectives offered in this book, and by the traditional ethical theories. Not all cases can be treated in non-committal terms, partly because interpretations are at the core of the issues. In such cases, the arguments can continue whatever the facts of the matter. This is particularly so in assessing the effects of aggregate economic policies, where the data are uncertain and capable of reinterpretation to fit preconceptions of the exponents of particular policies, or of the opponents.

7 SOME METHODS FOR ANALYSING CASES

The cases presented so far provide an indication of the range of values and value-related issues and topics that are found in business. In the early chapters I sought to explain why the cases are directly matters for ethical concern or are ethics-related. The aim was also to indicate the range of attitudes both towards the substantive ethical issues and the possibility of resolving them in rational, informed and defensible ways. Arguments about values tend to follow well-established patterns. Some of these have been explored. Broadly, they have been seen to involve a sequence in which claims are made, as assertions of fact or as affirmations of principles that are held, or assumed to provide ways of prescribing what ought to be done. The idea that business ethics is not possible, because business is supposed to be non-ethical, or inevitably driven by non-ethical matters such as the laws of competition, has been shown to be inadequate, because the allegedly amoral principles, such as profit-maximization and the essential self-centredness of individuals, can be seen to be ambiguous, and lacking in evidence. More importantly, perhaps, from the point of view of rational analysis of business values, it can be seen that values drive business, and are often affirmed and reaffirmed by business representatives.

I have argued that these values are generally impeccable, that it is possible to support or destroy arguments and claims in matters ethical in a variety of ways, from demonstrating consistency or inconsistency in claims, by showing that claims are clear (or ambiguous), or that they do not have the implications the bearers of the claim thought they had. Ethical arguments can be decisive when they show that people initially in disagreement actually hold the same values, but differ on the factual premises needed to reach a conclusion. A typical example of the last kind of argument concerned the European Social Charter, where the one country which did not sign, did so on the grounds that the principles themselves were not in dispute, but that the labour market in fact operates in such a way as to render the agreed principles inoperative. This, too, is a form of argument in ethics

124

that is very common. Issues surrounding the truth or otherwise of factual claims, and the lengths to which people will go in order to reinterpret, discount or ignore inconvenient evidence or counter-evidence, are unambiguously ethical in themselves, and are connected at many points with the unofficial and intervening processes discussed in Chapter 4.

We showed further that many ethical claims, accusations and issues remain unresolved because the crucial, factual (including statistical) evidence is often withheld, manipulated, or otherwise obscured. This was seen to be the case in matters as wide-ranging as the supply of official statistics and the genuineness or otherwise of technical claims for some 'green' products. Some ethical arguments, such as can be seen in Case 21 on trade policy, follow the line that there are circumstances in which an apparently sound ethical principle can bear more heavily than is appropriate, because there are structural differences sufficiently large to introduce a new principle into the argument. Thus, Italian representatives argued that the size of the Italian public sector made competition-control rules, designed for a largely private sector, unduly repressive, catching legitimate activity in a net designed to catch trading malpractice.

It is important to note that ethical argument can proceed at levels which do not require different 'sides' to be opposing each other with irreconcilable, 'subjective' ethical principles. Indeed, it is possible to conduct an ethical argument in order to judge the merits of claim and counter-claim without holding any of the substantive (first-order, or 'ethics 1' principles) in common with any of the parties. This is often what arbitrators and judges are required to do.

In short, business ethics involves arguments about values and arguments about facts, and about their interrelationships. It can involve both the championing or disapproving of ethical rules or principles (ethics 1), and the detached analysis of the values, for meaning, consistency or applicability. Virtually all the 'sceptical' arguments designed to show that business ethics is impossible are addressed to the 'ethics 1' issues, and with few exceptions, are not even aware of the 'ethics 2' issues. It is possible to conduct ethical arguments without recommending any course of action. This is the stock-in-trade of many philosophers. It is nevertheless possible to conduct high-level ethical arguments designed to arrive at a proper and defensible set of values. Thus, rational conduct of ethical argument and rational defences of different value-positions are equally possible.

In Chapter 7 I attempt to show:

1 That there are rival sets of ethical principles and theories. (The expression of some of these dates to classical antiquity.)
2 These rival theories are to some extent irreconcilable, in that if any one of them is wholly true, the others must be at least partly false.
3 This provides a strength for ethical arguments, rather than a reason for dismissing them.
4 That the ethical theories are at once necessary for defensible ethical practice, incomplete and irreconcilable.
5 That there are workable procedures for assessing and establishing the ethical defensibility of current or proposed practices, codes and decisions.

The chapter draws upon the arguments of Chapters 3, 4 and 5 of *Key Issues in Business Ethics*. It adds to the ideas presented there concerning the notion of 'techniques of evasion' by which ethical duties are sometimes evaded (not always intentionally). These techniques are often successful. Their success rate will only be reduced by an ability to recognize them and to develop counter-strategies. The concepts and language necessary to develop these counter-moves are underdeveloped, and much more needs to be done if the techniques of evasion are to be recognized for what they are when they occur, and their baleful effects are to be reduced.

I attempt to provide a method by which the rival doctrines in ethics can be put to service in analysing the case material presented in the book, with a view to reaffirming the proper and acceptable values that drive business, and also reaffirming the practices, or redesigning them to meet defensible ethical criteria where appropriate. This, for want of a more elegant term, I call an 'analysis matrix for ethical issues'.

It can be seen from the cases that arguments, criticisms, justifications and defences are not merely plucked from the air. The arguments appeal, typically, to what are assumed to be shared principles of duties, expectations, obligations and rights. They use ancient lines of argument, many of which require the weighting of different principles. An action may be expedient towards meeting some shared principles, but objected to on the grounds that others will be broken. For example, it is sometimes in a company's interests to pretend that rigorous product-testing has been conducted according to contract, when it has not. Any employee who is required to lie, or to be 'economical with the truth', may object on a variety of grounds, from upholding the law (a duty of citizens) to personal integrity and an obligation to perform duties properly. The assumption that companies can sometimes get away with such short-cuts is often true, as shown by Velasquez (1988, p. 58ff.). The principle of profit maximization is then in conflict with the principle that contracts should be honoured in both spirit and letter, even if it is possible to evade them with impunity. Other cases have shown that a person's obligation to tell the truth can be in conflict with the obligation to promote the employer's interests, and to defer to the employer. There are, of course, arguments to the effect that in general, in the long run, it is in everyone's interests to obey the spirit and letter of contracts, because otherwise the system will break down.

It is by no means obvious that widespread abuse over a long period of time does typically destroy any system. All systems degenerate eventually, and not necessarily from abuses. Long-term misconduct that is well-rewarded is by no means rare, but the long term is a vague concept. This vagueness vitiates many attempts to show that firms are 'profit maximizers', and to show that people with low ethical standards typically get their just deserts. Managers at the top of corporations are themselves usually in that position for only a short time, and may be long gone before their 'just deserts' catch up with the corporation. What is in the collective interest all too often is patently not in the interests of all individuals. The arguments of Thrasymachus in Plato's *Republic* demonstrate the difficulty in convincing on prudential grounds anyone who could get away with breaking the rules that they ought not to do so.

Among other things, theories serve to make explicit the implications of and interconnections between principles, hypotheses and other ideas. In ethics generally, there are many rival theories, and many rival methods of classifying them (*Key Issues*, pp. 80–2). Each one can be applied to each of the cases in this book. The exercise of doing so will show clearly that some theories do better than others in explaining and analysing the cases, but more importantly, in providing clues for constructive ways forward. Three very common ethical theories can serve to illustrate the point. As described in the Glossary, these theories are: utilitarianism, deontology and natural rights. For convenience, the accounts of these given in the Glossary are reproduced:

deontology The doctrine that ethics is grounded in notions of duty; that some acts are morally obligatory regardless of consequences in terms of practice. One of the major doctrines in ethics.

rights A person's entitlements as a member of society, and including liberties such as the right to use a public highway, and 'claim rights', such as the right to a defence counsel (Flew, 1984). Few people would deny that rights exist; but the sources are in dispute. Views range from rights as grants from the sovereign or from the law, to natural rights upon which the law is thought to be based.

utilitarianism In general, the notion that an action, state, process, etc., is good or right insofar as it causes more good than ill to be produced. Some see the end as pleasure; Bentham saw it as utility. This last has a profound effect on economic theory, with frequent changes of alias. One of the major doctrines in ethics.

These are 'ethics 1' theories, addressed to the question: On what grounds should an action, decision, process, state of affairs, etc., be judged to be good or bad, right or wrong, ethically defensible or reprehensible? In addition, there are many 'ethics 2' theories, addressed to such questions as: How can we know the truth or otherwise of the 'ethics 1' theories? How can we appraise their consistency and applicability? How can we be sure that the 'ethics 1' theories address topics that are real as opposed to imaginary? This last question is added because there have been many attempts to show that *all* moral or ethical concepts are 'literally nonsense' (Ayer, 1936 and various editions), or are 'known by intuition' (Moore, 1903), or are restricted in application in principle to particular times and places, thus being invalid as means of comparing one time or culture to another (MacIntyre, 1985). This last doctrine has many aliases, such as relativism, cultural relativism or historism. Even more radical versions exist, in some forms of subjectivism: the doctrine that all moral judgments are no more than a matter of personal taste.

From time to time, one or other of these doctrines has been dominant in some circle or nation, frequently with baleful effects: Sir Isaiah Berlin saw the reign of terror in French revolutionary times as substantially caused by 'natural rights' doctrines as explained by Jean-Jacques Rousseau (1762). The misery of the Poor Law in Victorian England, graphically described by Charles Dickens, and the handling of the Irish famine in the 1840s, have been attributed to the practical application of utilitarianism. It is not difficult to find moral justifications offered for excesses throughout history: 'Every evil can be justified by moral standards or by a law to the person who perpetrates it' (Gotbaum, 1978, p. 168).

If the excesses are likely to be generated, or even encouraged, by acting out the principles of the particular doctrines, it should at least sound a warning against the over-enthusiastic adoption of any of them. As it happens, they are all flawed, as well as useful. A standard and, in my view, decisive objection to utilitarianism as the single principle for ethics or policy, is that it requires the promotion or maximization of goods such as economic growth, 'the greatest happiness of the greatest number' (utility) and this maximization may require the use of such means as scapegoating. It permits the sacrifice of individuals 'for the greater good'. This permits punishing the innocent, and allowing people to starve, for example, because the market mechanism is convenient for everyone else. It allows lying to protect the reputation of the corporation. In short, it begins with the impeccable principle of 'beneficence', and ends with the malevolence of the Victorian workhouse and the inability to prevent punishment of the innocent, or discriminatory application of the law, so that favoured groups are virtually immune, while disfavoured groups pay the price, as tends to happen in incomes policies and, sometimes, in the control of ethnic groups in the labour market.

The chief rivals to utilitarianism have their own problems. Deontological theories do not permit scapegoating. They insist, for example, that only the guilty may be punished. They do not allow discriminatory policies towards enforcement of rules. Nevertheless, the logic of the deontological principles leads inevitably to the conclusion that 'criminals will their own punishment' and indeed have a right to it which may not be denied. Even the greatest exponent of deontological ethics, Immanuel Kant, could find no escape from this harsh doctrine. Its harshness varies, of course with the harshness of the consequences for rule-breaking or law-breaking, but the implications of deontological principles move them inexorably towards the conclusion that ethics exists for the purpose of enforcing rules, rather than to serve defensible purposes. Doctrines of rights, as Berlin showed, incline towards powerful resentments when rights are, or are thought to have been denied. Rights doctrines are usually, and for good reasons, connected with doctrines of freedom. A standard problem for such doctrines is how the existence of rights can be proved. If they are 'natural', they run up against Hume's argument that values cannot be derived from facts, and vice versa (*Key Issues*, p. 71ff.). A practical illustration is given by the examples in which motorists drive dangerously and injure or kill pedestrians. The doctrine of freedom requires us to applaud the freedom of the motorist, to deplore the extinguishing of freedom for the pedestrians, and to seek to balance one against another. This rapidly leads to issues such as the traditional 'doctor's dilemma': how to measure the value of one life against another.

If, then, the main doctrines assert impeccable principles, but are flawed in the areas in which their rivals are strong, what are we to make of it? My own answer is that in ethical matters (as in economics, mathematics, scientific theory and method, for example), the theories are partial, expressing some, but not all of the truth. That they are necessary is a plausible conclusion from their longevity, as they are all ancient doctrines. Taken together, they are incomplete for many reasons. One of these is that the grounds for asserting that 'good' be promoted, that 'rights' be respected, or the 'duties' may not be ignored, are not part of the doctrines themselves, but are part of the class of theories that I have called 'ethics 2', or the theories that allow appraisal of ethical arguments. These theories are sometimes called 'second order', 'meta-ethical, or 'methodological'. Which of these labels is preferred is not important. A more important set of issues is raised in some of them, though. It concerns the matter of the status of ethical language, and the problem of how anyone could know that a principle, such as telling the truth, keeping promises, or honouring contracts, is ethically sound, obligatory or, more simply, ethical in the sense of ethics 1? Currently unfashionable doctrines, such as intuitionism and the idea that some or all people possessed or were capable of developing a 'moral sense' amounted to the view that moral principles were basic, and incapable of further analysis. Unfashionable though they are, these doctrines did at least address the questions of the grounds on which ethical principles could be asserted. As can be seen from the case studies, it is rare for drafters and users of codes of ethics or of laws or of economic policy makers to address them. It is, I venture to say, unknown for corporations or for the drafters of the chairmen's statements given in Chapter 1, or the critics and defenders of claims to be producing 'green' products, to declare whether the assumptions on which they judge their own stewardship are known by intuition, relative to time and place, utilitarian or deontological. It is less rare for the values expressed in the statements to be clear examples of a utilitarian, deontological or rights-based theory. They are often mixed. This leads to a method for an ethical analysis of the cases, and indeed of past, current or future decisions, policies, practices or structures in business and industry. Before doing so, there is a set of issues concerned with the language of ethics in general and of business ethics in particular that needs to be addressed.

The language of business and of ethics

Classic texts on the theme of the language of ethics in general are A.J. Ayer's *Language, Truth and Logic* (1936), C.L. Stevenson's *Persuasive Definitions* (1937), and R.M. Hare's *The Language of Morals* (1956) and *Freedom and Reason* (1963). Summaries of these works will not be attempted here. Two topics that do merit more attention than has been given recently are the nature of definitions, particularly definitions of ethics and of ethical terms, and what can be called 'techniques of evasion'.

The first of these topics is important because it is usually thought of as marking out the scope of ethical argument, and providing the most general rules, or basis upon which decisions can be made. In the Glossary, the definition of 'definitions' is given as:

definition A process or expression that provides the precise meaning of a word or phrase (Flew, 1984). Much has been written on the nature and value of definitions, occupying much time in formal and informal logic. In moral matters, the precision of definitions can sometimes be preserved only at the cost of rendering them worthless in practice, or of making them so broad that they are hopelessly ambiguous or empty. Three kinds of definitions are worth nothing:

lexical reporting on how expressions are in fact used.

prescriptive recommending a use for an expression (a procedure that is often difficult to maintain consistently).

persuasive a definition in which emotive overtones dominate the logical or factual content.

Much moral reasoning is at cross purposes as a result of confusion between the various kinds of definition, and as a result of popular misconceptions such as that moral argument must begin with definitions.

A number of related matters must be negotiated at this stage. The first of these is the meanings of the general terms 'moral' and 'ethical'. These are sometimes spoken of as though they differ, 'morals' being those matters relating to personal actions, character and values, and 'ethics' being pertinent to group expectations, norms or values. While it is important to maintain a distinction between what an individual believes or considers to be valuable, this particular one will not do. If people are individual moral agents, it is possible for them to decide for themselves what their values are, and if need be to accept and affirm or reject those instilled into them by parents or other influences. I cannot be held responsible for your values, nor you for mine. A nation state, religion, sect or group can affirm official values, but individuals are logically able to accept or reject them with or without reservations. It may be a duty to obey the law, but some particular laws may be held to be immoral in themselves or in their mode of enactment, enforcement and much else. Despite all this, a distinction between morals (as personal) and ethics as a kind of group characteristic is unworkable. It would be a logical fallacy to claim that groups are moral agents separate from their members. A group without members is no group at all. The shorthand expression 'group *mores*' or 'group rules' is useful, but it can refer to no more than a set of rules that the members of a group accept, or are claimed to accept, or have had forced upon them. More importantly, the *mores* or ethics of a nation or epoch are typically varied between groups (in the sense described above) and individuals. The ethics or codes referred to as those of a nation or epoch tend to be those of the most influential groups. They may be rejected in their entirety by other groups or individuals, and the fact that a group is more influential than another, or larger in number, does not make the values claimed by its members correct.

Similarly, even if everyone were agreed that 'ethics' and 'morals' were the same things, it would not *prove* that this was so. As John Locke put it in the seventeenth century: 'Universal assent proves nothing true.'

Whether ethics and morals are different is a matter for reasoned discussion. As it happens, many philosophers (rightly in my view) regard the terms as interchangeable. One (morals) is from the Latin and the other (ethics) is from the Greek, but this proves little, as they both referred to the prevailing customs of groups and tribes, including much more than we would now regard as moral or ethical. What (some) people meant two thousand years ago in any case has little bearing on the kinds of distinctions we are now trying to make. To accept the original meaning as all there is to it would be to commit a fallacy: just as an oak tree is not an acorn, so the modern concepts of ethics are not what they grew out of.

Some examples illustrate the point. From Frankena's *Ethics* (1973, p. *xi*):

My aim in this book is not just to introduce the problems and positions of moral philosophers, but also to do moral philosophy.

From Singer's *Applied Ethics* (1986, p. 1):

This book is about ethics or morals – I use the words interchangeably.

From Nowell-Smith's *Ethics* (1954):

The words 'morals' and 'ethics' are derived from words meaning 'customs' or 'behaviour'.

Similar uses can be found in Warnock's *Contemporary Moral Philosophy* (1967), in Grayeff's *A Short Treatise on Ethics* (1980), and in the Concise Oxford Dictionary. The practice of using the words interchangeably is thus well-established, but more importantly, less confusing than trying to force a distinction where none is to be had.

Even more complex problems arise in attempts to define or encapsulate the meaning of major ethical terms such as 'good' and 'bad', 'right' and 'wrong', 'authority', 'power' and 'freedom', to mention only a few examples. To consider only one of these, 'good' has been taken to mean 'whatever is approved of', and 'whatever tends or is intended to promote pleasure or avoid pain'. These uses are clearly capable of coinciding or conflicting, depending on the circumstances.

A better solution is to abandon the quest for precise definitions of the key terms, and to recognize that they are used in order to justify actions or claims, and in order to play many other roles. These other roles include attempts to persuade, to obscure issues, and to provoke actions, for example.

The concept of persuasive definitions is not new. An early use was by C.L. Stevenson (1937). Flew's (1976) *Thinking About Thinking* gives many examples of ways in which people protect their preconceptions from counter-argument and from evidence by redefining , relabelling, or ignoring arguments and evidence. In the social sciences, there has been much research on 'the self-fulfilling prophecy', the idea that, for example, rumours of war cause wars, or that if people act as though all others are out to cheat them, they will cause to happen the very thing they are trying to avoid. Related to these are well-researched examples of people acting down to the low expectations of them held by others. The freedom fighters/terrorists are the same persons: how they are labelled determines the reactions of others to them. At political conferences, the mention of 'trigger' words such as 'democracy' can cause delegates to cheer, stamp their feet or give standing ovations, and stay together as long as they do not discuss the implications of the terms with much detail.

These persuasive uses of language are part of the methods by which individuals are controlled, and by which dominant values are ingrained in people's thinking. In business and industry the persuasive words that produce the warm glows tend to have a 'switched-on', 'hard-nosed' quality about them. If an action can be labelled as necessary for 'wealth creation', 'efficiency', 'strengthening the bottom line', 'effectiveness', or 'excellence' (to mention but a few) it stands a good chance of being approved. In very many cases, the claims are accurate enough, and are justified by the evidence. In some cases they are not. These persuasive uses of language, together with the informal processes discussed in Chapter 5 and the secrecy associated with most bureaucratic decisions, make a very powerful combination of forces, generating and keeping in place the gap between impeccable aspirations at the top of organizations and the actual outcomes.

There are some common methods of using persuasive and evasive language. Their improper uses trade upon their proper ones. For instance, 'labelling' is often useful, so that different things may be distinguished from each other. In the preparation of medicines, poisons are clearly labelled to avoid their being consumed in error. In business, claims to have followed a procedure properly, or to have prepared accurate accounts, are much easier to make, and more difficult to verify, or to correct if false, as many of the cases in the collection demonstrate.

The following list of 'techniques of evasion' has been gathered from my own observations over the years. Some of the works referred to above identify some of the processes, under different terms.

1 **Labelling**: persuasive and pejorative. Examples: freedom fighter/terrorist; pay demands/claims. Power (if used against you) authority (if used by you).

2 **Category restriction**: the idea that moral actions are either self-centred or foolish, or that inflation can be controlled only by controlling the money supply or restraining wages and profits. (A more complex route is by raising output.)

3 **Stereotyping**: the insistence or assumption that people or actions that have one characteristic must necessarily possess another. A key factor in issues of sex or ethnic discrimination.

4 **Hit-and-run**: making claims to which there is neither time nor opportunity to reply. A potent source of reinforcing the other techniques.

5 **Definitionism**: requiring a definition of complex ideas, on the grounds that the absence of a definition invalidates the ideas.

6 **'X is Y'**: an example from economics is the insistence by some schools of thought that evidence is to be described as 'empirical' (roughly equivalent to experiential), and that only statistical series be allowed to count. This permits investigators to ignore processes, viewpoints, production methods, methods for determining decisions and objectives, processes of price

and pay determination, etc.

7 **Enthusiastic dichotomizing**: a kind of category restriction. An example in economic reasoning involves the use of a distinction between 'positive' and 'normative' modes of thought. The distinction is a useful one, but is not exhaustive. Some ideas are neither one nor the other, but are logical implications, or judgments. For instance the idea that a statement is vague or misleading is in part normative, in part descriptive, and in part indeterminate. 'The long run' can be either normative or positive, depending on what agreements are made on the uses of the words.

8 **The technical theory-value slide**: Again from economics – 'the optimum inflation/unemployment equilibrium'.

9 **The straw man move**: a move in which an imaginary and false argument is attributed to an opponent, so that the real argument need not be engaged.

10 **Base changing**: the argument/ground shift. In this, a doubtful factual proposition is continually amended until it becomes true by definition, or otherwise untestable.

There are very many such techniques.

The significance, as I see it, is that although values drive business and are largely held in place by a rich variety of persuasive uses of language, these persuasive uses can be as easily used to keep unexamined or unjustifiable values in place as to keep the constructive and justifiable ones in place. For a variety of reasons, an objective (in the sense of unbiased) language in which to raise, analyse and solve moral issues in business is under-developed. The use of some standard moral terms, such as authority, responsibility and the like has tended to be diverted into descriptions of bureaucratic practice. Other value-terms, such as 'effectiveness', 'excellence', 'integrity', 'democracy' or 'quality' appear to be used, whatever the original intentions of their authors, as mere techniques, or worse, as empty rhetoric. Others, such as 'moral' and 'ethical' themselves sound, to many industrialists, to be embarrassing, or at least to be tempting fate if performance should falter, or if allegations should be made of hypothetical skeletons in corporate cupboards.

Given, then, that there are rival theories, conflicting attitudes, and many uses of persuasive, but by no means always justified language in business: how do we pass from analysis to prescription, if improvement is sought?

The first requisite is a set of criteria for improvement. Once these are chosen, it is possible to test past, current and future business decisions and practices for the extent to which they satisfy the criteria. In *Key Issues*, three criteria were offered: pluralism, autonomy and the golden rule. These ideas are of great antiquity, and crop up from time to time in different contexts. The criteria are not substitutes for the general ethical theories, such as utilitarianism, deontology or natural rights theories. They cannot guarantee that false claims will not be made that they are satisfied by a particular practice. If they are accepted, the main problems are then to do with distinguishing genuine applications from false ones. This will inevitably require a mixture of methods, likely to include the formal methods, as used in codes of practice, reforms of bureaucratic structures and procedures by additions to memoranda of association, and the exposure of practices to public judgment through the market, as proposed by Huddy (Chapter 3). They are also likely to include personal development through training and management development programmes, and the development of a constructive language for ethics in business that neither flatters managers into embracing the latest gimmick, nor assumes that no improvements are possible.

Autonomy is the right of self government. It applies to nations and to individuals. In business ethics its primary use is in determining the extent to which individuals at all levels are able to put into practice their own values, or to operate those of someone else, whether employer, peer group or union. As with that other abstraction, freedom, one person's autonomy might be won at the expense of someone else's. In practice, being able to operate one's own values requires the ability to make one's own mind up. It implies an appropriate level of knowledge and a supportive institutional framework. A typical practical issue is whether or not individuals have the factual knowledge and the concepts with which to make up their minds on an issue, and put their case. The practice of legal representation in courts is an acknowledgement that individuals may not possess these attributes. Much of business activity is conducted in secret, or at least in private, leaving open many opportunities for restricting the autonomy of others.

From analysis to prescription

So far the cases have been presented on the basis that they express values, technical, prudential and moral. We have seen that they are interrelated, though logically distinct. In expressing values, speakers do not always make direct appeal to principles, and almost never to those of theoretical ethics. Indeed, to do so, outside philosophical discussion seems at least to be affected, if not in bad taste. Nevertheless, the values do drive business, and the values expressed in actions and in what have been helpfully called 'performatory utterances' can be seen to fall into various patterns: some are based in utilitarianism, as is the case with virtually the whole of economic theory and policy: appeals are made to the 'trickle down' effect of providing money incentives for industrialists. The theory that others will gain through sharing in the creation of new income and wealth is not only clearly utilitarian, it appeals to values which everyone else is assumed to hold: that if everyone is potentially a little better off, this is to be preferred to a more egalitarian system in which reward is more clearly seen to be proportional to merit, or preferred to a rights-based doctrine in which people are held to be entitled to certain incomes, goods or claims, irrespective of merit.

It is not uncommon to attempt to support the general utilitarian stance by declaring that an economic system based on the incentives that can generate inequalities is also fair (a rights-based idea) since everyone has a chance of becoming 'winners' in the game. Anyone can be a millionaire, and every soldier carries a field-marshal's baton in his knapsack.

An opposing, rights-based doctrine is that despite the merits of industry being viewed as a system of competitive endeavours, some 'losers' lose because the rules bear unfairly upon them. To satisfy the demands of economic justice, the rules need to be freed from advantages. Everyone must start from the same point, and if that cannot be done, losers ought to be compensated to the extent that they are disadvantaged by the rule. This leads to doctrines of positive discrimination in favour of some ethnic groups in the labour market. The matter has been exhaustively discussed in the literature (Tawney, 1931/64; De George and Pichler (eds), 1978; Beauchamp and Bowie, 1979; Rawls, 1971). The issue is relevant also to the operation of 'the firm'. Standard hierarchical bureaucracies, in which authority to act is invested in top management, at whose discretion authority to act is granted or withheld from other employees, are defended on the grounds that they are the most efficient possible ways of running and administering industry (a utilitarian argument), and are proper, because they clearly set out the lines of authority, and base them in clear principles of law (a deontological doctrine), and permit all to play the game: every employee carries the potential to earn the key to the executive washroom.

Moral arguments, and the moral defence of actions in business can thus be seen from the cases to be in constant use. They are based firmly in well thought-out theories in philosophical ethics. Unfortunately, the arguments are rarely 'pure', and tend to be mixtures of the different doctrines. As it happens, these doctrines are incomplete individually and together, and are incompatible in that a utilitarian can consistently argue from a different set of principles from those used by, say, a deontologist. That they are often used together by the same company or the same speaker demonstrates that it is common to assert commitment to incompatible 'first principles'. This leads to the standard dilemmas exemplified in the cases. They are clearest, perhaps in the codes of practice, in which professional employees are required to demonstrate loyalty to the company, to pursue the company's lawful interests, and to ensure fair dealing with employees and clients. In the frequent cases of conflicts of interest the codes cannot provide much guidance, and tend to remain silent. This is particularly important in cases in which the law itself is uncertain, and in cases in which the evidence of possible law-breaking by a company cannot be had except by breaking confidences, or by illegal means. In some cases, the individual is advised to resign rather than resolve conflicts of interest in ways which might be seen as disloyal by employers. Such solutions may sometimes be the best options, but are likely to be so only when the checks and balances on abuses of bureaucratic power are weak, or non-existent. As can be seen from 'whistleblower' cases, sometimes the support for a rationally justified solution is not forthcoming from victims, colleagues or profession (Irvine, 1988; Newbiggin, 1984; Adams, 1985; Hughes, 1985a and 1985b; Dunfee, 1990). While it is perhaps true that 'who stands alone is morally strongest', the most defensible reason why ethical systems and doctrines exist is to provide practical guidance for people faced with moral issues or dilemmas. I see very little merit in a system whose prime purpose is to test individuals in difficult decisions, or to provide permanent beds of nails. As against these considerations, there is little merit in doing the right thing only because it is safe and cost less.

Ethics being, among other things, practical philosophy, it is suggested here that progress is likely to be easier to achieve when people have available for use:

1 some criteria for improvement;
2 a wide enough range of cases in which alternative principles, viewpoints and conflicting evidence are exemplified;
3 an adequate method for analysing the issues objectively and constructively;
4 some procedures for improvement. It is to the last two that we now turn.

Cases in business ethics: an analysis matrix

The ingredients for analysis have all now been assembled. They are:

Criteria for improvement Autonomy, pluralism and the golden rule.

Rival theoretical outlooks e.g. Utilitarianism, deontology, and rights theory.

Analytical distinctions that allow different categories of ideas to be recognized for what they are, and untangled where necessary: factual matters or kinds of evidence (statistical, direct observation, statement of reasons on which claims to justification can be checked); values: those of skill, prudence and moral principle.

They can be represented as a matrix. Any case can be analysed for the presence and importance of each element. The case used is a composite of the codes of practice in Chapter 4. Also see over the page. (It is useful to place several cases, each at the head of a column. This illustrates the configuration of ethical elements in each case.)

The framework is not intended to imply that the analytical categories form a closed set. There are many ethical outlooks other than the ones discussed in this collection. They include agapism (from the Greek, meaning 'love'), the idea that ethical behaviour is derived from the prescription or principle of beneficence or love; egoism, or the idea that action not only ought to, but *must* inevitably spring from self-seeking; existentialism (the notion that we are all responsible for and control our own development); intuitionism (the idea that moral concepts are known directly by intuition); emotivism (the claim that moral concepts do no more than express emotions). There are many more. They all share some of the principles of the main theories and approaches discussed here. They are also incomplete, and in conflict one with each other. Some depend more heavily on factual evidence than others. Some require people to assent to rules more on the basis of the authority of rule-makers or rule-interpreters than others. All have strengths and weaknesses.

Some prescriptive approaches

The present book is a case collection and not a prescriptive handbook. The subject of what I have elsewhere called 'procedures for improvement' (*Key Issues*, Chapter 9) merits separate treatment. As a matter of sequence, it is useful to establish the

Ethical principle or theory	Case or example
	Codes of practice
Facts/accuracy	'To encourage investigation and research'
Utilitarianism	'To meet the interests of clients and members' 'Without profit, we will not survive, and all will lose'
Duties/Deontology	'The guardian of standards of practice'; 'wish to be a good corporate citizen' 'Anti-bribery stance' (see also below, under 'moral')
Rights	'Irrespective of differences in race, religion or nationality'; (employees') 'right to be consulted on work that directly affects them'
Values	
Skills	'To develop and maintain professional standards of competence' 'To encourage investigation and research'
Prudence	'We cannot break the law, or deviate offensively from local custom in pursuing the goal'
Moral	Anti-bribery stance; 'will operate with legitimate groups such as trade associations'
Criteria	
Autonomy	'A say in matters that affect them'
Golden rule	'Defined procedure in order to ensure for consistency'
Pluralism	'Will operate with legitimate groups'

Handwritten margin notes: "Rival theoretical outlooks" (bracketing Utilitarianism, Duties/Deontology, Rights); "Criteria for improvement" (bracketing Autonomy, Golden rule, Pluralism)

kinds of theoretical principle to which appeal is made, and to add some supporting or limiting evidence. These have been the aims of *Key Issues* and of the present collection. It is worth rehearsing the kinds of procedures for improvement that have been used in the recent past. Some well-used methods have been presented and analysed in the cases presented here. They include:

- Factories legislation.
- Safety legislation.
- Codes of practice: official, supportive of laws.
- Codes of practice: voluntary, or self-regulatory.
- Individual business and management training and development.
- Participative systems.

- 'Quality of working life' studies.
- Matching individual and group values to business strategies (few offer the reciprocal).
- 'Mission-oriented companies', such as the early Cocoa companies, the Scott-Bader Commonwealth.
- Cooperatives.
- International charters and declarations.
- Professional institutions.
- Educational charities.
- New management systems or training systems, such as 'total quality', 'management by objectives' (new in the 1960s).
- Quality circles.
- Inspirational texts under such titles as *A Passion for Excellence* (Peters and Austin, 1985); *The Human Side of Enterprise* (McGregor, 1960). Many of these offer a mixed prescription for reassertion of legitimacy of managerial operation and an offer of technical improvement in performance, the last often rather vaguely described.

Some few of these sources claim explicitly to deal with moral, ethical or value matters. All have strong ethical contents.

Contemporary developments among individuals and institutions expressing a specific concern for business ethics appear to be concentrated upon:

- Meetings and conferences aimed at identifying like-minded institutions and individuals.
- Development of new codes of practice.
- Attitude surveys.
- Discussions of specific issues, such as 'insider trading', safety matters, takeover codes and methods for teaching business ethics.
- Indications of ways in which 'good practice' is 'good business'.
- Collaborative case studies such as those now in preparation in collaboration between industrialists and researchers through the medium of EBEN (the European Business Ethics Network).

The collection of case material, collaborative studies and surveys of attitudes and practices is in my view a necessary preliminary to the establishment of generally agreed standards of conduct in and of business. At least as important are studies of the 'intervening processes' and of the legitimate acceptance of outcomes. Values do drive business, and drive the people who have to do with it. The possibilities for pseudo-ethics are stronger than the possibilities for pseudo-efficiency. The outcomes of efficiency-related practices are difficult enough to establish with much confidence:

evidence of gaps between actual and potential performance are well enough known (Taylor, 1911; Argyris, 1974; Cohen and Cyert, 1975). Short-term improvements in 'the bottom line' can be won by a variety of means, from asset-stripping to efficiency drives. Some are short-lived, others are merely cosmetic, and others so lost in technical complexity that the outcomes are, at the least, far from clear. Internal and external politics can and do influence the data available, as when in Britain, 'uneconomic' collieries came under intense scrutiny in the mid-1980s. Whether they were or were not economic bore directly on the legitimacy of the decisions to close them or keep them open. In strictly technical and financial terms, performance can be dramatically influenced by judgment. That judgment in turn can depend upon the real or perceived need to secure a particular decision. The dependence upon ethical evaluations is clearly even more at risk from misrepresentation and wishful thinking than the more simple technical matters. The establishment of criteria for improvement seems to me to be relatively simple in theory: the principles of autonomy, pluralism and the golden rule are ancient, and have stood the test of time. As we have seen, no official company statements insist or even assert that ethical values are irrelevant or unimportant. The claim is always to legitimacy, and the technical and profit measures are only part of the claim.

There are, then, powerful reasons why ethical claims are made that cannot be tested. The criteria for improvement need to be supplemented by methods for testing claims to have satisfied these criteria. In short, the problem is less one of persuading business to adopt ethically impeccable values, than of identifying what keeps the many that are now both widely accepted and uncontroversial securely in place. This is a matter of searching out and analysing the evidence. The process is under way. At this point, it is conventional to enter a plea for more research, and in this area, such a claim is amply justified. There is, though, a supplementary point, that the terms on which research is currently conducted need re-examination. A standard solution is to institutionalize it through officially-funded institutions and programmes. It seems inevitable that this will remain so, but the process itself is also subject to the intervening processes, and this leads to frequent criticisms of the priorities, direction and value of research and funding processes. This in turn, raises all the ethical issues of the formation and legitimacy of values, and the proper separation between the factual and various kinds of value matters.

With all these reservations, it is still possible to identify some promising lines of approach to the generation of prescriptive work.

In *Good Business* (1989, pp. 122 and 124) Carmichael and Drummond highlight two propositions:

It is time to stop feeling helpless, and to see that there are ways in which you can bring together the kind of citizen you want to be in your private life and the kind of citizen you want your company to be in its public life . . . .

. . . The easiest way to avoid a corporate tragedy is not a strong culture and a slick PR company. It is a weak culture and an open communications system.

Carmichael and Drummond emphasize the scope for combining defensible ethical rules with standard performance criteria: 'ethics' can be good business in both what I have called 'ethics 1' and 'ethics 2'. My own view is that there are cases in which this synergy is unlikely to 'work', but that does not imply that those areas in which it will 'work' are not capable of yielding substantial and fully legitimate rewards.

In *Good Intentions Aside* (1990, p. *ix*), Laura L. Nash of the Institute of Economic Culture in Boston, USA observes:

Many management books have ended with a paean to ethics. Forty years ago, Philip Selznick's classic *Leadership in Administration* finished with a thoughtful essay on the moral responsibilities of leadership. Today, Donald Trump's best-selling self-portrait of a deal-maker ends with a few remarks on philanthropy and working in the service of others. Tom Peters's latest work *Thriving on Chaos*, ends with the prescription to 'Demand Total Integrity'. Successful organisations, claims Peters, must shift from 'an age dominated by contracts and litigiousness to an age of handshakes and trust'. His advice: 'Set absurdly high standards for integrity – and then live them, with no fuzzy margins'.

While such testimonials are important and inspiring, they seem to imply that business integrity is simply a matter of 'really meaning it'. Such advice fails to help the already well-minded manager who nevertheless finds the ethical aspects of business sometimes painful, frequently confusing, and occasionally a matter for personal disappointment – in oneself or in one's company.

In the work from which the quotation is taken, Nash concentrates on the individual manager, as a logical starting point and as a necessary condition for development. As with Carmichael and Drummond, Nash offers checklists. She adds the reminder that understanding how ethical assumptions can be made to work effectively in the marketplace requires attention to the reasons why the normal moral values of private life seem to break down or be ineffectual in a business context, and that, in part at least,

The answers lie in the analytical frameworks that managers use, the goals they set, the organizational structures they adopt, the language they use to motivate others, and their personal assumptions about the intrinsic worth of other people.

In an earlier article 'Ethics Without the Sermon' in the *Harvard Business Review* (November–December, 1981), Nash produced the following checklist under the heading, 'Twelve Questions for Examining the Ethics of a Business Decision':

1 Have you defined the problem accurately?
2 How would you define the problem if you stood on the other side of the fence?
3 How did this situation occur in the first place?
4 To whom and to what do you give your loyalty as a person and as a member of the corporation?
5 What is your intention in making this decision?
6 How does this intention compare with the probable results?
7 Whom would your decision or action injure?
8 Can you discuss the problem with the affected parties before you make your decision?
9 Are you confident that your position will be as valid over a long period of time as it is now?
10 Could you discuss without qualm your decision or action to your boss, your Chief Executive Officer (CEO), the board of directors, your family, society as a whole?
11 What is the symbolic potential of your action if understood? If misunderstood?
12 Under what conditions would you allow exceptions to your stand?

There are many indications that business ethics has at least arrived on the business agenda. The ingredients for producing effective and acceptable prescriptions for business conduct are at least partly assembled. What is needed is a series of recipes which use ingredients of the right quality in the right proportions.

There are limitations on proceeding direct to practice (for example in producing codes of ethics or codes of practice). To coin a phrase: practice without theory is blind. But theorizing in ivory towers has sometimes been wholly ineffective, and sometimes devastating. Research without guidance from issues and research paradigms is likely to produce volume without content. Analytical methods without business cooperation remain merely potential. Business, as a whole, seems to expect to see the 'bottom line' healthy as a result of any excursion into ethics. The last requirement is a tall order — but the scope for combining efficiency and equity appears to be very great, through voluntary and pluralistic methods as well as through legislation and regulation.

We are now in a position to address directly the traditional question: Why should anyone or any company be 'ethical?'

There are two groups of reasons. The first of these is that in terms of 'ethics 2', there is no choice. No activities of individuals and companies are logically exempt from evaluation in ethical terms. The second group of reasons can be explained by the logical proposition that the requirement to hold to ethical values is no different from the requirement to hold to non-ethical values. When people express belief in Science or Scientific Method, they are expressing commitment to a value system in its own right. 'Why should companies be ethical?' attracts the same kind of answer as the question, Why should firms be competent, skilled and lawful? Inconsistent factual claims and prescriptions are equally logically invalid. Self-contradiction is irrational. The consequences of inconsistent factual beliefs about how production lines work, for example, can show up in breakdowns, industrial disputes and much else. The consequences of the irrationality are soon made plain. Inconsistency in ethical claims in industry destroys the validity of the claims. Since companies do make such claims, they are under an obligation to be consistent. The obligation can be ignored, overlooked, misunderstood or rejected successfully, but the pressures against doing so are mounting. Improvement is possible, and is increasingly expected. Criteria with which to recognize it are available. The rest requires acceptable procedures for recognizing rather than inventing 'hard realities', and giving at least equal weight to matters of efficiency and equity, rather than pretending, as is common, that what is expedient for some is equitable for everyone else.

To the extent that improvement, set against these criteria, does occur, it will come, as always, through a mixture of technical skill (knowledge of ethical concepts and arguments), prudence (sometimes it pays, sometimes inattention to ethics produces unwelcome repercussions), and the force of other people's expectations. People are more driven by values, including moral values than they are usually willing to admit. It takes a strong individual or company to withstand pressures from groups and associations whose membership they value. Ethical systems survive because they are practical, and not because they provide beds of nails, dilemmas and tests of character. The huge variations in standards and expectations over time and place demonstrate that 'what is' is not necessarily 'what has to be', still less 'what ought to be'.

8 EUROPEAN ENVIRONMENTAL ISSUES

Environmental issues and welfare economics

Cases 10 to 15 in Chapter 1 provided evidence of recent general concern within and outside Europe with environmental protection, pollution and public safety issues. The concerns are not new and have been expressed over centuries, if not millennia. References can be seen in the late eighteenth and early nineteenth centuries in the ideas, for example, of the economist Thomas Malthus, that population tends to increase to the limit of subsistence, precipitating cyclical disasters. The removal of major woodland areas for charcoal and shipbuilding in late medieval times has long been noted as providing a stimulus to and hence depletion of resources. Growth in size of deserts has been clearly identified causally with removal of trees, and non-renewing agricultural practices.

Environmental issues enjoyed a vogue in the 1950s and 1960s in the context of recognition of the harmful effects of over use of compounds such as DDT. Welfare economists showed interest through cost-benefit analysis and ingenious schemes for compensation, aimed at removing what were thought of as hidden subsidies to polluters who were allowed to emit noise and smoke and to discharge pollutants into rivers. (In the event, however, despite lingering interest in cost-benefit analysis, 'welfare economics' came to be seen as an effete luxury, promising much and delivering little, and probably standing in the way of economic growth, to which most observers were committed, as indeed were most governments.) Nevertheless, some dissenting voices were heard from time to time:

Underlying the notions of continued economic growth is the assumption of a dwindling role for Government. The public services are increasingly seen, as Galbraith says, as an incubus; an unnecessary doctrinaire burden on private enterprise. The act of affirmation, the positive political decision about equality and its correlate, freedom, becomes harder to make as the majority of voters (and not just the top 10 per cent) grow richer. Negatively, they assume – in so far as they are helped to think about these matters at all – that the unseen mechanisms of a more prosperous market will automatically solve the problems of the poverty

147

of dependency, the slums of obsolescence, the growth of irresponsible power and all the contradictions that flow from undirected or misdirected social policies. (Titmuss, 1960)

Titmuss was here referring to Galbraith's *The Affluent Society* (1958).

In *The Costs of Economic Growth*, (1967) Mishan puts a similar point:

While his father thought himself fortunate to be decently employed, the European worker today expresses resentment if his attention is drawn to any lag of his earnings behind those of other occupations. If, before the war, the nation was thankful for a prosperous year, today we are urged to chafe and fret on discovering that other nations have done perhaps better yet. Indeed with the establishment of the National Economic Development Council in 1962 economic growth has become an official feature of the establishment. To be *with* growth is to be manifestly 'with it', and, like speed itself, the faster the better.

Twenty-five years on, economic growth rates are mostly lower and seem not to yield much to the sophisticated economic management techniques now available. But even the lower rates of growth are associated with what is widely believed to be a series of crises in the physical environment. Low rates of economic growth and high rates of environmental destruction are no longer trade-offs in many areas – they seem to be inseparable companions.

An excellent summary of the basic ethical issues surrounding the topic of business and the environment was provided in 1989 by Robert E. Frederick, of the Center for Business Ethics, Bentley College, at Waltham, Massachusetts. It provides an introduction to environmental issues generally, as they are increasingly, and rightly, being seen as ethical matters of concern to the international community as a whole, rather than merely matters for individual counting.

The Eighth National Conference on Business Ethics marked a departure from many other discussions of business and the environment since the major focus was not on the monetary costs or benefits of environmental protection. If there are such obligations, then companies are morally required to consider them when business adversely affects the environment. But are businesses obligated to protect the environment? Should private enterprises take an active and leading role in solving this national problem? Or should the solution be entirely a matter of public policy, not involving business except to the extent that businesses are required to act by law and regulation?

Many of the speakers addressed these and similar questions. It was noted throughout the conference that problems with and concern for the environment are not new. Warnings came out in the 1960s that lakes and rivers were dying from industrial contamination. Our foodstuffs were tainted with methyl mercury and radioactivity. The World Health Organization even warned of the DDT contamination of mother's milk. It was reported in 1969 by the Atmospheric Sciences Research Center that there was not a breath of uncontaminated air anywhere in the North American hemisphere. In 1970 Thor Heyerdahl found no oil-free stretch of ocean during his Ra II crossing, and a 1971 report to the United Nations stated that oil dumping, lead exhaust and mercury pollution would soon render the oceans incapable of sustaining aquatic life. (Frederick, 1989, p. 2)

CASE 31   Environmental issues and business policy

The whole area of environmental protection provides powerful illustrations of the need to work with clear conceptual frameworks, such as those set out in Chapter 7. This is so because the scientific and technical arguments are complex and often uncertain. There are other reasons – it is virtually impossible for most people to acquire expertise in the whole range of technical disciplines involved. Even if they did, the factual data, say in nuclear power, atmospheric deterioration, water and ocean pollution are difficult to come by, and in many cases are jealously guarded. Experts can pronounce a process safe or dangerous according to which data and information they favour. Suspicions that officials in companies and in government are sometimes excessively 'economical with the truth' are not hard to come by, and relate as often to published data, offered as 'objective', as they do to denials that events or cover-ups have actually occurred. On issues such as those concerning environmental matters, where interests, principles, ideals and ideologies provide powerful motives, it is inevitable that facts and values become entangled. Even the nature of arguments themselves is often unclear and sometimes evasive, whether intentionally or not. Technical, moral and prudential values are often mixed up as though they were all of the same kind, and of equal force.

The environmental issues thus are mixtures of technical, prudential and moral arguments. No one can be an expert in all of them, but experts disagree, often over fundamentals, and as a group can exhibit confidence in a set of propositions at one time and in its contradictory or even its converse at another. To say this is to say no more than that experts are human, and are often faced with very complex issues. The major ethical concern, in my view, is not that experts and authorities in whom a good deal of trust and privilege are invested, can sometimes be wrong, as individuals or collectively; it is rather that the processes by which the propensity to defend collective misjudgments can be corrected are, to say the least, rudimentary and grossly under-researched. Indeed, the proposition can be offered that the volume and resources devoted to research is often inversely proportional to the importance of the topic. Parkinson's Laws (Parkinson, 1981), provide early explanatory frameworks, but in general, once major policy decisions have been made, often based on 'gut feeling', any doubts as to their wisdom and validity call the 'intervening processes' (discussed in Chapter 4) into action in defence of the decision, and serve to discourage doubt. The case studies provide many examples of these processes.

For these reasons, the approach to the environmental and 'green' issues in the present case is to provide examples of the debates, theses, counter-theses, and illustrations of the general points made above. The various facts and figures cited cannot always be checked, or their ultimate sources traced. Where possible, attributions are given. It should be borne in mind that one of the major ethical issues in environmental debates in so far as they affect business is the reliability and trustworthiness of the data and information provided by the various sources.

It should be clear from the extracts that all of the traditional ethical matters are raised by the environmental debates. These include the need to reconcile utilitarian considerations (costs and benefits) with those of duty-based principles (avoiding the use of scapegoats, distributive justice, telling the truth even when inconvenient, etc.) and rights-based principles (of even-handedness, natural justice, decent living standards, etc.). Where these are clearly in conflict (as is often the case), there is a need to develop procedures for defensible choices. In the public domain, these are, as yet, as rudimentary or lacking as are 'juridical processes' in corporations. It should also be clear that matters of technical skill, prudential management of resources and moral imperatives do become entangled in the debates, and need to be disentangled. Finally, the processes that intervene to produce environmental disappointments need to be clearly identified and seen as problems to be jointly solved. At present, the research skills, paradigms and resources seem to be in short supply.

Cases 10 to 15 in Chapter 1 raise many claims. These relate to damage or alleged damage to people and environment, as well as relating to claims and counter-claims of forward-looking, ethically sound 'green' and environmental practices and policies. They include:

- Explosions at chemical plants, and dangerous emissions from chemical and nuclear plants.
- Disputes as to the nature of the risks and consequences and the responsibilities for them.
- Claims to produce 'eco-friendly' products, and counter-claims that they lack independent validation, and are in fact, often spurious.

- Non-disclosure of risks, allegations of cover-ups, and litigation surrounding the use of asbestos, and of insurance practices relating to it; also allegations of improper refusal to hold formal enquiries to ascertain the relevant information.
- Accusations of insider trading and conspiracy in the above matters.
- Allegations of 'shameful' lack of public investment in roads and in public transport, leading to unnecessary congestion and pollution. Such allegations are by no means confined to public transport pressure groups, and include representative motorists' organizations, who are willing to apportion some responsibility to individuals and irresponsible use of motor cars.
- Accusations in respect of toxic waste and its control, from industrial effluents and farming, that the responsibilities and costs are being improperly passed on, to consumers, neighbours, other countries, and, in global terms, from the prosperous North, to the impoverished South. Whether all of the 'North' is prosperous, and whether the whole of the 'South' is impoverished is a separate issue which is often raised. The distributive ethical issues are difficult, if not impossible to distinguish from each other in practice, although in much of the debate, recognition of this seems to be minimal.

Further examples of recent claims and counter claims in various European countries are as follows:

On 26 September, 1990, under the heading, 'Gas Guzzling Cars Could be Penalised in the next Budget', Nicholas Schoon reported that 'Environmentalists identify transport as key area for action because of damage caused by road building and exhaust fumes' (*The Independent*, 26 September, 1990) – but that there would be no reversal on the trunk road and motorway building programme, costed at £15 billion. In the same issue, the British government is cited as forecasting traffic growth of between 80 and 140 per cent by the year 2025.

A British government White Paper published that day had pointed out that:

1 Transport, especially road traffic is a major source of air pollution, and produces a fifth of carbon dioxide, the main global warming gas.
2 Car ownership is relatively low in Britain, compared with other Western nations.
3 The Government welcomed widening car ownership, on the grounds of personal freedom and choice.
4 New regular vehicle testing rules were being considered, as were tighter pollution control and stricter enforcement of speed limits.
5 The Government was 'exploring the possibility' of a code of practice for advertisers which would 'encourage car manufacturers to lay less stress on power, speed and acceleration, and more on efficiency,

economy and safety'.
6 The White Paper defended government levels of investment in public transport and made no promise to raise them.

New roads were to be kept away from areas of outstanding natural beauty and sites of special scientific interest 'wherever possible'.

Stephen Joseph, director of Transport 2000, was quoted in the same source as saying that the White Paper did little to mitigate the colossal damage caused by the forecast traffic increases. He called the White Paper 'a woolly wish list of what the government might like to see happening towards the end of the century.'

Simon Foster, director of the Society of Motor Manufacturers and Traders, was reported as saying, 'we are pleased that the government recognize that more and more people want their own cars.'

Three months later, under the heading 'False figures blamed for spread of new roads', claims were reported that 'False assumptions about journey times and traffic forecasts are used by the Department of Transport to justify road schemes that damage the environment', P. Brown, *The Guardian*, 28 December, 1990, p. 2.

The Department of Transport, however, was quoted in the same article as not accepting that new roads generate more traffic. The issue, it seems, is dependent upon the assumption that saving a motorist a minute on some journeys is worth 3p. It is this figure, when multiplied by the estimate of the drivers who might use the new road, which is said to form the basis upon which a proposed new road is considered to be worth paying for.

On a wider European level, an article in *The European* indicates that companies that 'go green' can make a large profit from doing so, citing The Body Shop, which sells natural cosmetics (i.e. not tested on animals) and saw profits rise 50 per cent over the previous year.

- Volkswagen advertise their 'Golf' and 'Polo' ranges as clean cars (eco-friendly diesel/petrol cars fitted with catalytic converters).
- Spanish glass maker; Lorente-Massons, promotes its product as 'glass that has nothing to hide'.
- German chemical giant Bayer offers the message of 'responsible efficiency' (*The European*, 13 May, 1990).

The import of toxic waste is a major issue: According to the government, importing toxic waste for disposal by burying, 'landfill', or incineration is providing an environmental service while earning foreign currency.

Environmentalists and green campaigners, however, claim that it is not only dangerous to transport toxic waste over long distances, but dumping it is turning Britain into a 'potentially poisonous dustbin.' Some environmentalists claim that only a small quantity of highly toxic waste imports can be justifiable at present, because there are few companies that can deal with it safely.

Government estimates of imports of toxic waste, last calculated in 1989, stand at 40,000 tonnes. This figure did not include chemical solvents and non-ferrous metals. Toxic materials have also been found entering the country marked only as 'goods in transit' (*The Independent*, 19 September, 1990).

There are, of course, many different kinds of costs incurred in reducing the harmful environmental impact of industrial production practices. There are also many ways of mitigating them. An example is the impact upon employment. Under the heading, 'TUC wants green stewards at work', the following passage provides an illustration. In Britain, Mr Edmunds (chairman of the environment action group of the Trades Union Council), was reported as claiming that:

the argument that there must be a choice between jobs or the environment is false. You need a change in existing industrial processes not a shut down of dirty plants. [The TUC proposed a plan] . . . to create a 250,000 strong network of green workplace representatives. [The plan included] . . . environmental audits covering everything from resource use to waste disposal, to be agreed by employers and unions in every workplace in the country. (*The Guardian*, 21 August, 1990)

Three days later, on the topic of 'global warming', the same source quotes Dr Mustafa Tolba (executive director of UNEP), in preparation for a conference to discuss the United Nations Report into climate change:

The stabilization of atmospheric greenhouse gas concentrations at present levels demands – in most cases – a reduction of 60% in global greenhouse emissions. This is not the conclusion of ecological prophets of doom, these are facts, and they demand that we act now.

Politicians are viewed as reluctant to act on the causes of global warming because of the economic consequences of reducing oil and coal consumption. In the same source, Brazil and Indonesia are cited as refusing to accept any proposed action that will limit their destruction of forests unless the developed world does something about carbon emissions from power stations and cars.

It is the poor and underdeveloped countries that are expected to suffer most from the effects of global warming. The effects will be most drastic there, when the sea levels rise, reclaiming land, and they cannot afford the sea defences and other means of protection that richer nations can (*The Guardian*, 24 September, 1990).

Several separate spillages of oil into the sea have been seen to have had serious effects, not only on the environment (polluting water, killing marine life, birds, etc.) but also in straight cash terms. For example, in 1989 when the *Exxon Valdez* spilled eleven million gallons of oil off the coast of Alaska, the monetary costs of the clean-up were estimated as running into a sum in excess of two billion dollars (*The Financial Times*, 13 June, 1990). In addition there are costs associated with the wasted oil, and the cost of extracting it in the first place, and of the lost tanker.

The release of carbon dioxide into the atmosphere is estimated as being responsible for about half of the damage to the 'Ozone Layer' (the layer that screens out the sun's harmful rays). Other gases that cause depletion of the layer include methane, nitrogen oxide, and CFCs (Chlorofluorocarbons). The effect is that these gases eat away the ozone, which in turn allows harmful ultra-violet rays to penetrate the atmosphere.

There are held to be two major causes of global warming: the burning of fossil fuels and deforestation. The latter is probably the most serious, and needs to be dealt with most urgently, although it is not the main contributor of harmful gases. In 1988, up to eight billion tonnes of carbon are estimated as having been added to the atmosphere – well over five billion tonnes by fossil fuel combustion, and perhaps half of that figure by deforestation. Deforestation has many effects on the environment, since trees, like all vegetation, absorb carbon dioxide and release oxygen. Trees provide important wildlife habitats as well as many useful materials, including medicines. They prevent desertification and soil erosion by physically holding land together, providing shade, and retaining moisture at ground level.

The following ways of controlling pollution are widely canvassed:

1 Energy efficiency on a global scale, to reduce carbon emissions.
2 Reforestation and revegetation on a global scale.
3 It may also be suggested that market forces could be harnessed through the 'polluter pays' principle, and the transfer of money thus collected for use in reforestation.
4 Investment in efficiency, and gas converting chambers, e.g. catalytic converters for factories.
5 A legal requirement for the fitting of all new cars with catalytic converters.

An example of the importance of securing accurate and balanced factual information is the accusation that some large companies have been destroying areas of natural beauty by clearing large areas of peat, thereby destroying natural habitats for plants and animals, risking the possibility that yet more species are lost forever. Targeting any particular company for criticism risks missing other equally important removers of peat, and at least in one case, has drawn the rejoinder that some of the large companies also put a great deal of research into alternative sources of plant bedding material, and in any case do not completely destroy any sites (*The Independent*, 21 May, 1990).

Such claims and counter-claims risk turning joint, constructive solutions to issues in environmental ethics into win-lose adversarial stances, in which the main losers could easily be third parties. The main mediating processes between competing claims of this kind (i.e. those that cannot be handled by private negotiation or impersonal processes such as market forces) are the law, and quasi-legal institutions.

The somewhat kaleidoscopic list of issues and views examined above illustrates many general points:

1 Many environmental issues are now urgent and are very major matters for concern, but are far from being new, or newly-recognized.
2 They are typical of issues in applied ethics, in that the necessary items of factual information (the 'minor premises' in moral arguments) are not straightforward, or easy to come by, or universally agreed by educated or informed people.
3 They are typical also in that the value matters and technical matters often become so entangled in debate that what ought to be rational arguments end up as mere assertions by 'sides' who become 'camps' and engage in conversations in which neither side listens to the other, or is willing to concede a point. The game becomes one of winning at all costs, rather than attempting to discover the truth or reach agreement.
4 They are typical in the sense also that the different kinds of values are not distinguished, and criteria for deciding what is really important, to whom and why, are rarely if ever discussed.
5 The public cannot acquire expertise in all the disciplines necessary to participate on equal terms with the experts, and thus have to rely on the experts, or to ignore them.
6 The experts often disagree and individually or collectively can be biased, as a result of conviction, training (which can produce methodological biases), commitment to others, and for many other reasons.
7 Even if experts do agree, the consensus can easily be wrong, as can be seen in such matters as the relentless pursuit of combinations and permutations of simple forms of wage and price restraint throughout Europe and in America in the 1960s and 1970s.
8 Experts can and do change their consensus views, so that intellectual fashions emerge. Examples include fads as to which foods are good for people and which are bad. Starch, butter, sugar, and even tobacco have enjoyed the 'in favour–out of favour' cycle. Economics experts declared the trade cycle dead in the 1960s, just as it was returning with renewed vigour. The world dollar shortage of the 1940s and 1950s was declared to be permanent, but no

longer exists. The population of many countries in the 1930s was projected as falling at alarming rates. It has been rising at alarming rates ever since.

9 The 'environment' debates are characterized also by an absence of agreed or visible methods for disentangling the 'false' facts from the 'true' facts, or facts from values, or different kinds of values from each other.

10 Following from this, it is rarely clear what the ethical component of the environmental issues is. For instance it seems to be assumed that, if it could be shown that a particular policy served the interests of all, then it would be ethically justified. It depends, of course, on whether 'the interests of all' could ever be identified in relation to a specific action or policy, and if they could, whether an authentic representative could be found to articulate them. Many claim to be able to speak with such authority. It also depends on whether criteria used to identify 'the interests of all' include the method by which the decision is reached. This is, of course, a version of the old argument that the end does not necessarily justify the means. Would it be in everyone's interests to lie, or suppress data if it were judged to be the only way to save the planet from a major ecological disaster? Could such a judgment ever be correct?

Is this just another example of an artificial moral dilemma? Or should we say that it is permissible sometimes to break moral rules for the greater good? Would it be better to say that it is sometimes justifiable to break some ethical rules in order to preserve more important ones?

11 The above questions have been asked in various forms throughout the history of moral thought, and have spawned many moral theories and theoretical debates (cf. Mahoney, 1990, p. 39).

Environmental issues: control policies

Although not initially covered by the Treaty of Rome, a European Community Environment policy has gradually become a reality. Such a policy has emerged thanks to the growing awareness of European citizens, the commitment contained in four European Community action programmes on the environment and a legislation policy implemented since the Seventies.

The Community has adopted more than 120 legislative acts mainly concerning the environmental problems of trade and industry and there has also been scientific collaboration on a number of major problems under the Eureka project and more recently the European Year of the Environment. (*The European*, 17–19 August, 1990, Supplement p. II)

The article in *The European* from which the above quotation is taken describes three principles of EC policy:

1 Prevention is better than cure.
2 Subsidiarity (specification of the appropriate level of responsibility for action).
3 The polluter pays.

In the same source, the report of a special Commission task force is cited as recommending eco-taxes and charges 'to shape the EC's economic development'. Ecological issues are also live at wider international levels than the EC: According to a headline in *The Independent* in November, 1990, there will be 'International Law to Protect Climate By 1992.'

The headline referred to the Second World Climate Conference in Geneva, attended by prime ministers, ministers and officials from 137 nations. However, real disagreements continue:

Representatives of various West European states, Australia, New Zealand, Japan and Canada express commitment to the view that stabilizing then curbing emissions of CO_2, the most important greenhouse gas, are of great urgency. The USA, USSR and Saudi Arabia, three of the world's biggest oil producers disagreed. (Loc. cit)

Dr John Knauss, administrator of the US Oceanic and Atmospheric Administration, told the conference:

My country is not prepared to make any commitment on any reductions which we are not able to guarantee to fulfil.' (Loc. cit.)

Even with massive reductions and stabilizing of carbon dioxide emissions, the effect of the industrializing Third World will be devastating. The declaration recommends that the Third World be given extra financial aid and technology to help minimize the effects of industrialization.

Simon Roberts of Friends of the Earth is reported as saying,

'There remains a very great risk that the lack of drastic action by rich industrialized nations will blow the final whistle on the planet.' (*The Independent*, 8 November, 1990)

Notwithstanding the 'Year of the Environment' initiatives, indications are that even among industries whose environmental impact is clearly visible to the public, the provision of corporate policies is very patchy. An example is provided by a survey of British companies and professional institutions by the National Materials Handling Centre at Cranfield. The report, 'Environmental Policy: Standards and Development' (P. Davis, 1991) found that:

... 56 per cent of all firms and 90 per cent of all professional and trade associations surveyed had no written policy on the environment. Firms had very few standards in operation beyond those imposed by parliament, with 73 per cent of firms reporting operating no voluntary codes on the environment and

70 per cent reporting no monitoring of their environmental impact beyond statutory requirements . . . and 75 per cent of all firms reported no plans to introduce environmental programmes in the near future. (*Procurement Weekly*, 14 March, 1991, p. 2)

As is often the case, American experience with major legislative and control policies predates that of Europe, but the results, in some areas, have been seen as disappointing:

In the 1970s, beginning with President Nixon's famous message to Congress, the United States was the state of birth and the world leader in environmental policy. It was the mecca for hundreds of environmental politicians, lawyers and members of citizen groups who consulted American policy documents and visited the United States for inspiration. It was the United States that coined the terms 'environmental policy' and 'environmental law', and enacted various model laws and programs for environmental protection. These statutes and programs included the National Environmental Policy Act, with its environmental impact assessment procedure; the technology-forcing car exhaust emission standards adopted under the Clean Air Act; stringent ambient air quality standards to be achieved within short deadlines; the goal of zero water pollution set under the Federal Water Pollution Control Act; the notification and testing requirements under the Toxic Substances Control Act, and citizen suits provided in major Federal laws. Together they constituted the highlights of the American environmental decade under the presidencies of Nixon, Ford and Carter.

In the 1980s, US environmental policy suffered from a severe environmental crisis . . . . And it is no secret that in this decade, adversarial competition between a Congress responsive to pressures from well-organized environmental groups and an executive branch responsive to business interests has often resulted in environmental policy deadlocks. . . . many important, urgent, or at least long-term problems like acid rain have not been tackled. Moreover, independent of the conflict between the Congress and the executive branch, various policy goals contained in the legislation of the 1970s had to be delayed because it was not possible to achieve them (zero water pollution or the achievement of secondary air standards). (Rehbinder, 1989)

Contrasting the US and EC policy styles and contexts, Rehbinder points to the sheer size of many American pressure groups (sometimes with several million members) facing a single government (albeit with separated powers), adding that by contrast, EC environmental policy is a bureaucratic, member-state based policy that – even after the coming into force of the Single European Act – lacks political legitimacy. These institutional factors have an impact on the content of environmental policy, and make it 'impossible simply to transfer American solutions to Europe' (Loc. cit.).

Both in the US and in Europe, policy contents include the 'polluter pays' principle, but in both contexts, self-imposed restrictions in scope (e.g. exclusion of state as a legitimate instrument), and the operation of powerful pressure groups have diluted it, and in Europe, enforcement by the Commission has been rendered highly uncertain by the paucity of resources devoted to supervising and implementation.

However, American policy has included buying dollar bonds issued by Latin American countries in exchange for promises to protect tropical forest areas permanently. This very practical form of 'paying for one's principles' does not, so far, seem to have commended itself much, if at all, in Europe.

Some conclusions

Environmental issues are ethical issues in the 'ethics 1' sense in that they generate moral obligations and affect the well-being and rights of people, and involve the 'categorical imperatives' of providing accurate and truthful information. They are also ethical in the 'ethics 2' sense in that they can be analysed, evaluated and treated, using standard moral concepts and logic. It would seem that, on environmental issues, Europe has lagged. The reasons why this is so are not immediately clear, given that the issues have been well-known for at least a century, and were the subject of considerable discussion in the 1960s, in the context of social policy as well as welfare economics. Clues are to be found in the discussions of 'growthmania' and the belief that the application of scientific method rendered all discussion of values unnecessary, or even perverse. These no doubt played major roles. The general lines of my own approach are given in Chapter 7, and are summarized there as including:

1 Methods for encouraging participation in discussion, rather than merely going through the motions. In this, all participants are encouraged to become well-informed, rather than fed predigested 'informed opinion' (the autonomy principle).
2 Recognition of issues for what they are (technical, prudential, moral). This is easy enough within a company or department of a company, even if it is rarely achieved. It is more difficult in terms of, say, the debate on the future of energy generation, but it is by no means impossible. It is a challenge for business in the late twentieth century.

This approach avoids undue narrowing of the terms of debate, and dispenses with techniques of evasion.

The elements of an ethically-informed debate and policy on environmental issues would thus involve:

1 Legislation and realistic control aims and procedures.
2 Rules or codes for extending participation in the formulation

and encouragement of ethically justifiable policies and actions, avoiding undue restrictions of the agenda.

3 Extension of teaching on the environment from mere technique and lists of what are to be considered 'good' and 'bad' actions.

4 Visibility, through publication of the debates and arguments in an informed way, using third party commentators and researchers. This means publishing accessible and authentic arguments from various viewpoints (avoiding, or at least recognizing the 'techniques of evasion' discussed in Chapter 5) as opposed to the hit-and-run debates that dominate public discussions in the broadcasting media, and the method-bound research of a good deal of social science. Procedures on the lines of the Register suggested by David Huddy (Case 23) have a potential role in this context.

5 'Good practice' cases which are commonly used to spread ideas through what is sometimes called 'the demonstration effect' tend to be filtered through one case-study writer or team. Authentic statements of various viewpoints could be sought, rather than the more common, and more convenient, search for single representatives, who may in fact be far from representative.

6 Recognition that ethical conduct needs to take account of rights (see J. Donaldson, 1989), as well as duties and obligations, and that the processes of the recognition and distribution of rights, duties and obligations are crucial to their outcomes.

9 | THE CONTROL OF INCOME, INFLATION AND THE LABOUR MARKET

Business operates within a framework of rules. These rules originate from a variety of interconnected sources, including law, custom and practice, professional standards of analysis and of 'good practice', government policies and, increasingly, international law. Earlier case studies have illustrated the mode of operation of many of the rules. The rules are transmitted and filtered by the institutional framework, including opinion-forming institutions such as the Churches, universities, and the various pressure groups that are representative of people in various occupations. The framework of rules is also profoundly influenced by the 'intervening processes' of unexamined assumptions, narrowing of agendas, and the tunnel vision provided by specific disciplines.

Persistent efforts in many countries to control the general levels of pay and prices merit inclusion of the topic as a case study in its own right. Case 32 identifies the ethical context of policies for the control in the aggregate of pay and prices, which are generally (and correctly) seen as interconnected.

CASE 32 | The control of incomes and inflation

The body of specific topics relating to the control of pay and prices has been intensely, if not exhaustively, analysed and debated in the economic and political literatures. The essence of the subject can be had from any standard macroeconomics text, such as R.G. Lipsey's *Introduction to Positive Economics* (various editions since 1963), Bell and Kristol (1981), or any dictionary of economics.

As might be expected of topics which refer to important matters such as people's incomes, the literatures contain many overt and hidden values which seek to persuade those whose actions influence pay and prices to adopt sets of beliefs and practices that it is hoped will render control by the proper authorities (i.e. governments) easier and more predictable. In the event, different countries, and even groups of countries, exhibit long-term and characteristic patterns in incomes and prices. Some countries, such as Germany, for example, have been able to maintain a low rate of increase in prices, and a relatively high rate of increase of incomes. The distributional rules that govern pay differentials and pay movements vary between countries, as a result of differences in culture and institutions. Income is viewed as effective command over resources, goods and services (sometimes called 'real income'). Other countries, such as Britain, have maintained generally higher levels of inflation and money wages, but lower levels of 'real income', despite many policies pursued with great determination, and many changes of policies. Britain was widely held, in the 1980s, to be emerging from a long period in which no policy had been sustained for long enough to be effective. After a period of more than a decade, in which many previous options had been ruled out, the inflation rate nevertheless had continued (with temporary aberrations) almost unchanged (source: Great Britain, National Economic Development Office, *British Industrial Performance and International Competitiveness* 1987, 1990).

To note these effects is to say no more than that the control of incomes and inflation is a difficult and uncertain matter, and that historically no set of institutions has maintained control for very long. The German experience from the 1950s was probably one of the most effective and long-lasting. It is not the purpose of this case study to speculate on the possible longevity of any particular set of policies or policy effects. A purpose more relevant to the theme of the present book is the identification of the ethical issues involved in controlling incomes and inflation. The topics have not, to my knowledge, been systematically treated by the use of the concepts and methods of ethical reasoning, but have tended to be seen as primarily technical: statistical, mathematical, or as relevant only to the design of economic and industrial relations institutions. A critique of these methods of conceptualization is beyond the scope of the present work. The methods were analysed in some detail by the contributors to *Pay Differentials* (1985), edited by John Donaldson and Pamela Philby.

Expertise in these matters is not easily gained. Much of the topic turns upon what is actually happening at a particular time, but the factual and statistical information available is at best sketchy, and often gathered and presented by authorities and others for particular purposes, especially to justify or advocate particular policies. Factual assertions often draw accusations of manipulation of data:

An important sector of the information industry has grown up around official economic statistics – predicting, analysing and disputing them. Financial analysts and traders in the City can add or wipe off billions of pounds from the value of shares and currencies by their reaction to these economic indicators. Politicians attempt to interpret them so as to favour government or opposition, particularly in the run up to elections. Employers and trade unions fasten upon such key numbers as the inflation rate as an essential input into pay negotiations. (Johnson, 1988)

Johnson quotes the Select Committee of the House of Commons as showing concern that judgments about the state of the British economy are seriously hampered by the unsatisfactory state of official statistics, commenting that the government's competence and motives are in question, but leaves open the question whether the deficiencies in the figures themselves and their availability are due to lack of coordination skills in official circles, or to deliberate intent.

Another commentator (also referring to Britain) adds:

What we can say with certainty is that the much-publicised two-year fall of 800,000 in the unemployment figures is a statistical illusion. There is no consistent definition of the phenomenon that yields those figures. On the other hand an increasing number of people have jobs; a decreasing number of people want work but cannot find it. An honest figure would look less dramatic than the distorted impressionist painting we are offered each month, but would still look tolerably bright. (Kellner, 1988)

Even if the basic figures were unproblematic and agreed, the method of handling them to give 'objective' results presents further, unresolved problems. Whether income as a result of any policies or developments is becoming more or less widely dispersed, or whether this is true only temporarily and for some sectors of the population, is not known. Different methods yield different results, even with agreed data. To my knowledge, there are no agreed principles at the technical level as to whether effective control is to be achieved by means of technical – statistical and mathematical – analysis, or by the design of economic and industrial relations institutions. Some helpful sources of information and ideas on the debate about the distribution of income are: Atkinson (1980), Royal Commission on the Distribution of Income and Wealth (UK, 1977); Pen (1971), Lydall (1967) and Phelps Brown (1977).

To summarize the problem: issues of incomes and inflation are important enough to attract intense, even obsessive policy attention by governments and commentators. The last fifty years have seen regular patterns of price behaviour between different countries. Germany, for example, has typically had the lowest rates of inflation, while Italy and Britain have typically been among the highest. There are no sets of data upon which agreement on comparisons could be sought, and there are no agreed 'research paradigms' by which the 'right questions' could be identified and tackled. This is characteristic of major topics in business ethics and economics. These are not merely technical matters whose chief interest is in providing amusement for academic problem-solvers. If, as some claim, the distribution of income in each country is very stable, then policies aimed at changing it, or bringing it into line with general notions of fairness or rights, are hopeless, and pretences at doing so are false. If, on the other hand, the distribution *is* changeable, and government policy action changes it, then the possibility of gross unfairness in policies remains open. As it happens, it is traditional to criticize authorities' policies on grounds that they are unfairly redistributive. It is also traditional for authorities to attempt to give the impression that they are fair, either because they redistribute in directions opposite to those claimed by their critics, or because they provide incentives to generate more wealth to share out.

These topics matter because people do have strong views on the fairness of policies. Historically, in periods when there has been growth in income, the issues have been masked or have become less visible. Thus, in prosperous times, authorities can say something like, 'You've never had it so good. Incomes will be doubled in ten years, we have maintained the external value of our currency, and kept a surplus in the balance of payments. We have kept the inflation and unemployment rates low, and have no significant environmental problems.'

In some circumstances governments can make claims such as those above for several consecutive years, without much fear of contradiction. In other contexts, few, if any of the claims can be made without fear of contradiction, whether or not such contradiction is justified.

The above introduction forms the background to a series of propositions which illustrate the ethical content of policies for the control of incomes and prices (inflation). These are:

1 **Income is one of the most potent distributors of the goods that most people actually do prize.** This is not merely a matter of the supply of consumer durables, or holidays in the sun. Researchers have long noted that individual health expectations and 'life chances' and lifestyle are greatly influenced by occupation, and hence depend on income level. This holds for rich as well as poor countries, even though the incidence of poverty-related diseases and disasters is both absolutely and relatively higher in poor countries.

2 **Most people accept that the general features of income distribution are justifiable.** That is, that people do not, on the whole see a need to question seriously the distribution of income, except when required, either through natural disasters or major policy decisions to accept a fall in income. Even in developed economies in Europe and America, 'incomes policies' have been relatively easily accepted, until people become aware of 'anomalies'. These have included situations in which some group with which other people compare their own situation appears to have gained relatively, without meriting the gain. When, as is inevitable, this happens to enough groups the 'incomes policy' becomes untenable, and is abandoned.

3 **The ethical content of incomes policies is by no means**

confined to the 'ethics 1' issues. By this, I mean that the distribution and redistribution of income have such a profound influence on people's lives – and hence on their values – that the matter does not depend wholly upon whether people have enough to eat. This is manifested in the great lengths that governments, trade union leaders, and, often, individuals go to to justify their stances on matters relating to incomes and incomes policies. It is also manifested in the explanatory moves that are used to support ill thought-out or under-researched policies. This leads to proposition 4.

4 **The pursuit of ethically unexamined 'macro' policies by ethically unexamined means is a major source of missed opportunities as well as of unnecessary conflict.** What this amounts to is the obvious point that a policy that can be seen to be manipulative generates equally cynical and evasive behaviour. This explains the demise of some incomes policies (though not all). A more important point is that lack of recognition of the ethical content of policy in such an important area is symptomatic of lack of ethical awareness generally. The missed opportunities relate to the huge discrepancy between what industry is capable of producing, with proper attention to values, and what is actually produced. The British experience of the 'three-day week' in 1974 demonstrated that many companies were able to produce in the three days in which they had supplies of electricity as much as they normally produced in five days with overtime. After making due allowance for the fact that people can make supernormal efforts only for a short time, the event provided a brief glimpse of what can be achieved when due attention is paid to shared values.

5 **There is, traditionally, a 'policy cycle' which can be usefully analysed in terms of ethical theory.** The features of the policy cycle are as follows:
Stage One: Policy preference. (It should be noted that the mechanisms for control are sometimes designed to be staged, or phased.) In this stage, the holders of positions of responsibility recognize a need for action. Normally, the action will be as close as possible to previous actions on what are thought to have been structurally similar matters. Sometimes the expedient works, to the extent that the problem seems to go away, but in the case of incomes policy this stage rarely lasts for more than a few months.
Stage Two: Reinforcement. This sometimes takes the form of converting a 'voluntary' restraint (all incomes policies are primarily restraint, rather than expansion or redistribution policies). The reinforcement also involves mobilizing support from those who are expected to be influential allies, lampooning critics and opponents (when it is not possible to ignore them).

Stage Three: Alternative forms of reinforcement. For instance, British incomes policies have traditionally gone through a process of varying stages of voluntarism, enforcement, abandonment and relabelling and repackaging, e.g. from 'wage freeze' to 'wage norms', 'nil norms', 'guiding lights', 'planned growth of incomes', codes, repairs of 'anomalies', 'social compacts', and, subsequently, unannounced policies of restraint, repackaged as controlling public spending to set an example to the private sector (this is, in fact a return to an earlier stage). Most critics have held that the policies bear unfairly on the public sector.

Part of stage three involves an evaluation, usually forced upon the government of the day by its critics, of the actual operation of the policy. Usually, the news is bad from the point of view of the authorities. There is, at this stage, a temptation to refuse to accept the inevitable. This is described below in terms of 'moves in justification'. The purpose of the analysis is to demonstrate *not* that the designers of such policies are dishonest or 'unethical' in the sense of 'ethics 1', but that given the starting point, the technical assumptions and the absence of systematic handling of values, the cycle is inevitable, and is liable to begin again more or less as soon as it is generally pronounced to be finished forever. For instance, in Britain, 'incomes' policy was abandoned in the late 1970s, followed immediately by cuts in public spending. By the late 1980s calls for restraint in wage settlements in the interests of 'the fight against inflation', the 'need to remain competitive with trading partners', with assertions that excessive pay settlements are against the interests of the settlers and everyone else, because they lead to even higher levels of unemployment. This return is illustrated in the following comment in late-1990 concerning the Confederation of British Industry conference:

The Confederation of British Industry last night clashed with the government on the twin policy issues of interest rates and wage restraint by calling for an immediate cut in the level of borrowing and defending the high level of pay awards . . . .

As the [British] government struggles to control inflation and public sector pay rises in a bid to prevent the economy tipping into recession, the CBI's position is unlikely to be welcomed by ministers. (*The Independent*, 20 November, 1989, p. 22)

It is worth noting that these formulae demonstrate:

1 particular views of causality;
2 assumptions that specific values are near universal, and are not questionable; and

3 that redistributive issues can properly be ignored.

The ethical and technical matters become, as is typical in these matters, hopelessly entangled.

Reference has already been made to debates about the reliability of statistical series, and the merits or otherwise of changing the basis of collection, but the value issues do not end there. Events can be interpreted favourably by supporters and unfavourably by antagonists. Thus, even if the figures were agreed, their meaning and importance is open to reinterpretation. Circumstances can change, so that, say a balance of payments deficit (a traditional trigger for 'incomes policies') of the equivalent of 100 million dollars, can in one year be a crisis level, and in another year a deficit of fifty times its size may not. This could be so, for example if in the second case, major resources with which to pay for the deficit were about to come 'on stream'. Where it is not the case, or where the size of the problem and of the resources to relieve it are uncertain or hidden, and the cause-effect relationships are merely matters of speculation, situations tend to produce their own imperatives. One set of these is the search for convenient explanatory and supportive interpretations. The case concludes with some explanatory options that have been chosen from time to time to take the sting out of what appears to be 'bad news'.

The ethical content of the matters raised is in both the 'ethics 1' and 'ethics 2' fields: which of the relevant values are in fact truly representative of a consensus that goes at least some way to meeting the criteria for ethically defensible decisions? Which issues are in the 'ethics 2' field, which deals with whether the facts and values have been properly disentangled? I offer no assessment here, but list below some of the 'explanatory-justificatory' moves. As indicated, the potential factual content of these explanation sketches is greater than that of the 'techniques of evasion' discussed in Chapter 7, making them, in principle, more testable, given the will and the resources. The technical testing does, nevertheless, appear to exhibit a cycle of confidence and abandonment of conclusions, many of which are beyond the reach, for assessment purposes, of all but a few specialists. An example is the career in the economics and econometrics literature of the 'Phillips Curve' (Bell and Kristol (eds), 1981).

Policy uncertainties: explanatory options

The expansions of the options are real arguments. The anonymity of the authors has been preserved:

Option One
'Things would have been worse if we/they had not done what we/they did.'
'In evaluating incomes policy the crucial question is what would have happened if there had been no such policy. Incomes must surely have been higher, and statistical tests have been inconclusive.'
Option Two
'The figures show a real improvement. Things admittedly appear, from the mere figures, to be moving in the opposite direction from the one predicted, but they are doing so at a diminishing rate. This vindicates the policy.'
Option Three
'We were right on course until things happened abroad. Some things you cannot predict, such as the outbreak of wars, sudden rises in raw material prices.'
Option Four
'Powerful and irresponsible groups have thwarted our policy.'
Option Five
'Things would have been worse if our competitors had been in office.'
Option Six
'Any other action would have been wrong [or impossible, or unthinkable].'
Option Seven
'There will have to be some sacrifices. There are tough times ahead. We never said it would be easy. It will take time. Your unemployment is a price well worth paying, for the benefits it brings the rest of us.'
Option Eight
'For every level of inflation there is a natural level of unemployment.'

A widely held view is that a more efficient labour market would reduce inflationary pressures. One way in which this is thought to happen is to reduce the 'monopoly power' of the unions. The assumption is that pay, and therefore prices, are held at artificially high levels if there are restrictions of movement of workers from places where there is a surplus of labour to places where there is a labour shortage. It is widely recognized that hardship and exploitation can occur in the labour market, whether or not there is freedom of movement. This provides a rationale for what has become known as the European Social Charter.

It would appear that the contents and provisions of the Charter are not widely-known outside the circle of labour market specialists. They are included here, with some indicative attitudes and issues.

The Community Charter of Fundamental Social Rights for Workers

CASE
33

(The full text of the European Social Charter is reproduced below. Reproduction is authorized by the Commission of the European Communities. The text was completed in January, 1990.)

At the meeting of the European council in Strasbourg on 8 and 9 December 1989, the Heads of State or Government of the European Community Member States, with the exception of the United Kingdom, adopted the Community Charter of Fundamental Social Rights for Workers. The signatories intend the Charter to be at once a solemn statement of progress already made in the social field and a preparation for new advances – so that the same importance may be given to the social dimension of the Community as to its economic aspects, in the construction of the large market of 1992. In the preamble to the Charter, the Heads of State or Government also underline the priority which they attach to job creation, the importance of the social consensus as a factor in economic development and their rejection of all forms of discrimination or exclusion. They also declare that, far from justifying any regression from the very diverse situations prevailing in the twelve member countries, the Charter demands a series of initiatives to develop workers' rights: responsibility for these initiatives will sometimes lie with the social partner, sometimes with the Member States and sometimes with the Community itself.

Accordingly, the Commission of the European Communities has drawn up an action programme for the parts of the Charter to be implemented at community level. The programme sets out about fifty proposals which the Commission will bring forward by the end of 1992. The Council of Ministers should pronounce on these proposals within two years, having first consulted the European Parliament and the Community's economic and social committee. The aim of these proposals will be to develop the social dimension of the large market, thus increasing the economic and social cohesion of the twelve-member Community. They will address only those points in the Charter which require new initiatives and which fall within the responsibilities of the Community institutions, as defined by the Community Treaties and by the principle of subsidiarity, whereby the Community acts when the set objectives can be reached more effectively at its level than at that of the Member States or the social partner but which arise in similar terms in all countries of the Community. The Commission has promised non-binding measures to encourage some convergence of efforts while respecting national practices.

The rest of this case consists of the full text of the Charter, apart from its introductory remarks, together with an account of its various measures announced in the Commission's programme.

Title I – Fundamental social rights of workers

Freedom of movement

1   Every worker of the European Community shall have the right to freedom of movement throughout the territory of the Community, subject to restrictions justified on grounds of public order, public safety or public health.

2   The right to freedom of movement shall enable any worker to engage in any occupation or profession in the Community in accordance with the principles of equal treatment as regards access to employment, working conditions and social protection in the host country.

3   The right to freedom of movement shall also imply:

(i)   harmonization of conditions of residence in all Member States, particularly those concerning family reunification;

(ii)   elimination of obstacles arising from the non-recognition of diplomas or equivalent occupational qualifications;

(iii)   improvement of the living and working conditions of frontier workers.

In the Commission's programme

Revision of the regulation on the right of workers to remain in a member country after having been employed there.

Extension, to cover all insured persons, of the measures which enable workers to continue to avail themselves of social security benefits when they move from one member country to another.

Study of the problems involved in the transfer from one member country to another of rights acquired under supplementary social security schemes; opening of a debate on this subject.

Proposal on the working conditions of workers from one member state who are engaged in the provision of services (subcontracting, etc.) in another. Also a proposal to include in public contracts a labour clause to ensure equal treatment for workers detached by a firm from another member country.

Examination of the living and working conditions of Community citizens living in frontier regions and of frontier workers in particular.

Employment and remuneration

4   Every individual shall be free to choose and engage in an occupation according to the regulations governing each occupation.

5   All employment shall be fairly remunerated.

To this end, in accordance with arrangements applying in each member country:

(i)   workers shall be assured of an equitable wage, i.e. a wage sufficient to have a reasonable standard of living;

(ii)   workers subject to terms of employment other than an open-ended full-time contract shall benefit from an equitable reference wage;

(iii)   wages may be withheld, seized or transferred only in accordance with national law; such provisions should entail measures enabling the worker concerned to continue to enjoy the necessary means for him or herself and his or her family.

6   Every individual must be able to have access to public placement services free of charge.

In the Commission's programme
Publication of an annual report on employment in Europe.

Creation of an 'employment observatory' for the Community, to forecast trends in labour supply and demand.

Development of the research and action programmes already launched on job creation for specific groups (long-term unemployed, young people, local initiatives etc.).

Improvement of systems for international exchange of vacancies and applications for employment which have not been satisfied at national level.

Evaluation of the effectiveness of the European Social Fund's activities in helping to find jobs for young people, and for the long-term unemployed.

Opinion on the measures taken by the Member States to guarantee the right to an equitable wage.

Proposal for a directive setting minimum requirements for contracts and employment relationships other than full-time, open-ended contracts (part-time working, fixed-term working, casual work, etc.).

Improvement of living and working conditions
7   The completion of the internal market must lead to an improvement in the living and working conditions of the workers in the European Community. This process must result from an approximation of these conditions while the improvement is being maintained, as regards in particular the duration and organization of working time and forms of employment other than open-ended contracts, such as fixed-term contracts, part-time working, temporary work and seasonal work.

The improvement must cover, where necessary, the development of certain aspects of employment regulations such as procedures for collective redundancies and those regarding bankruptcies.

8   Every worker of the European Community shall have the right to a weekly rest period and to annual paid leave, the duration of which must be progressively harmonized in accordance with national practices.

9   The conditions of employment of every worker in the European Community shall be stipulated in laws, a collective agreement or a contract of employment, according to arrangements applying in each country.

In the Commission's programme
Proposal for a directive on the adaptation of working time and of essential working conditions, particularly in regard to the well-being and health of workers.

Proposal for a directive to establish on a general basis a form of written proof of an employment contract and of its principal conditions.

Revision of the directive setting out procedures for information and consultation prior to collective redundancies, in particular so that it applies in cases of transfrontier restructuring.

Drawing up a memorandum on the social integration of migrants from countries outside the Community (education, housing, etc.).

Social protection according to the arrangements applying in each country
10   Every worker of the European Community shall have a right to adequate social protection, and shall, whatever his status and whatever the size of the undertaking in which he is employed, enjoy an adequate level of social security benefits.

Persons who have been unable either to enter or re-enter the labour market and have no means of subsistence may be able to receive sufficient resources and social assistance in keeping with their particular situation.

In the Commission's programme
Recommendation on convergence of Member States' objectives in regard to social protection.
Recommendation setting out common criteria for the guarantee given by Member States of sufficient resources and social assistance for the least advantaged citizens.

Freedom of association and collective bargaining
11   Employers and workers of the European Community shall have the right of association in order to constitute professional organizations or trade unions of their choice for the defence of their economic and social interests.

Every employer and every worker shall have the freedom to join or not to join such organizations without any personal or occupational damage being thereby suffered by him.
12   Employers or employers' organizations, on the one hand, and workers' organizations on the other, shall have the right to negotiate and conclude collective agreements under the conditions laid down by national legislation and practice.

The dialogue between the two sides of industry at European level which must be developed, may, if the parties deem it desirable, result in contractual relations in particular at inter-occupational and sectoral level.
13   The right to resort to collective action in the event of a conflict of interests, shall include the right to strike, subject to the obligations arising under national regulations and collective agreements.

In order to facilitate the settlement of industrial disputes the establishment and utilization at the appropriate levels of conciliation, mediation and arbitration procedures should be encouraged in accordance with national practice.
14   The internal legal order of the Member States shall determine under which conditions and to what extent the rights provided for in articles 11 to 13 apply to the armed forces, the police and the civil service.

In the Commission's programme
Continuation and development of dialogue with the social partners and a communication on their role in collective bargaining, including collective agreements at European level.

Vocational training

15 Every worker of the European Community must be able to have access to vocational training and to benefit therefrom throughout his working life. In the conditions governing access to such training there may be no discrimination on grounds of nationality.

The competent public authorities, undertakings or the two sides of industry, each within their own sphere of competence, should set up continuing and permanent training systems enabling every person to undergo retraining, more especially through leave for training purposes, to improve his skills or to acquire new skills, particularly in the light of technical developments.

In the Commission's programme

Proposal for measures to improve access to training for all workers throughout their working lives.

Revision of the general principles for vocational training originally established at Community level in 1963.

Rationalization and better coordination of Community programmes in the field of initial and continued vocational training.

Development and rationalization of Community programmes for youth exchanges and exchange of young workers.

Continuation of work on comparability of vocational training qualifications of the member countries.

Equal treatment for men and women

16 Equal treatment for men and women must be assured. Equal opportunities for men and women must be developed.

To this end, action should be intensified to ensure the implementation of the principle of equality between men and women as regards in particular access to employment, remuneration, working conditions, social protection, education, vocational training and career development.

Measures should also be developed enabling men and women to reconcile their occupational and family obligations.

In the Commission's programme

Preparation of a third action programme on equal opportunities for women.

Proposal for a directive on the protection of pregnant women at work.

Recommendation on methods of child care.

Recommendation setting out a code of good conduct on the protection of working women in pregnancy and maternity.

Equal treatment for men and women

17 Information, consultation and participation of workers must be developed along appropriate lines, taking account of the practices in force in the various Member States.

This shall apply especially in companies or in groups of companies having establishments or companies in two or more Member States of the European Community.

18 Such information, consultation and participation must be implemented in due time, particularly in the following cases:

(i)   when technological changes in which, from the point of view of working conditions and work organization, have major implications for the work force, are introduced into undertakings;

(ii)   in connection with restructuring operations in undertakings or in cases of mergers having an impact on the employment of workers;

(iii)   in cases of collective redundancy procedures;

(iv)   when transfrontier workers in particular are affected by employment policies persued by the undertaking where they are employed.

In the Commission's programme
Proposal on the information, consultation and participation in undertakings of European or transnational scale.
Proposal on equity sharing and financial participation by workers.

Health protection and safety at the workplace
19   Every worker must enjoy satisfactory health and safety conditions in his working environment. Appropriate measures must be taken in order to achieve further harmonization of conditions in this area while maintaining the improvements made.

   These measures shall take account, in particular, of the need for the training, information, consultation and balanced participation of workers as regard the risks incurred and the steps taken to eliminate or reduce them. The provisions regarding the implementation of the internal market shall help to ensure such protection.

In the Commission's programme
Proposals for directives on minimum health and safety requirements in a range of sectors: transport, shipping and fisheries, temporary or mobile work sites, the drilling industries, quarrying and open-cast mining.
Proposal for a directive on minimum requirements in regard to exposure of workers to certain physical agents (vibration, electromagnetic radiation, etc.).
Revision on the directive on exposure to asbestos at work.
Proposal for a directive on safety and health signs at the workplace.
Proposal for a directive on specific information for workers exposed to certain dangerous substances and industrial agents.
Revision of the European schedule of industrial diseases and recommendation on its adoption by the Member States.
Proposal to create a special European agency to provide scientific and technical support in the fields of safety, hygiene and health in the workplace.

Protection of children and adolescents
20   Without prejudice to such rules as may be more favourable to young people, in particular those ensuring their preparation through vocational training, and subject to derogations limited to certain light work, the minimum employment age must not be lower than the minimum school leaving age, and in any case, not lower than 15 years.
21   Young people who are in gainful employment must receive equitable remuneration in accordance with national practice.
22   Appropriate measures must be taken to adjust labour regulations

applicable to young workers so that their specific development and vocational training and access to employment needs are met.

The duration of work must, in particular, be limited – without it being possible to circumvent this limitation through recourse to overtime – and night work prohibited in the case of workers of under 18 years of age, save in the case of certain jobs laid down in national legislation or regulations.

23 Following the end of compulsory education, young people must be entitled to receive initial vocational training of a sufficient duration to enable them to adapt to the requirements of their future working life; for young workers, such training should take place during working hours.

In the Commission's programme
Proposal for a directive approximating the laws of the Member States on the protection of young people in regard to employment (minimum age, working hours, etc.).

Elderly persons
According to the arrangements applying in each country:
24 Every worker of the European Community must, at the time of retirement, be able to enjoy resources affording him or her a decent standard of living.
25 Every person who has reached retirement age but who is not entitled to a pension or who does not have other means of subsistence must be entitled to sufficient resources and to medical and social assistance specifically suited to his needs.

In the Commission's programme
Communication and proposal for an action programme to suit pilot projects, exchanges of information, etc.
Proposal to organize a year of the elderly in 1993.

Disabled persons
26 All disabled persons, whatever the origin and nature of their disablement, must be entitled to additional concrete measures aimed at improving their social and professional integration.

These measures must concern, in particular, according to the capacities of the beneficiaries, vocational training, ergonomics, accessibility, mobility, means of transport and housing.

In the Commission's programme
Preparation of a third community action programme on integration and equality of opportunity for the disabled.
Proposal for a directive to promote better travel possibilities for workers with motor disabilities.

Title II – Implementation of the Charter
27 It is more particularly the responsibility of the Member States in accordance with national practices, notably through legislative measures or collective agreements, to guarantee the fundamental rights in this charter and to implement the social measures indispensable to the smooth operation of the

internal market as part of a strategy of economic and social cohesion.

28   The European council invites the Commission to submit as soon as possible initiatives which fall within its powers, as provided for in the treaties, with a view to the adoption of legal instruments for the effective implementation, as and when the internal market is completed, of those rights which come within the Community's area of competence.

29   The Commission shall establish each year, during the last three months, a report on the application of the Charter by Member States and by the European Community.

30   The report of the Commission shall be forwarded to the European Council, the European Parliament and the Economic and Social Committee.

The ethical principles underlying the Charter, as was seen in Case 27, have not been controversial. The strongest critics, in the British Government, have directed their objections to the predicted consequences (an expected rise in unemployment). The entanglement of moral and technical values is clearly visible, as commitment to one prediction rather than another appears to have become, in this case as in many others, a test of loyalty to group preferences.

10 THE ETHICS OF THE MARKET

The market and freedom

A common argument for free competition and free markets is that they expand both choice and potential welfare. The word 'welfare' is itself an ethical expression, although it remains an empty one until some meaning is imported into it. 'Choice' has many ethical overtones, although in many uses the idea is ethically neutral. It is not value-neutral, because choosing implies a basis for choice, and that can be evaluated as good or bad, fit for its purpose, aimless, or as an example of an infinite number of values. In 'free' markets, choice is expanded because anyone can set up in business, and succeed by supplying what consumers want. Competition keeps prices down to levels that make it just worthwhile to stay in business. Monopolies (private or state) are held, in general, to restrict output and keep prices higher than they would otherwise be. Because demand for a product or service will call it into existence, and lack of demand will cause it to disappear, resources are not wasted. If, in the process, some people are richer than others, then that provides an incentive for people to use their initiative to catch up.

Some of the expressions above began life as descriptive expressions, but have taken on emotional and even combative ballast. Consider, for example, the use of 'competition' at political party, trade or trade union conferences.

A standard argument against the above case for the market is the view that there is a natural tendency in competitive systems for the more efficient (or more fortunate) to drive the less efficient from business or to swallow them up, to produce a monopoly or monopolistic practices. This negates the efficiency gains of free enterprise, and allows the rich and powerful to dictate to everyone else. The case against monopoly has never been other than a moral one, however much it is clothed in technical-sounding language. Further, some people can be victims, not of their own inefficiency, but of arbitrary decisions made by powerful people elsewhere, as in the case of a plant closed as part of a rationalization plan carried out for absentee owners of a factory. Others can be excluded from the benefits of free competition on grounds of colour, race, sex or religion. Given that the free market system can produce 'losers', and the losers may be so for reasons other than their 'just deserts', they are under no moral obligation to applaud a system that has cast them in the role of victim. In short, the ethical economic principle of the free market is in direct conflict with the ethical principle that no one should be harmed deliberately or through neglect without just cause. In essence, the free market system is ethically justifiable only to utilitarians, and it is not surprising that economic theory only permits the use of utilitarian concepts from the whole range of possible moral concepts.

In general, if the free market is efficient for some and unjust for others, how can these conflicting values be balanced? One solution, perhaps the most common one, is to ignore the issue altogether, or shrug it off as a matter for welfare economics, even though welfare economics is in a moribund state. A second solution is to mitigate the harms done by legislating to prevent their occurrence, thus interfering with the free market in order to make it free.

A third solution is to claim that the free market produces the moral goods generally attributed to it only in some circumstances, and within limits. An example of the first is the strange case of the supply of blood for medical use. Donors supply blood in the United Kingdom. It is bought on the market in America. The supply and quality is greater when given than when bought.

A fourth solution is to recognize that analytically there are several distinct concepts of 'the market'. This has nothing to do with traditional attempts to measure the degree of monopoly in a market, or to classify market structures. Each of the separate concepts has different ethical overtones or implications.

In Chapter 2, the role of the concept of the market as an ideology-supporting myth was explained and illustrated by means of some case studies in trade policy. A reasonable conclusion is that, at best, markets are only relatively free, and need constant regulation to guide them towards satisfying the many values expected from them. At best they do satisfy many of these requirements, and in fact frequent intervention by the authorities continues. This can be seen in health and safety legislation, consumer protection, accounting standards, investor protection, environmental protection, labour market legislation and regulation, enforcement of technical standards and much else.

The following case studies illustrate the operation of normal values in widely different industries. It will be seen that pressure for regulation does not always come from the 'losers' in the system, and indeed can come from 'winners'. The cases illustrate that neither content nor procedure alone can provide a satisfactory basis for justified business values, but that both are necessary.

The first case (BREL) illustrates the operation of ethically defensible, accepted, but tacit values. The second case, the proposed code for the gambling machine industry, indicates a set of proposals still in the process of development, but industry-led, for a mixture of reasons. The third case, Sedgwick James, illustrates a set of normal operational principles that do not set out explicitly to be 'ethical', but in which the influence of many of the standpoints listed and discussed in Chapter 7 is clearly visible.

CASE 34 **BREL – economic restructuring, employment and community**

This case was written by Dr Peter Davis, Senior Consultant, NMHC, Cranfield Institute of Technology. Agreement to publish has been granted by BREL on the understanding that the choice of materials and the interpretation are the responsibility of the author, and do not necessarily represent an official company view. References in this case study are detailed references to internal minutes. They are numbered consecutively in the text, and listed as an addendum to the case study.

The role and limits of collective bargaining

The closure in 1986 of its Swindon workshop by British Rail Engineering Ltd (BREL) was perhaps the most emotive and dramatic closure in the whole series of workshop closures that a mixture of government policies, changing circumstances of transport, and world market conditions for locomotives and rolling stock forced upon BREL. The whole management exercise represented a very substantial rundown in employment by a single company, involving, in addition to Swindon, closures in parts of Scotland and the North of England, areas which were already depressed, with high levels of unemployment. Management was operating in an industrial relations environment with very high levels of union organization in unskilled, white-collar and craft grades. It is a remarkable achievement for which both sides deserve some credit that despite the very tough decisions that were taken, cooperation was maintained and not a single day's work was lost in industrial disputes arising out of the closure programme. How this was achieved is of course of general interest to personnel management and industrial relations specialists, but an additional and possibly crucial dimension involves an examination of this success within the wider terrain of business ethics.

Background

The 1960s saw a dramatic reduction in the number of railway lines and stations. This could be seen as the result of government policies emphasizing road transport in the 1950s, and the general trend towards car ownership. The cuts themselves may have speeded up the transfer of traffic from rail to road in both passenger and freight services, but there was no doubting the prevailing trend in the post-war period.

In November 1977, recognizing the potential adverse consequences for employee relations that could result from these changes, the BREL management established a Joint Consultative Committee (JCC) for all staff, involving representatives from the NUR (National Union of Railwaymen), CSEU (Confederation of Shipbuilding and Engineering Unions), TSSA (Transport Salaried Staff Association) and the Transport Officers' Guild. The Committee was to meet four times a year. A central item convern of the JCC was BREL Workload and Manpower Forecasts. Detailed information was presented to the union side at virtually every meeting. The Chairman '... expressed the company view that it would provide a useful forum for *in-depth* discussion on an informal basis of matters of joint interest concerning BREL'[1] (author's emphasis). The management presentations in the late 1970s, whilst not hiding the adverse trading environment, showed growth for wagons, carriages and locomotives, with levelling-off or turndowns not predicted until the late 1980s. Manpower forecast curves reflected the investment forecasts. However, the forecasts for British Rail, virtually BREL's sole customer at this time, were hit by the winter recession which reduced iron, steel and coal-carrying capacity, lowering demand for wagons and locomotives. At the same time, because the government funded British Rail's new-build programme, British Rail's labour-intensive maintenance and repair requirements were reduced. New build was less labour intensive than maintenance, and in any case BREL did not receive all the available new-build contracts from British Rail. BREL management, faced with a radical decline in the level of work from British Rail, identified a wider international market for its products. Management forecasts of the size of BREL's share in this new market proved to be optimistic.[2] Clearly, the decline in rolling stock and increased investment indicated that British Rail, BREL's biggest customer, was embarking on a twin process of rationalization and modernization.

Throughout the late 1970s, and until the autumn of 1980, the picture presented by management was one of growth hindered by manpower shortages and some industrial disputes: 'The Chairman reported . . . in 1980, the growth situation which the company was in.'[3]

What was to be the last JCC meeting for over eighteen months, however, produced some portents of the overmanning crisis that emerged in the 1980s. The first of these was the revised forecast figure for locomotives, wagons and carriages, which were all significantly down.[4] The repercussions on manpower were that all overtime was stopped on locomotives and wagons, with a small surplus of staff appearing, and reduced overtime working on carriages. The Chairman of the JCC stressed to the unions that, despite the downward revision of the figures, 'The objective was to preserve the capacity of the company for future growth.'[5]

The second portent was the appearance of PA Management Consultants to look at productivity within BREL. The unions expressed concern at this development, and management agreed to provide them with a copy of the terms of reference.[6]

Some preliminary ethical issues

1 What information needed for the management of the business is it fair and reasonable to share with employee representatives?
2 How does timing impact on the ethical issue of when to share the information?
3 What is the responsibility of management to stress the assumptions and potential variability of the figures presented to employee representatives?
4 What is the responsibility of the trade union to examine proactively management's figures, rather than simply to react to the information at face value?
5 How are the trade unions to balance their need to protect their members' interests between short-term and long-term perspectives, i.e. how ethical is it to attempt to preserve the status quo by mortgaging the future?

Some readers may be surprised that the question of the rights and wrongs of enforced redundancy (as opposed to voluntary redundancy) is not posed as an ethical question. The point is, however, that in the end none of the parties had control over this issue once the political decision not to subsidize BREL was taken. The macroeconomic forces and the finite investment resources available to management meant that redundancies were inevitable. How to manage the process and limit the damage to BREL itself, the individual workers and their local communities did of course raise many practical issues with heavy ethical resonances.

The crunch

Although the JCC did not meet for eighteen months, an informal liaison committee for workshop staff existed between management and trade unions, that had continued to meet. Hence the unions were kept up-to-date with what can be described as a deteriorating situation. The unions had responded with calls for '*in situ* slimming', rather than shutting down whole facilities. The management responded by going along with this in the short term, but then confronted the unions with the results of such a strategy – namely a substantial shortfall of volunteers for redundancy, and the loss of economic viability in a number of the workshops. The process of '*in situ* slimming' created diseconomies, leading inevitably to the need for closure – the logic of which the trade unions were forced to accept over time on a piecemeal basis.

At the first of the revised JCC meetings, the new chief executive of BREL put the problem of resolving the 'substantial over-capacity' at BREL at the top of the agenda. The Swindon workshop was earmarked at this meeting for a 'slimming' exercise.[7] The trade union was offered a five-point action plan and a joint working party to examine the results of the management analysis and to look at a range of options for responding to the crisis (a potential deficit of £23.5 million in 1983). The options to be reviewed included:

1 The reallocation of workload (i.e. a closure of some workshops).
2 Reduced working week to three or four days.
3 Local redundancy discussions.
4 Leasing arrangements between trades. (BREL still had some skill shortages and was not inclined to lose skilled people if they could be leased to other work, giving greater flexibility and labour productivity.)[8]

By this time management estimated, after volunteers and natural wastage were accounted for, an overall manpower surplus of around five thousand employees by the end of 1983. Of this total, almost four hundred were situated at the Swindon works. During the following four months an internal management report making reference to the closure of the Swindon works had been leaked to the trade unions, and the matter was raised by them at the March 1983 meeting. Management dismissed the document as an 'internal management exercise to investigate potential solutions',[9] conceding, however, that by the end of 1986 there would be a need to reduce capacity by a medium-sized workshop, and that the signs 'pointed to Swindon'.[10]

Management was anxious to make a clear presentation and dispel any ambiguities or misunderstandings on the part of the unions, before the unions visited the workshops to discuss with their members the BREL management programme of workload transfers.[11] The NUR indicated that '[the] Union would produce a positive reaction to management's future strategy in the form of an alternative future plan'.[12]

The series of workshop meetings was followed by a further JCC meeting in June 1983, at which management expressed satisfaction at being able to put their case direct to the shop floor. The management felt that no real alternatives had been presented to their plans, but the unions felt they should be given more time to respond. Management agreed to this and the trade unions put their alternative proposals at the following JCC in July 1983. By these strategies the trade unions bought some time, but they produced little by means of alternative policy. They wanted surplus capacity to be viewed as 'under-utilization', but provided no strategy for improving on management's predictions for throughput, and no solution to the £17.7 million deficit that their proposals left BREL to carry.[13]

Management then unilaterally declared the consultation processes at an end and said that there was no alternative but to implement the closure and reallocation programme. The trade unions rejected the programme and said that they would block its implementation.[14]

Management from this point on, whilst maintaining the consultative process with the trade unions, adopted a unilateral strategy, bypassing the national representatives and dealing with their staff on a workshop-by-workshop basis. That they succeeded may be attributed to three factors:

1 Essentially the workforce recognized the economic facts of life as they experienced them in the workshops.
2 Management produced relatively generous severance terms and ensured that the under-sixties who were displaced were offered alternative employment and relocation expenses if they preferred this to redundancy.
3 Management worked positively with the local community to establish job-creation schemes which helped to mitigate the adverse effect of the closures on local economies and helped to divert energies that might otherwise have been spent on resisting the closure. These community-based economic development projects also presented a valuable public relations exercise at a critical point in BREL's rationalization programme.[15]

The trade unions cooperated at local level with the management's proposals, and some officials were actively involved in supporting the new employment initiatives. At the national level the trade unions concentrated their efforts in three directions:

1 Scrutiny of management efforts to get new, non-British Rail business, and offering some suggestions and leads themselves.
2 Trying to put pressure on British Rail (BR) and the government to give BREL more work. This latter strategy appeared to be doomed by the policies adopted by the government to make BR profitable. Faced with a declining market, this could only be achieved by cuts. There was new investment in rolling stock, but not enough to maintain BREL at its existing capacity. The introduction of new stock also meant a further decline in maintenance and repair work for BREL.

3 Gaining marginal (but not inconsequential) concessions from management concerning the arrangements relating to severance payments, the management and distribution of work between the workshops, the operation of notice periods, relocation allowances, etc.

Far from British Rail being able to respond positively to the requests of the unions, BR found it necessary to remove from service certain old units which had provided considerable asbestos-stripping and refurbishment work for BREL. In the event, the suddenness of this decision meant that BREL management was forced to announce further redundancies to the trade unions without prior consultation:

... earlier consultations had not been held because the company had hoped that the realization of the effect of the decision would have brought about a change of mind, but unfortunately, subsequent confirmation of policy was received from BRB [British Railways Board].[16]

This situation was extremely provocative from the trade union perspective, but given the limitation of their position in a period of recession, they were powerless to prevent the decision from being implemented, despite protests to BREL and British Rail.

As the general rationalization programme progressed during 1984 and 1985, the issue of the Swindon works position was raised by management in May and October 1984, April 1985 (extended alternative policy at Swindon) and May 1985, when management projected (due to the continuing rundown of repair work), the closure of the Swindon works on 31 March, 1986. The union responded by deploring the decision to close the Swindon works, pointing to the efforts put in by Swindon employees to meet the company requirements.

The trade union side pointed out that 'Swindon Works had done everything in their power to arrive at present day requirement', and that 'it was deplorable to consider the closure of the Works'.[17] The trade unions asked for a copy of BREL's five-year plan, 'in order that they might know what to expect in the future'.

However, management refused on the grounds that forecasts over five years were too unreliable, but that they would give the unions Management Projections until 1987/88. In accepting this compromise, the unions argued that they did not want 'bad news in small doses as has tended to happen over the last four years, preferring to receive as full a picture as was avaiable.'[18]

The unions returned to this complaint at the next JCC meeting, suggesting that 'BREL's management had carried out a policy of disclosing limited amounts of information at any one time to avoid revealing the real depths of the problems BREL faces.'[19]

From this point on, the principal trade union strategies moved from collective bargaining to political pressure, with BREL management meeting local Members of Parliament, and trade unions claiming that the decision to close Swindon works had involved government pressure.

Management's response to these pressures was to announce that it was actively evaluating the possibility of maintaining a presence at Swindon. Local management was instructed to establish whether such a presence could be viable in December 1984, but British Railways Board's announcement of a further thirteen per cent cut in BREL's repair workload in April 1985 made the closure of the Swindon works inevitable.[20] BREL management argued convincingly that if more repair work was allocated, this would create diseconomies in the new-build work, which would prevent BREL from tendering competitively.

Management presented two detailed papers discussing the possible basis for maintaining a presence at Swindon, and hired a consultant to explore the possibility of selling parts of the works as a going concern that could ensure the future employment of BREL employees. As a result of the report by the consultants, Leslie Hays and Associates Limited, BREL announced the intention to retain the brass foundry, the spring shop, and the associated machining activity at Swindon at least until 31 March 1987, keeping around 150–60 men employed. Beyond this point it was felt it would be difficult to integrate economically these residual activities in BREL's business. By October 1985 BREL was able to report positively to having four enquiries expressing interest in the foundry at Swindon.

After 1985 the trade unions had effectively given up trying to prevent the closure of workshops, including the Swindon works, and concentrated their efforts on extracting the best possible terms for redundancy and exploring all the possibilities for ensuring the maximum benefit to their redundant members from the establishment of Swindon Holdings Limited and the job creation subsidies put in place by the Secretary of State for Employment.

With the cooperation of the trade unions established, management's concerns were primarily to ensure the success of Swindon Holdings and to minimize any public relations damage locally, particularly arising out of what was a hostile local press and a vociferous local campaign to save the works. (The issues arising from this stage in management's closure programme are to be discussed in a forthcoming study.)

Industrial relations lessons

The first point to come out of this study is that the trade union will to prevent large-scale redundancy is likely to be undermined when the trade unions are satisfied that management is presenting them with the full facts and giving them an opportunity to examine the facts and the management proposals for dealing with them.

Trade union complaints that more time was needed to review management's plans if the trade unions were to develop a viable alternative were less convincing than might have been the case, simply because management had given a number of earlier signals of where its thinking was leading concerning the closure of the Swindon works, over a period of two years prior to the closure. One is forced to conclude that the trade unions had reviewed this threat and failed to find a viable counter-strategy during the 'notice period' management had provided, or else had refused to face up to the position until it became an immediate prospect.

The management had clearly worked hard to present the facts that supported the decisions during the establishment and operation of the joint working party, and had been able to use this period as an opportunity to ensure a common message both from national trade union working party representatives and management when the time came to take the issues 'on the road' and hold the workshop meetings. This strategy of early cooperation with the unions clearly paid off. Paradoxically, it may be that the BREL Swindon closure demonstrates that, particularly when the news is bad, it can be shared effectively with the trade unions.

Information sharing was only one element in eliminating negative employee relations consequences. The compensation package itself was recognized to be reasonable and BREL management was able to offer a level of compensation that ensured that the numbers preferring the relocation option were minimized. The offer of relocation for the under-sixties took the sting out of redundancy notices, even if to some extent this offer may have been more a cosmetic than a realistic option from the perspective of the workers faced with the choice. The age profile of the BREL workforce may also have worked to management's advantage here.

Collective bargaining as a means of managing drastic rationalization programmes comes out in a remarkably positive light, from the management perspective, in the BREL case. The closures and manpower reductions were effected on time and without strikes; improvements in productivity and flexibility at the remaining workshops were achieved, and the future of BREL secured.

The trade unions did not have the management resources effectively to challenge management, and their ability to exert political pressure was negligible in the climate of the 1980s. The twin realities of the declining demand for labour in their industry and the decline in demand for labour in the local communities did not deflect them from responding through the established collective bargaining machinery to management and the established political machine, but the positive results that followed from this path were disappointing in terms of protecting jobs and trade union membership within BREL. The trade union merely secured 'the best terms that could be achieved under the circumstances', to quote a standard trade union expression in justification for acceptance of a negotiated settlement.

It is too easy to say with hindsight simply that the management position was strong and that of the unions weak, as being enough to explain the industrial relations success embodied in the closure programme. Had management overplayed its hand, and tried to push too fast or shave some extra savings from the compensation package, for example, the closures might not have gone so smoothly. Had a long and bitter strike or lock-out resulted, BREL might not have survived the way it did.

The unions too could have lost the support of their membership and undermined their position in BREL had they adopted a tougher stance than they did. Both sides recognized the legitimacy of the other's objectives and the boundaries of their power to influence those objectives. Many industrial relations failures are the result of one or both sides failing to recognize both the boundaries of their own power and the legitimacy of the other party's objectives. In the BREL case neither side made this mistake.

Conclusion: the role of values in the process of collective bargaining

The degree of homogeneity in underlying values between the two sides, despite the radically different objectives being taken as the best solutions to the problems of overmanning and British Rail's changing volumes and type of investment, was essential to ensuring a peaceful and constructive resolution of the crisis.

Examining and comparing the objectives of the two sides it is clear that management scored highly in the realization of its objectives, whilst the unions lost out almost entirely on objective 3 and substantially on objective 1, with their best results being realized in objective 2.

On the values comparison there is a good deal of congruence, with the main friction coming on the issues of timing of information release and on the role of government. This latter union value may have helped management by deflecting union anger from BREL and on to British Rail and ultimately the government. The most substantial complaints the unions were able to levy at the BREL management related to its failure to provide information early enough.

The issue of timing was one on which the management could respond swiftly, by providing the information once it had been identified, which meant that ruffled feathers could soon be smoothed.

That management values and strategy were appropriate to the use of collective bargaining appears well established in this case. The surprising and paradoxical question that the case study raises is to

Objectives and values of BREL and the unions

BREL	The Unions
Objectives	**Objectives**
(1) Eliminate losses.	(1) Preserve manpower levels at BREL.
(2) Improve capacity to tender competitively (including satisfying BR as main customer).	(2) Expand scope for collective bargaining.
(3) Manage employee relations effectively.	(3) Rail investment should ensure full utilization of BREL's capacity.

BREL	The Unions
Values	**Values**
(1) BREL should survive and management must do what is necessary to ensure that it does.	(1) BREL: has skills that produce good quality products.
(2) We should share information with the unions.	(2) Craft grades are the pillars upon which quality depends.
(3) Be positive in presenting information.	(3) Collective bargaining is the best means of security for employees.
(4) Honestly present the facts but not always as soon as you know them.	(4) Management should share all information at the earliest opportunity.
(5) Be helpful and cooperative to the unions commensurate with achieving objectives.	(5) Government should spend more on the rail system.

what extent trade union investment in the value of collective bargaining resulted in too narrow a statement of objectives – reflecting an inadequate definition of trade union value for the late twentieth century. The lesson of the 1980s, as elaborated in the Swindon plant closure and the recession of the early 1990s, suggests that the organization of labour to defend employees facing unemployment due to industrial decline requires the basic values of collective bargaining to be subsumed under a broader set of values, permitting a wider range of options and strategies to be applied at the level of the labour market in general. The defence of yesterday's skills against today's technology will always present the trade unions with a practically impossible task, and in public relations terms their image as a reactionary force preventing technological development and change will be reinforced.

The value of training and research gave rise to the craft-based mechanics' institutes in Britain in the nineteenth century, and reflected the more general prevailing belief in education and self-improvement. Trade union efforts to protect their members' interests clearly have not been broad enough to provide a more flexible response to changes in labour market conditions than those adopted by the unions in this case. The unions' demands for more government investment was a partial recognition of this point, but it was clearly an inadequate one. Trade unions have not seriously reviewed what alternatives there may be to collective bargaining and government intervention.

The BREL case illustrates management's responsibility to manage the change process, however painful, within its organizational remit. The unions played (as well as could be expected) the role of 'loyal opposition' (Davis, 1988). The trade unions and the process of collective bargaining based on prior joint consultation enabled a difficult situation to be managed effectively by the management, with a level of autonomy and involvement in the process that would not have been available in a non-union and/or paternalistic environment.

In general, the case illustrates the benefits to management of maintaining a pluralistic approach to employee relations, whilst recognizing sufficient common ground to make candid information-sharing a positive advantage in the pursuit of management objectives. It may well be true that in a share-capital based organization the common ground reduces, but even here the reality of the need to maintain dividends and share prices to avoid hostile takeovers is no longer likely to be lost on workforces.

Methodological note

The values identified by the author have been based on analysis of the documented statements and actions of the parties, as recorded by the agreed minutes of the JCC and the informal liaison committee for workshop staff. Clearly each of the three ethical theories discussed in this book and at more length in *Key Issues in Business Ethics* could be used to justify the values that the parties clearly held.

What has been attempted is an evaluation of how helpful to the parties their adopted values were. It maybe worth observing that in this case the trade union 'right' to be involved was not necessarily one accepted by management. It may have been that management felt an overriding duty to save the business. The trade unions were there, and dealing with them made sense at the time. Formal agreement on fundamental philosophical principles or ethical theories is not necessary within a pluralistic system, where there are real alternative sources of power that can act as checks and challenges to each other. The resolution of conflict within the system may be possible, utilizing a wide range of values for the justification of action. It is equally true that arriving at acceptable accommodation within a pluralistic framework can be made easier or harder for the parties by the value-set that they choose to adopt. Nor is this an argument for relativism. It is rather an acknowledgement of the reality of change in our environment as a permanent condition, requiring that we constantly check out the values we bring to the problems we confront in handling the process of change itself.

Case references

1 JCC Meeting 25.11.77, Minute 1
2 *Ibid.* Appendix (iii)
3 JCC Meeting 30.10.79, Minute 79/17
4 JCC Meeting 25.11.80, Minute C80/17
5 *Ibid.*
6 *Ibid.* Minute C80/18
7 JCC Meeting 8.6.82, Minute C82/5
8 *Ibid.*
9 JCC Meeting 30.3.82, Minute C83/1 & 2
10 *Ibid.*
11 *Ibid.*
12 *Ibid.*
13 JCC Meeting 21.7.83, p. 3
14 *Ibid.*, p. 4
15 JCC Meeting 12.4.85, Minute C85/1
16 JCC Meeting 10.11.83, p. 1
17 JCC Meeting 29.5.85, Minute C85/4, p. 3
18 *Ibid.*, p. 4
19 JCC Meeting 19.6.85, p. 1
20 *Ibid.*, p. 3

A chance to change policy for the better: ethical codes in the gambling machine industry

This case was written by Rob van Es and Dirk Lindenbergh.

In this case we outline the development of ethical codes and moral regulation in the gambling machine business. Primarily this concerns the Netherlands, but there is an intertwinement with developments on the European level. After a short characterization of the sector, we present the Dutch national ethical code, along with some comments. This is followed by an examination of a single corporation that is at the forefront of national developments, and the Dutch initiative to develop strategically a European code. Finally we provide some conclusions and suggestions for the making of codes in the gambling machine business in other countries.

Sector intentions in a sector in tension

The gambling machine business is a relatively young branch of industry, which has repeatedly come under intense scrutiny, since the start of its development in the 1940s. In the past, public morality was never very enthusiastic about the gambling machine. On the other hand, there was always an obvious demand for playing this type of machine. The tensions between public disapproval on the one hand, and the apparent demand on the other, have brought this branch of industry into frequent conflict with authority. It was, and sometimes still is, a sector in tension.

One of the things gambling machine entrepreneurs came to realize in the 1980s was the impossibility of going outside the law, politics or morals. Instead of fighting and circumventing regulations, they gradually changed their strategy and nowadays most entrepreneurs in the gambling machine business view proper legislation and an ethical code as being necessary to avoid undesirable situations. These situations concern the operators, who would otherwise be kept permanently in a state of suspense, but they also concern the players, who would have to do without sound legal and moral protection and could easily fall victim to illegal operators as a result of it. In the Netherlands these changes within the industry resulted in legislation, the Law on Games of Chance, which came into effect in 1987.[1] It was the result of a process of discussion and negotiation between government officials and the representative organization of the sector, 'Vereniging van Automatenhandelaren Nederland' (VAN) (Gambling Machine Trade Association of the Netherlands). The points of departure of this law are:

- the existing need of players to make a bet;
- the desirability of giving entrepreneurs a sufficient return to permit well-founded management;
- the need to protect players from excessive losses;
- the need to bring about a regulation which can be enforced.

These points already show moral consideration. Each party is given an equal share of freedom, while the less powerful are given extra protection. During the series of meetings between officials and the VAN, several other moral points emerged. They required a more detailed examination in a different context. This was the impulse for the development of an ethical code.

Towards a national ethical code

In the course of 1990 the VAN accepted the draft of a national ethical code. The key word in this code is self-regulation. Within the parameters set by the Law on Games of Chance, there is still scope for questionable behaviour and consequences. The question here is how much further one must go in regulating freedom of action by designing rules that go beyond the judicial. Probably this will always be a point for discussion, and that is why the code will not be fixed, but will remain a working code for years to come. This means that code and practice will be compared regularly and, after discussion, the VAN members must decide to modify their practices according to the code, or adjust the code to their practices. The draft code can only be understood as a compromise between different intentions and different interests. The accepted draft code runs as follows:

Article 1
In as far as they operate arcades, the VAN members agree to their personnel undergoing the 'Jellinek education', geared to the early recognition and tackling of gambling addiction.
Article 2
The VAN members who operate arcades agree to maintaining a ban on advertising.
Article 3
The VAN members agree to introducing and then maintaining a minimum age of 18 for playing gambling machines, and to imposing this obligation on their fellow operators in the catering industry.
Article 4
The VAN members agree to introducing and maintaining a voluntary ban on entering an arcade for players who request that or have another person request that.
Article 5
The VAN members agree to applying warning stickers on all gambling machines, in consultation with the NMI.
Article 6
The VAN members agree to loyally carrying out a restriction on the number of gambling machines, whether or not differentiated as to the establishment or duration of placement, imposed by the central government or a local authority and to obliging their fellow operators to act accordingly.
Article 7
The VAN members agree to carrying out loyally a fixed restriction on the life of machines – in consultation with the NMI, and to obliging their fellow operators to act accordingly.

Let us first classify these restricting articles. The first article concerns internal education: a matter of personnel and organization. The second concerns a restriction on advertising or marketing while 5, 6 and 7 restrict the product. Articles 3 and 4 represent a restriction to the public or client: not everyone is allowed to use the machines.

The motives behind these articles and their orders of appearance remains unclear, or at least it is not made explicit. For instance, why exactly is there a ban on advertising? And what is the idea supporting the fixed minimum age? Apart from that, some formulations are dubious. Should one, according to Article 4 really ban a player at another person's request? *Any* other person? What was the intention here? We don't know because the underlying values and arguments are missing. This code is very much a draft. It is no more than a collection of specific norms, very much standing alone and apart from values and purposes. The draft code clearly needs to be the subject for many meetings.

One of the participants in that discussion is already a step ahead on this national level. Because it has already set the moral trend, focusing on that corporation will give us an impression of things to come in this branch of industry.

A single corporation: Errel

Within the Errel corporation, one of the five largest corporations in the Dutch gaming and gambling machine business, the moral regulations enjoy a special status. Of course Errel complies with the rules of the national draft code, but apart from that, it tries to develop moral rules and moral procedures that fit the morality of the market. In its own way the corporation tries to match theory and practice in business ethics. This means that Errel recognizes the moral responsibility of corporations in the market-place. But this responsibility is not without limits, and surely cannot be compared with the moral responsibility of, say, a political party. The latter obviously tries to make values and to change policies for the better. A corporation is not charged with that duty; it is directed to provide products and services. It strives for continuity and has to make a profit to do so. The moral obligations of a corporation are less ponderous than those of a political party or a political pressure group. The market, then, is characterized by a limited ethics in which 'transactions of interests' and 'recognition of basic rights' form the main parts. Errel as a corporation is situated in the market and therefore adheres to the morality of the market. In accordance with this morality, the corporation tries to develop a consistent ethical policy. In its *Business Policy 1991*,[2] Errel for the first time set down in writing moral considerations and moral arguments to throw some light on its policy principles. We have selected a crucial part of a section that is called 'Games of Chance in a Changing Society'. This text gives us a broad view of the gambling business, focusing, finally, on gambling addiction.

Moral responsibility
Errel Holding is very much aware of its position in an ever-changing society. It cannot limit itself to reacting to social developments, but has to be ahead of

them. This is possible by conducting a policy expressly geared to the long term. In such a policy, the company's moral responsibility is also expressed. But what do we understand by that?

Boundaries

We presuppose that Errel Holding naturally makes use of its freedom of entrepreneurship. This constitutes the scope to operate as a company in accordance with one's own view. This freedom of entrepreneurship is not unlimited, however. First of all, there are boundaries which the law lays down with regard to a company's acts in the field of covenants, contracts, taxes and terms of employment. It goes without saying that Errel Holding stays within the boundaries of the law as far as those are concerned.

Secondly, there are the imperative directives for good entrepreneurship. Reliability and approachability are the key words in a well-considered policy for the long term at Errel Holding. They are operative in the contacts with colleagues, suppliers and purchasers, and in the production and maintenance of, among other things, gambling machines. They are especially important for the cooperation of over 200 employees, and are central to further expanding personnel management.

Finally there are the gradually changing moral standards of Western culture within which Errel is working. Particularly with regard to societal judgements on the products marketed by Errel, and the effects and their side-effects.

View on gambling addiction

The most problematic side-effect of gambling machines is gambling addiction. Since every employee of Errel Holding is tackled on this issue at some point in time, it seems right to formulate our views on it once more.

Errel Holding forms part of the Dutch amusement business and provides products and services, especially in the field of gambling and gaming machines. We strive to guarantee the quality of those products and services. Many people gain a lot of pleasure out of using them. A smaller number of people with limited self-control use them too often. This can lead to gambling addiction with all the special and financial miseries connected with it. The primary responsibility for gambling lies not with Errel Holding, but with the individual user who has too little self-knowledge or self-control. It is not the game of chance itself that is harmful, but the way in which the user handles it.

Responsibility

In this context, Errel Holding has a secondary responsibility. It is up to the company to alert the players to the fascination of their gambling behaviour, so they can remain aware of the hazardous character of the game. This feedback takes place by means of signals: introducing in every gambling location a financial limit for each gambling machine, and offering, also at each gambling location a leaflet, developed on the authority of our company, 'Feel free to make a bet, but don't play with yourself!' By means of these signals, the player is given the opportunity to take his or her own responsibility.

An exception must be made for a group of adolescents, because these players generally do not have enough experience in taking responsibility. This group must be protected from itself. This can be achieved by decreasing the accessibility of gambling machines for adolescents in years to come. One way of doing this is by refusing 16-year-olds and 17-year-olds (and under) access to amusement arcades. Another way is limiting the number of gambling machines in the 'dry' catering industry. Errel Holding will take the initiative to discuss these and other measures in the branch of industry in order to reach nationwide agreements.

Of course, this text is part of a subjective and promotional business plan, but nevertheless a moral stand is taken with serious arguments. One can disagree with the argument developed here, but the fact that a corporation has values, norms and arguments justifies a claim for attention. Here we have a contribution to a sound societal debate on the problems of gambling addiction and responsibility. In such a debate all parties have a say, and this company uses its say quite clearly. Hopefully, this way of taking moral stands will find support in the sector, and in the end, will change the existing draft code into a mature national ethical code.

Impulse to an ethical code for Europe

At the European level the moral developments run one step behind the Dutch national code. Naturally, the legal and moral situations in Britain, Belgium, Denmark, Germany, France, Spain and Italy differ considerably, as do their contributions to the European association for the sector. Still, the normally effective point of impact has to be EUROMAT, the European Coin Machine Association. In 1989 and 1990 the members of this association discussed the content of different draft codes. They did not succeed in reaching a full educational code: there were too many differences in interests and contexts. For this reason the VAN, in the autumn of 1990, proposed a different approach. Basically, it is to use a strategic framework for the development of an ethical European Code.[3] What follows is the middle part of that proposal:

What we want is clear. We want to develop a European code of ethics for our profession. Why do we want to do that? We want our profession to be trustworthy and we want our businesses to be known as responsible. A code of ethics is a landmark in the development of moral responsibility in our profession. This, in short, is our vision.

Some draft codes have been written, for example a Dutch one and an English one. But of course on the European level there are many differences between the countries. One cannot expect to develop a full ethical code in Europe within two or three years, so we have to follow a special strategy.

Our proposal is: try to develop a European aspirational code for our profession within two years. Such a code will include the values and ideals of our profession in a European context. In this way we develop an umbrella code: it covers the European gambling machines business, but it is not as comprehensive or fully detailed. Every country has to develop its own code underneath this umbrella code. Possibly in five or ten years we will succeed in developing a more educational code, a code with interpretations and advice on how to handle problems of application for all European countries. Meanwhile, we have to be content with a smaller but in the long run more effective approach.

We therefore recommend the installation of a special, small, but international working group that will do the job for us. The group will need to do some research and coordination on empirical data. It will need to produce a concept/aspirational code that can be used as the subject of discussion among all members. The group will need to report regularly on the development of a more definitive aspirational code, to be completed in 1992. This means that the problem of implementation will be left to the individual countries until then. This provides time to develop national codes, or at least to do some research on the subject.

The proposal for a strategic plan of action was accepted at the EUROMAT meeting on Brussels on 25 October, 1990. The development of this umbrella code will thus appear frequently on the agenda in years to come. The working group (England, Spain and the Netherlands) has been installed and has received some points of departure for social considerations that can supply the structure of an ethical code (1). It also received guidelines for the approach to opposition from governments and interest groups (2). These are:

1 The gambling machines business must recognize its moral co-responsibility to players, by a number of self-regulating measures concerning:
    (i) gaming machines;
    (ii) modes of playing machines;
    (iii) players;
    (iv) measures imposed by operators on their own businesses;
    (v) measures imposed by operators on the owner/managers of the establishments to which they supply machines.
2 The way we approach opposition to our business from government and interest groups is, in principle:
    (vi) we are open to reasoned discussion with all interested parties;
    (vii) such discussion must take place on an equal footing;
    (viii) all arguments put forward in such discussions must be taken into account, and only the best solutions are to be used;
    (ix) the basis of all such discussions will be to seek consensus, while compromise remains a good alternative.

It is not difficult to recognize the VAN draft code in the proposal under (1), but it is quite unusual to see, under (2), the influence of German philosophy. Jürgen Habermas will be surprised to know that some basic rules of his 'Diskurs-ethik' reached the meeting of the European Coin Machine Association![4] Whether his ethical theory is the appropriate one for the gambling machine industry remains to be seen. But it is an improvement to see an attempt to combine theory and practice in this area of business ethics.

Some conclusions and recommendations

The gambling machine business operates under considerable social and moral pressure. Compromises between the interest of corporations and the 'common good' are possible when corporations focus on their long-range policy and recognize their moral responsibilities (and their limits).

It is important to gather the entrepreneurs in a national association. The problem with such a gathering is: which entrepreneurs? All of them, or those who are especially concerned with moral considerations? It depends on the political situation, the pressure of public opinion and the time one has to develop a national policy. The national association will be the platform for further developments.

First, legislation has to be formulated in discussion and negotiation with government officials. In the process of formulation, moral questions inevitably arise. An inventory of these questions will provide a good start for an independent moral debate. It is preferable to have parallel processes for the legal and moral issues, but this is not easy. It takes much time and draws heavily on the relevant functionaries of the association. Therefore it is wise to involve from the start both a legal and a moral adviser in the process.

With regard to the ethical issues, the association concentrates on moral self-regulation. This probably will lead to an ethical code. It is important to see this code not as a static pronouncement, but as a recurring device of self-confrontation and self-education. Ethical codes offer each player the chance to take his or her own responsibility, while each manager is offered the chance to change the company's policy for the better. In the process the manager will develop further insights into the morality of the specific market with which the manager deals. At one pont in time this market morality will be integrated in the corporate policy and, perhaps later, the code will become redundant. But in the gambling business, and especially at the European level, this will take more than a decade.

Case references
[1] The Law on Games of Chance, 'Hertziening Wet op de Kansspelen', was published in Staatsblad 600 (3.12.85) and Staatsblad 589 (28.11.86), The Hague.
[2] The business policy of Errel Holding was published as 'Beliedsplan 1991' (December 1990, Den Bosch).
[3] The proposal for a strategic plan of action on a European level is called 'From a reactive to an active Association', and was delivered and accepted at the Euromat meeting on 25 October, 1990 in Brussels.

[4] Jürgen Habermas develops the 'Diskursethik' in *Moralbewusstsein und kommunikatives Handeln* (1983). This is an elaborated part of his theory of action, outlined in J. Habermas (1981) *Theorie des kommunikativen Handelns*. These are available in English translation. The effect of Article 7 implies a voluntary restriction on operators, over and above the requirements of the law.

CASE 36

What worries New Europe's executives most? A study of social issues and mixed priorities

This case is my summary of a paper presented to the American National Academy of Management in 1991, by David L. Mathison and David Boje of Loyola Marymount University College of Business Administration, Los Angeles. The summary is produced here with permission.

The authors of the paper address the question, 'Have European chief executive officers' social and strategic priorities changed with the "New Europe"?' The research took the form of a questionnaire survey in France, the United Kingdom and Germany.

In the Abstract of the paper the authors explain:

EC Europe is currently experiencing significant changes. This study reports preliminary questionnaire findings of French, UK and German CEOs' reactions to these changes. The focus is on both what issues will most strategically impact on their operations and executives' recommendations on how the EC should prioritize these same social and business concerns. Included also is a five-question section which compares EC executives with US counterparts on ethical concerns. The results are extensive. The paper concludes with insights for both corporate planners and social issues scholars.

The background issues identified in the study included what the authors see as an uneasy partnership of 322 million EC consumers, who give the Community the potential to become the leading economic world power by serving as the most lucrative market-place in the 1990s. The problems they identify are, principally, the instability in Eastern Europe and the USSR, a new and untested unified Germany, questionable mergers, an unpopular Social Charter, and costly ecology initiatives.

The preliminary report referred to 107 initial participants in the survey, being chief executive officers representative of the top two hundred corporations in France, the United Kingdom and Germany.

There have been at least some comparative studies of attitudes. Becker and Fritzsche in 1987, for example, concluded that US managers were noticeably more concerned with ethical and legal questions while their French and German counterparts appeared to worry more about maintaining a successful business posture.

The Mathison and Boje study included three major sections:

1 social issue questions;
2 issues that 'will most impact your operations'; and
3 questions concerning which issues should be the EC's top priority.

The questionnaires were constructed in three languages, scaled for strength of agreement or disagreement with the ideas in the questions, and analysed using conventional techniques of statistical analysis. Six hundred questionnaires were originally sent, producing a response rate of 29 per cent. Of these, 61 per cent were usable.

Social issue questions

- Women and minority opportunities.
- Separate career tracks for women.
- Drug testing.
- Corporate involvement in community problems.
- Fairness assessments of Japanese business.

Issues that impact company operations

The section covered thirty-five EC issues, including:

- 'Macro' issues, such as merger activities within the EC; economic instability in the USSR; and pollution.
- 'Micro' issues, such as 'non-white and women work opportunities'; health needs of employees; relocation of EC jobs to Eastern Europe.

The third section asked respondents to give priorities to the issues identified in the first two sections.

Results

On the social issues, the results indicated national differences. For example, both France and Germany tended to agree that businesses were unfairly blaming Japan for their difficulties; Scotland, Germany and the US saw a need for more corporate involvement in social issues; the US agreed with routine testing for Aids and drug abuse, while the UK strongly disagreed; all disagreed with career tracks for mothers; only the US and Germany believed that minorities had equal job opportunities.

On the 'impact' issues, France saw the increases in mergers, exploitation of Eastern Europe, and pollution, as important for company operations. The UK highlighted mergers, German unification and poaching of employees from the company by others. Germany emphasized poaching, mergers, and lower business and environmental standards in Eastern Europe.

Level of priority that the EC should give

The top priority issues reported by France were the USSR's instability, exploitation of Eastern Europe, and German unification. The UK's priorities appeared as German unification, USSR's instability, and exploitation of Eastern Europe. For Germany they were Soviet instability, pollution, and German unification. The combined order gives German unification, USSR instability, and pollution.

Some issues showed a combined high expected impact with a high priority for response policy. These included German unification, USSR instability, pollution, exploitation of Eastern Europe, lower business and environmental standards in Eastern Europe, and increase in EC mergers.

Some issues showed both low expected impact and low priority. These included non-whites and women lacking opportunities; corporations providing child care services; promoting by age and service, not merit; corporate power over labour; EC favouring corporations and minimizing social issues; and protection of whistleblowers.

In their discussion the authors comment:

Dunfee's (1990) discussion on Extant Social Contracts theory suggests that such contracts or behavior standards within a nation can be discovered through empirical evidence. As noted earlier, mid-1980s observations suggested that European executives as compared to Americans were more concerned about employee welfare, more long-run oriented, more tolerant of government intervention, more open to discussing social issues, and less concerned about formal codes of conduct. When Europeans had codes, employee conduct, community and environmental concerns and technology were typically priorities.

The authors express caution in interpreting the results of a preliminary study, but pose the plausible idea that there has been a shift in European business attitudes on some social concerns and policy matters. Using Dunfee's concept of Extant Social Contract, the authors conclude that a new understanding among European business leadership may be evolving, at odds with the EC's Brussels Commission and its Social Charter. Finally, the authors propose that:

During times of fast radical change the tendency is to focus on survival issues over less immediate problematic human issues. This appears to be the case with European CEOs facing the critical events of the new 12-member alliance. However, while European strategic concerns should be noteworthy to any multinational corporate planner, the emphasis away from a focus on employee welfare should also be a matter of awareness and serious concern for business scholars of international social issues.

The comments are well made. Whether we think of chief executives as originators of values or representatives of them, their position places them in leadership roles. If key values and issues are indeed subject to short-term concerns and expedients, this could be explained in a variety of ways. The economic pressure for short-term results could be seen to be strong in Britain, where, despite the sustained endeavours of government in the 1980s, the stop-go economic cycle showed little sign of yielding to policy initiatives. But this would not explain changes in German priorities, because the German economy has not been subject to the stop-go cycle except in a comparatively weak form. Nor has Germany been subject to the fluctuations in company fortunes associated with attempts to control the cycle, for example through interest-rate fluctuations around the high level used in Britain.

The issues surrounding German unification could go some way towards explaining shifts in German attitudes, but would not explain them all. The comparative importance of pollution issues was present in Germany long before unification became a reality, and long before the events that brought about the radical changes in Eastern Europe.

The shifts in values and priorities described in the Extant Social Contract can plausibly be seen to be partially, but not wholly determined by external pressures and short-term expedients. The absence of methods for the systematic handling of values suggests an openness to many pressures other than those of the stop-go cycle and external threats and opportunities in the market-place. The management fads, fashions and 'quick-fix' techniques are indicative of a perhaps chronic lack of clarity and stability in very many business values. A legitimate role for business ethics is to identify what the values are. Another is to examine the processes by which they change. In other words, values appear to be under a constant process of prescribing, reaffirming or abandonment. Part of the process is a political one, through representative systems. Another part is the instinctive, often unwritten and often improvisatory nature of the 'intervening processes'. This is reinforced in the case studies that show the limitations on the operation of the official values of companies, as expressed by their chief executives. The survey provides clear indications of the direction of shifts in values, and identifies some of the major determinants of the shifts.

Conclusion

The market as a mechanism or instrument for the efficient allocation of capital, goods, services and labour forms the basis for modern advanced economies. Much of economic theory and policy are aimed at freeing or controlling the market. There are in fact, many concepts of the market, ranging from the apparently very technical ideas developed in 'positive economics', to the practical controls asserted or recommended by national governments, the EC, the International Labour Organization and the

General Agreement on Tariffs and Trade. All of these theories and policies imply some very powerful values. As is typical of moral issues, there are major logical and factual matters which tend to be tangled, as attacks on or defences of the market take on ideological, and therefore partly irrational and emotional baggage. The market as a moral institution has had some attention in recent years (see, for example, Donaldson, 1989; Hospers, 1978; Sen, 1987), and a reasonable conclusion is that this side of the analysis is relatively underdeveloped, though arguably much more important than the merely technical topics.

The cases show the importance of administrative decisions on how the market can be viewed and is viewed, and suggest that for all the technical superiority of relatively free markets over all other systems, there are limits to the freedom with which markets are in fact allowed to operate. These limits to freedom reflect the complexity of values. They also reflect the recognition that powerful forces, such as those of the market, need to be restrained if the other values that are asserted in any country are not to be seriously compromised. The conflict of values is also reflected in the ambiguities visible in the various concepts of the market.

In practical terms, interference with market forces is necessary because some markets have an inherent tendency towards monopoly, or towards small group domination. It is necessary for a variety of other reasons, too. These include possibilities of exploiting consumers of those goods which can be addictive. Addiction annuls the concept of 'consumer sovereignty' which is crucial to free markets. Executives of large companies can affect, by their decisions, the interests and aspirations of others. They often do so on grounds which are highly defensible in ethical terms. When it is made, the pretence that decisions are forced upon decision-makers by the alleged 'brute facts' of the market or of individual psychology is unnecessary, and unworthy. The completely free market is an abstraction with little practical application. The key problem for the systematic handling of the values of the market-place and their effects, is how the factual matters can be effectively disentangled from the values and ideologies of policy makers, analysts and apologists, for or against the market. The sustained attempt by the positive economists in the 1960s have been seen to be useful, within limits. The nature of those limits needs to be explored if the values, facts and preferences are to be rationally disentangled. One starting point is the identification of the values that business people do live by, as opposed to those that they are required to have in order to makes one's assumptions work, or to prevent disturbance to old habits.

11 | THE PROPAGATION OF CORPORATE VALUES

In a chapter entitled 'Values: The Core of the Culture', Deal and Kennedy (1988, p. 21) comment:

Values are the bedrock of any corporate culture. As the essence of a company's philosophy for achieving success, values provide a sense of common direction for all employees and guidelines for their day-to-day behavior. These formulae for success determine (and occasionally arise from) the types of corporate heroes, and the myths, rituals and ceremonies of the culture. In fact we think that often companies succeed because their employees can identify, embrace, and act on the values of the organization . . . . In Part II of the book, we discuss in more detail how companies can avoid the risks and pitfalls of strong values by constantly tuning them to the business environment . . . . How do values come to be shared in a company? Through the reinforcement provided by all the other elements of the company's culture, but primarily by the culture's lead players – its heroes.

A different perspective is offered by Soler (citing Pastin) in Enderle *et al.*, 1990, p. 202):

Even though ethics and culture are closely related, however, the infatuation with culture does not extend to ethics. One reason is that those promoting organizational culture are now competing in a small, but profitable industry, *organizational culture consultancy*. Introducing ethics into the discussion is perceived as not at all likely to help sales. And those who sell culture, like the managers who buy it, have allowed themselves to become illiterate in the language of ethics, so they ignore it. But the truth is that the ethical ground rules are at the heart of organizational culture.

It is clear enough that 'culture' as described by the above authors is enforced and reinforced via taboos and rituals. This can often ensure that ethical issues are not raised.

Clients are relevant in so far as companies will not survive without a market for what they have to offer. Many principles of the 'customer is king' kind are promulgated, and acted upon. The increasing number of codes of practice aimed at the protection of consumers and investors suggests that the 'consumer sovereignty' values either do not permeate through companies' bureaucratic structures, or that they are more difficult to apply than is usually supposed; or, as I think most likely, that there is a fundamental incompatibility between the idea of managers as authors of company values and the expectation that they should be even-handed in the relationships with the various interest groups. Staff are regarded as relevant insofar as they are obliged to obey the rules, or, sometimes to embrace enthusiastically those values offered to them. If these offers do not 'work', there is always the possibility of finding out why, through employee attitude surveys, or encouraging compliance through participative schemes, profit-sharing, employee share ownership schemes and the like. The popular management literature contains many examples of insights gained in this way. Indeed the 'managerial orientation' of much of this work makes it unthinkable to many managers that the 'company values' could be anything other than those set for it by top management. To some, it may seem obvious that choosing and propagating a set of 'core values' is one of the principal responsibilities of top management. In the industrial relations sphere, conscientious and thoughtful managers often express surprise and deep disappointment when their efforts to promulgate rational and concerned values end in acrimonious disputes.

The problem with formulations of responsibilities is principally that there is a basic inconsistency with the notion of top managers as agents who neutrally adjust between the interests of identified 'stakeholders' and the recognition that they are 'stakeholders' in their own right. It is true that there are many expedients for guarding against abuses of powers. These include provision for re-election of directors, tests for financial probity through accounting and auditing practice, the power of the consumers to go elsewhere if their interests are not safeguarded, possibilities of litigation and much else. The fact is that boardroom battles are far from unknown, and there has been a rising tide of financial scandals in Europe and elsewhere in the 1980s. It seems improbable that companies and institutions will relinquish their myths, taboos and rituals. A conclusion for practical business ethics is that methods need to be established for objective evaluation of these myths, taboos and rituals. The history of attempts do so, from Socrates onwards, is not too encouraging, but working with them and 'exposing them to the air' could be helpful.

A recurring theme of this book is that official, normal business values are usually impeccable, and that their operation in practice tends to satisfy many of the criteria and principles identified. They do so to a much greater extent than perhaps might be gathered from the literature on business ethics. This is partly because when they are operating to the satisfaction of participants, there are no issues or dilemmas that people wish to raise. Where there is no issue, dilemma or problem, there is not usually much exciting news either. What this suggests is that much of the value-sending does not originate from the top of organizations, but is fundamental to the way of life. Value messages are received from a variety of sources.

The range of values from which top executives can choose is limited. It is true that new executives can implement policies previously thought impossible, as when new incumbents oust potential rivals or critics who had previously been thought of as secure, but bureaucratic conventions provide limits outside which new 'reporting' procedures cannot be officially adopted. This is one route by which the informal and intervening processes work, as various parties bypass the formal rules.

The values which are propagated are limited by the extent to which the product or service can be redefined, or the image to be reworked. There are many examples of marketing campaigns that work by tuning in to consumers' values so that their objectives are fulfilled and people begin to see a product differently. There are many campaigns that do not 'work' in the sense described. If the goods are not delivered, or are not up to expectations, the market reacts by sending signals back. All this is commonplace enough in cases in which the results are obvious, as in the collapse of a market, or a rising tide of complaints about a particular service.

Not all areas in which values are propagated provide the rapid feedback recognizable in falls in sales, or customer complaints. As was seen in the early cases in the collection under the heading 'When things go wrong', the values that top managers think are being propagated are not always the real 'operational values'. This can be because the official values are not made operational by middle managers, who are usually judged by their results (as defined by their immediate superiors), rather than by the sincerity of their commitment to official values. It is often because official values are vague, leaving choices as to which ones to pursue.

Examples are seen in investigations of transport crashes and the like, in which bureaucratic control and cost-cutting are suggested as having been in practice (unintentionally) the dominant values, while in theory, customer care and safety were held to be of the utmost importance. This is not a reason for assuming hypocrisy on the part of top management. It is more often the case that they are far less in control of the values operational in parts of the system than they think they are – the values of employees further down the hierarchy are normally held to be unimportant, except when something goes wrong, or is not working. Counsel in the inquiry into the Clapham rail disaster made the point that the sincerity of the managers could not for one moment be doubted, but that the true position in relation to safety lagged 'frighteningly far' behind the idealism of the words.

Value-sets often contain incompatible imperatives, as can be seen in some of the codes of practice, and members of professional bodies can have incompatible demands made upon them by the company and by professional institutions. When 'normal values' are not recognized or are rendered unworkable, the result can lead to corporate disaster, perhaps on the scale of Chernobyl (Chapter 5), Seveso (Chapter 1) or the 'Guinness affair' (Chapter 13), or to the collapse of an entire industry. But other possibilities exist. It is by no means impossible for 'normal' official values to coexist with chronic 'moral poverty', as some of the cases in the present (and other) collections illustrate. These symptoms can be manifested in the frequent recurrence of enquiries, for instance into low pay, frauds, or in the frequent appearance of some organizations in courts or industrial tribunals. In some cases, control at the top extends little further than protection of individual managers' places in the scheme of things – in management slang, known as 'protecting the rear end'. One problem is that the evidence and information tend to be filtered through the 'winners' ('heroes'?) and their control of information output, hence a below-the-surface examination is unlikely to be supported by any other than the most ethically self-confident companies and institutions. Companies and institutions, like individual people, are capable of error and of exhibiting both exemplary and reprehensible behaviour. Unlike individual people, however, these things can happen all at once in corporations and institutions, with no guarantee that the highest standards will win.

What needs to be eliminated is the assumption that errors may not be admitted to, unless forced by the courts or by public opinion, and that all differences of view are destructive of the corporate endeavour. This latter view tends to lead to managers seeing every disagreement as a battle to be won at all costs. This, at any rate, can be concluded from some of the cases presented so far.

The slightly negative portrayal of the propagation of corporate values is by no means universally appropriate. Not all ethical matters are controversial, nor are all corporate cultures driven by amoral imperatives or internal cynicism. As remarked earlier, goods and services often, if not usually live up to what they are supposed to do or to be. Contracts with suppliers and staff are, on the whole, honoured. Most companies do not make repeated appearances in court, or before industrial tribunals. The cases from here onwards illustrate a variety of ethical themes in business. Not all describe issues or dilemmas or solutions to them; by no means all are controversial. Some are presented simply to illustrate the theoretical content and backing for the operation of 'normal values'; others describe unresolved dilemmas, and demonstrate that particular solutions to certain dilemmas can raise new dilemmas. Typically of ethical issues, the evidence available is selected and filtered by some participants, and disputed by others, and the principles which conflict seem to be equally imperative. Also typically of ethical issues, they tend to recur in different formats and guises, once some sort of settlement has been reached.

In the following example, specific and self-conscious ethical stances and practices are described.

CASE	
37	**Electricité de France (EDF)**

In a paper to the 1989 Conference of the European Business Ethics Network, under the title 'Ethical Decision-Making in a National Utility: the Electricity Industry in France', François Ailleret identified the cornerstones of his own ethical convictions and those of his corporation, Electricité de France. They can be thought of as at least widely-shared in France as a whole. The first set includes:

. . . respect for the human person, whoever that person may be: citizen, customer, competitor, company employee, capital owner, trade unionist, politician; the obligation to fight against all narrow self-interests and selfishness . . .; and the acceptance of full responsibility for fulfilling our duties . . . while being entirely aware that no single person can have total control over his or her activities, nor escape the complex, turbulent and contradictory system of political, financial, social and legal constraints in our world – knowing, however that we have a duty to contribute towards making the system more efficient. (Ailleret, 1990, in Enderle *et al.*, p. 20)

Ailleret adds that the ethical outlook of Electricité de France is largely implicit, commenting that:

On the one hand, it derives from the customer, who, after all is the very *raison d'être* of the business . . . . On the other hand, the EDF ethics derives from the individual within the company who, regardless of his or her particular character or beliefs – has a basic right to a career structure and a professional future through the recognition of, and emphasis on his or her qualities and abilities. (Loc. cit.)

Ailleret sees the values that typify the French outlook as those of a 'transaction society', based on a market system. He points to strong principles of equality and justice. He sees the supply of electricity to the home as part of a package of basic essentials to which people have a legitimate expectation.

Five examples are given in the paper. The first is the traditional problem of 'bad payers'. Some who do not pay their bills cannot do so. Allowing any individual employee to make a disconnection decision is seen by the company as allowing that individual too much power over others. EDF subsidizes a fund to help those who cannot pay, but the decision on whether to help is referred to outside organizations, including charitable ones. Secondly, at the time of writing the article, EDF did not withdraw supply in winter, but the year-round extension was foreshadowed. A development is the notion of a Minimum Income Level, leading further to schemes for assisting subscribers.

The second example is that of discriminatory pricing policies. These are not used, unlike many other places, because they are held to be inconsistent with the principles of equality. (It might be added that the principle of equality of price paid for a product or service is a standard prescriptive, ethical element in traditional economic theory, and a part of the foundation of anti-monopoly policy.)

The third example is concerned with safety and environmental damage. A new high-voltage power line, deemed to be necessary is likely to scar the countryside. Objections will come from those who do not want the power line to be built at all, and from those who do not want it near them. The solution adopted is to aim for consultation, even if it means uncomfortable confrontations and, if necessary, recourse to arbitration.

Example four is the control of information, whether for normal operation or for emergencies and accidents. Information is to be made available immediately, or explanations given as to why it cannot; any errors are to be admitted (presumably to avoid the need for elaborate cover-ups) – own up and do not use scapegoats. EDF claim instances where this policy has produced an enhanced image, and potential conflict converted from win-lose situations to a combination of acceptable conduct and enhanced efficiency.

The final example is that of applying rules in selection procedure in relation to persons suspected of drug abuse, alcoholism, or who are HIV positive. Essentially the rules opt for strict medical controls in employment, rather than as a precondition for it.

Case 37 has been drawn from a single source. It has been chosen as a clear illustration of the interconnection between different kinds of values, and technical evidence, and their practical implications. The values propagated are clear, and feasible. The intervening processes appear to be enlisted in support of values thought to be acceptable to the various stakeholders that have been identified. The dilemmas

generated or solved, and in particular the use and support, neutraliza-
tion or destruction of intervening processes (assuming their presence
in the first place) would require a major research programme.

A research ideal proposed in this book requires the use of several
sources of information, and several perspectives from participants
or from people who have a legitimate aspiration in respect of the
corporation or institution. Case 38 moves closer to this paradigm.

CASE 38 | Propagation of values through the mass media

The Press

Ailleret's material draws attention to the interconnections between
internal values and their propagation, and the corporation's relationships
with the rest of the economy (or, if it is preferred, of society, or the body
politic). These interconnections are clearly visible in the operation of
the mass media, including radio and television broadcasting and the
Press. Some aspects have been intensively studied. Such studies have
rarely been in the sense of 'ethics 2', and have concentrated on how
preferred values can be made operational, rather than on the status of
the values themselves. In some instances, major formal claims of
responsibility for the moral education of nations have been made.
Freedom of the Press in its own right is seen as a mark of a mature
democracy, with all that that implies for helping to safeguard 'the liberty
of the individual' and other high-level values.

Press codes
By contrast, recent concern for the right level of the freedom of the
Press, and of publishing in general, has been exercised through issues
of censorship – political and artistic – intrusion of privacy, and the
bellicose patriotism of some newspapers. Attention has been drawn to
the inner workings of some sections of the mass media through state
controls, both financial and in regulating competition policy. The
suggestion that the internal workings of the Press profoundly affect the
nature and quality of their output was discussed many years ago in
America, where the operation of newspapers came under scrutiny
(Argyris, 1974). Some examples, mostly from the British Press, provide
an introduction to how the issues are seen and what that implies in
terms of values:

The spate of activity on the conduct of the press is based on the automatic
assumption that it is in the press's interest, at all costs, to stave off new
legislation. Self-regulation, good; legislation, bad . . . . So now we have an
editors' code of conduct and a new Press Council Code of Practice, fast-track

complaints procedures, readers' representatives . . . all kept cosily in-house, just like a general medical council or a law society. We journalists seem to be saying, we too, can be real professionals. All working journalists know how easy it is to make high-sounding promises. We promise to be good; we promise not to invade anyone's privacy unless it's in the public interest; we promise to be nice and not nasty; we promise to print the truth and not lies. (R. Lustig, *The Guardian*, 29 January, 1990, p. 23)

Lustig adds that he finds these promises unconvincing, with the suggestion that the public may share that view. As examples of what may be called 'values-in-action', he identifies the case of a boy labelled by one newspaper the 'worst brat in Britain'. The boy was thought to suffer from a severe behavioural disorder, and cites the case of an actor who committed suicide after being hounded by some newspapers. Lustig advocated a law which

. . . for the first time struck a fair balance between the right of people to a free press and their right to be left alone in privacy. (Loc. cit.)

This requires a sound criterion for identifying the 'public interest' in a particular situation, if the concept can be saved from becoming a 'weasel' expression: the solution could well turn on the procedure for making the decision as to whether the criteria apply in a particular case. One criterion for identifying the public interest in this context is attributed to Mr Lewis Blom-Cooper, QC, Chairman of the Press Council:

A public interest instantly arises by reason of some public office or position that an individual is holding or by reason of his conduct in the public domain or of his involvement in a public event. (Loc. cit.)

In the article the author proposes various forms of redress, ranging from speedy resolution by a Judge in the case of less serious matters with relatively small compensations sought, to scales of damages in more serious cases.

In the case of whistleblowing involving officials, Lustig concludes:

In Britain we do it all backwards. It is the mole not the official who is tracked down, hauled before the courts and charged. (Loc. cit.)

A later article, this time in *The Independent*, took up the theme of 'in-house appointees'. Commenting on the appointment of ombudsmen by individual newspapers, with the role of adjudicating between national newspapers and aggrieved readers, Michael Leapman put the point:

Most of the ombudsmen are from inside the newspapers that appointed them. Not all are experienced in journalism. Almost the only thing they have in common is that they are men. (*The Independent*, 28 March, 1990, p. 17)

Newspaper editors are reported as having issued a code of acceptable behaviour, with the intention of appointing readers' representatives. In

March 1990, the Press Council issued a code of practice, more detailed than that of the editors.

Leapman adds:

Codes are by themselves of merely symbolic significance. It has never been suggested that newspapers do not know how they ought to conduct themselves. The difficulty has been to hold them to decent behaviour in the face of powerful temptations to flout the rules. (Loc. cit.)

Views on the value of in-house appointees vary. Some newspaper people are reported as holding that what matters is the integrity of the individual concerned, rather than who employs that individual.

Others believe that it depends on the role expected of the ombudsman, and that a conciliator may be most appropriate from inside the organization, while an adjudicator would be better as an outsider.

In June of the same year, the Calcutt Committee reported. The Committee had been appointed by the Home Secretary, with the following terms of reference:

In the light of recent public concern about intrusions into the private lives of individuals by certain sections of the Press, to consider what measures (whether legislative or otherwise) are needed to give further protection to individual privacy from the activities of the Press and improve recourse against the Press, for the individual citizen, taking account of existing remedies, including the law on defamation and breach of confidence: and to make recommendations.

The report recommended further efforts to make voluntary self-regulation more effective, but proposed an independent Press Complaints Commission to replace the (voluntary) Press Council. The notion of a statutory right to reply has been widely regarded as unworkable, and was rejected by the Committee. The pressure for the enquiry had been mounting for some years. The appointment of the Committee followed a number of Private Member's Bills in Parliament that had attracted much support across party lines.

A main recommendation was the strengthening, not the abolition of self-regulation. A spokesman for the Guild of British Newspaper Editors is reported as commenting:

Calcutt's idea of self-regulation is to fit the Press out with a straight-jacket and invite us then to do up our own straps. This is not true self-regulation. (C. Wolmar, *The Independent*, 22 June, 1990, p. 2)

A representative of the National Union of Journalists is reported as taking the view that it was dishonest for the government to tell the Press to set up a new self-regulatory body which was government-controlled, and that

The present government has demonstrated how far it is prepared to abuse its powers of appointment in the case of the Board of Governors of the BBC. The greatest threat to press freedom in Britain today comes from government interference and the concentration of ownership. The Calcutt Commission has encouraged the one and entirely ignored the other. (Loc. cit.)

The new Press Complaints Commission, operated by the industry, started work at the beginning of 1990, replacing the Press Council. The Chairman announced:

The Commission needs people on it who carry the respect of their peers. It is also essential that there should be strong representation of tabloid editors so the Commission does not become a body of posh papers sitting in judgment on the rest. (G. Henry, *The Guardian*, 28 December, 1990)

It is clear from the discussions that the attention devoted to the Press has raised many ethical issues. The Press is made up of many different businesses. It could be said that they are not typical businesses, in that although costs are far from irrelevant, their owners are not single-minded pursuers of maximum profit, other considerations also being important. But if the Press is not typical, it naturally raises the question of what is a typical business? It is equally clear the discussions have applied much skill in addressing the issues, and that it is too early to be able to assess the effects of the new arrangements.

In terms of the analytical methods discussed in the book, it does appear that the agenda in the discussions has focused on only a limited range of issues and a limited range of stakeholders. The arrangements for ascertaining the authentic views of the various stakeholders are dependent upon the ability to identify who the stakeholders are. There are indications in the discussions that the participants have been aware of the operation of the 'intervening processes'. Public discussion of them has made much use of the mature judgements of skilled and experienced people, mostly from within the industry. This appears to satisfy the analytical requirements of applying skill and prudential calculations, fitting into a utilitarian framework, in that it promises more 'satisfactions' to aggrieved persons, without creating opportunities for new grievances to arise.

The influences on autonomy, reciprocity (the golden rule), and the recognition of a plurality of stakeholders and viewpoints do seem problematic. Any recognition of the operation of the 'intervening processes' would appear to be in danger of increasing the use of legal actions. As one observer put it:

The Press Complaints Commission will be a legal minefield. Without a legal waiver, the papers aren't going to turn up — they will send m'learned friends. (*The Independent*, 22 June, 1990, p. 2).

None of this would seem to be inconsistent with studies of the operation of the processes outside the context of specific actions and complaints. The choices of voluntary codes or statutory legislation do seem to rule out the possibility that some of the practices which gave rise to the debate may have sprung in part from internal causes. The general assumption seems to be that certain newspapers are obliged, in order to maintain circulation, to indulge in the practices which have been criticized. This could be so, but earlier cases have demonstrated the power of myths, of group assumptions, and of protection from exposure to the views of outsiders. There would seem to be scope for research informed by the systematic handling of values to supplement the political or social science methods already widely in use.

The corporate values of the Press are by no means obviously determined by the demands of the market-place, or of the niches occupied by individual newspapers. The values may even be major determinants of the beliefs about the nature of the market place, and the beliefs themselves can have a tenuous relation to the facts. Some industries have disappeared altogether as a result of false myths about the market. Research on the generation of beliefs about the market and their propagation remains to be done. Complaints of improper reporting are not confined to the tabloid press: elements of the 'quality Press' are caught in the same net from time to time. For example, in 1989 a very large and well-known company, involved in a (genuinely) 'friendly' takeover of a family firm, felt it to be imprudent to take corrective action on a report in one of the quality newspapers. The report made false allegations that several thousand staff of the family firm which had been taken over would lose their jobs, and that the owners of the family firm would receive well in excess of £100 million, having tens of millions of pounds in debt wiped out. The report turned out to be highly inaccurate, but no redress was available except through the courts.

One ethical point arising from this is that redress that requires a high price to be paid, financially and psychologically, should be a last resort only. Quicker means of redress, as advocated by the Calcutt Committee, have strong support from the principles of distributive justice. This support is even stronger in the case of those who cannot afford redress. A second ethical point is that the processes that give rise to the complaints are capable of improvement, so that far fewer complaints need be made. One way is to produce codes and legislation. Another is to influence the processes. The point that self-regulation can generate its own abuses is a serious one, and is made in many contexts other than the control of the Press.

Broadcasting

The agenda for discussion of the broadcasting media has been somewhat wider than that for the Press. As Lord Thompson put it, the Peacock Report and its reception (in 1986) provide illumination of the

way in which '... legislation for social and economic change in
sensitive areas of our national life finally reaches the Statute Book'
(Lord Thompson of Monifieth, *The Royal Bank of Scotland Review*, No
168, November, 1990).

The Peacock Committee was appointed to enquire into the effects of
the introduction of advertising and sponsorship on the BBC's Home
Services. Assessing the likely impact on the range and quality of
existing broadcasting services was part of the Committee's remit, as
was investigation of the financial consequences for the media
industries generally. The value background was a commitment by the
government to a free-market philosophy, and to the specific doctrine of
deregulation. Lord Thompson sees broadcasting as much more than
an economic activity:

It is a creative activity which has major influence – perhaps the major influence
these days – on our society's capacity to be well-informed, to provide in positive
ways for the increased leisure time of its people, to preserve and enhance the
rich diversity of its cultural life. (*Ibid.*, p. 7)

These values and their implications were not lost on the many pressure
groups with special interests in the values, or some subset of them.
Lord Thompson cites the ITV companies, the satellite corporations, the
Campaign for Quality Broadcasting, The Broadcasting Consortium and
the Voice of the Listener. Fears were expressed that the obligations to
provide educational and religious broadcasting were in danger of
becoming diluted, and the public service obligations of broadcasting
along with them. The mission to provide 'information, education and
entertainment' was dropped from the 1990 Broadcasting Bill, but later
reinserted into the Act. The new Act set up new institutions – the
Broadcasting Standards Council, the Broadcasting Complaints
Commission and the Radio Authority. Other existing regulatory
bodies include the Office of Fair Trading and the Office of Telecommunications.

Much of the subsequent debate included these values, especially
those relating to the quality of output, and the impact of different modes
of funding upon it. They also concentrated increasingly upon allegations
of bias (on the part of programme makers), and of interference by the
State in what is broadcast. Allegations of bias on the part of
programme makers included especially accusations of leanings to the
political 'left' or 'right', sometimes with accusations of both at the same
time. Apart from illustrating the powerful values involved in control over
information, education and entertainment, these accusations serve to
show the 'weasel word' qualities of 'left' and 'right', demonstrating that
they serve to transmit strong emotive meanings, with limited descriptive
or rational content. They provide strong examples of reasons why
some ethical theorists have been attracted to 'emotive theories'. These

assert that the meaning of moral or ethical expressions is no more than expression of emotion. It seems to be assumed that because holders of ideologies of the 'left' and 'right' often seem unable to discuss values objectively, it must be that values are non-rational. What it does indicate is not that values are non-rational, but that some value-holders are irrational.

| CASE 39 | **Propagation of corporate values: the 'bias' debate in broadcasting** |

The debate on the effect of funding methods on standards and on output has thrown up much information on how external forces affect internal 'values-in-use'. These values are the actual outcomes that result from the 'intervening processes'. As pointed out earlier, studies such as those by Argyris have demonstrated the existence of pressures in the other direction: internal organization and values can influence the output in many ways. One of these is the choice of 'campaigns' undertaken by crusading journalists. Another is the choice of events that are deemed to be worth reporting. Another is the choice of methods for presenting news. These latter aspects have been widely studied and debated, for example in the work of the Glasgow University Media Group (*War and Peace News*, 1985, Open University Press; *Bad News*, 1976; *More Bad News*, 1980).

The mass media provide good examples of the propagation of corporate values, because they are large corporations in their own right, as well as professional propagators of values to the public at large. In some cases, strong claims to ethical superiority are made before international audiences. The claim is widely accepted. As Lord Thompson put it in a letter to *The Guardian*:

Professional broadcasters have a heavy responsibility to ensure vigorous but objective and impartial presentation of public issues. The answer is not to put them in a straightjacket, but for the Government to sustain the courage, integrity and independence of the broadcasting authorities on which the high international reputation of British broadcasting has been built. (*The Guardian*, 31 August, 1990)

A letter from Hilary Dawson on the same day in the same newspaper put some practical points:

I was interested to read the report concerning proposals to 'stiffen' statutory requirements for broadcasters to make balanced and impartial programmes.

I was to appear on LWT's Six O'Clock Live programme to criticise British Telecom and Oftel. Both BT and Oftel refused to provide spokesmen. This apparently left the programme 'unbalanced' and my appearance was therefore abandoned. Organisations can effectively censor all broadcast criticism by no greater effort than refusing to appear to rebut it!

Reference to 'the broadcasting authorities' reflects the fact that the number of channels is limited, as are the skills, equipment and finance to propagate values. Because access is necessarily limited, those to whom the control of the channels is entrusted inevitably have a major responsibility for avoiding bias. But the stewardship of public resources clearly does not end there. The claims to high standards, and to the (moral) mission to educate, inform and entertain imply a wide range of obligations, not only to the owners and customers ('the public'), but also to suppliers and employees. The 'public' includes very many people whose values are not restricted to those offered by the political 'left' and 'right'. If, as seems to be the case, the internal values and practices have profound effects upon the quality and impartiality of the output values, it is proper that internal investigations and review be undertaken. Decisions internally and externally are taken that affect others. As with codes, such decisions need effective juridical processes such that, in particular, the opportunity is denied for the managers of a corporation or company to be 'judge and jury' in their own cause. In other words, the problem of external validation is particularly acute in the situation in which control over information and over the propagation of values is so great. These 'validating processes' come under frequent scrutiny, for a variety of reasons which are discussed below. Their occurrence appears haphazard when discussed in context. Calls for enquiries often appear to arise from particular whims of people in the privileged position of being able to add items to the corporate agendas, from corporate crises, or the passage of time, such as an impending annual general meeting, or the statutory duty to produce an annual report.

The connection between sources of income, standards of (internal and external) conduct and quality of output has received little systematic ethical analysis to date. It is an area in which the familiar entanglement of facts and evidence, values of various kinds, assumptions, myths and corporate propaganda is particularly dense. The first step in the disentanglement process must be to consider with care the various viewpoints, complete with their biases. Bias-free discussion of claims and counter-claims of bias has its own problems. One line of thought is that, like discussion of pedantry, attempts to discuss the area objectively can do no more than reveal the authors' own biases. Another line of thought is that pessimism about the possibility of objectivity in discussion is itself representative of a particular bias. In some instances, the connection between the source of an organization's income and its standards of conduct is obvious enough. If a corporation is going through lean times, competition for dwindling resources rises. The tendency towards 'devil-take-the-hindmost' attitudes is intensified, as is the tendency towards in-fighting and office politics (sometimes called 'micropolitics').

But, even if resources are not diminishing, people seem to have a limitless capacity for creating 'positional goods', that is, those goods that one person only can have to the exclusion of other people. The chief executive's job, or the President's or Prime Minister's are positional goods. In addition, managers at all levels, when new to a corporation need to prove themselves. One easy way to do this is to take 'tough' decisions, demonstrating their loyalty to the corporation, even if it is at the expense of selected victims. Many unfair dismissals arise this way.

Examples of views of bias are provided by interchanges occasioned by the publication of the BBC's annual report in July, 1990. According to the *Daily Express*:

The boss of the BBC last night warned his TV and radio producers to cut out bias in programmes. His blunt words came as he made a surprise admission that the BBC had fallen below its proper standard of political neutrality. (*Daily Express*, 27 July, 1991, p. 1)

One critic is reported as welcoming the 'ready and free acknowledgement that programmes are biased' (loc. cit.).

In the Chairman's Foreword to the BBC's annual report, Mr Marmaduke Hussey included the following observations, following a reference to the old BBC/ITV 'government protected duopoly':

Now that comfortable arrangement has gone once and for all and the BBC is part, albeit the largest and most wide-ranging part, of a multinational, highly competitive and increasingly market-directed industry . . . . The BBC has welcomed this new broadcasting environment. Much has been achieved by everyone in the BBC over the past year, and I believe that we are now a more confident and better-managed organisation. Our structures have been rationalised. The Board of Governors and Board of Management work harmoniously together. Our staff has a much clearer idea of the BBC's objectives and they are better equipped to face the Nineties. Last Summer's dispute, though, focussed our minds on the challenges which confront the BBC. The fundamental issue we face is to reconcile an adequate and competitive staff remuneration with the investment necessary to retain and continually to improve the quality of our programmes. (BBC, *Annual Report and Accounts*, p. 2)

He added:

The guiding principle of the BBC must be what it has always been – to provide the widest range of quality programmes right across the full range of licence-payers' tastes, interests and enthusiasms, or as the Charter outlines, to inform, educate and entertain. (Loc. cit.)

In the same passage Mr Marmaduke Hussey reaffirmed the dictum of Lord Reith, the first Managing Director of the then British Broadcasting Company, appointed in 1922: 'The BBC's role is to bring the best of everything to the greatest number of homes.'

The Foreword continues with references to many values, including 'continuing commitment' to Lord Reith's vision, to current 'unrivalled authority and immediacy', 'unbiased news and information', 'dissemination of truth', the public's 'loyalty and affection' for the programmes, and their 'extraordinary value for money'. The funding through the licence fee is seen as 'the best system available for ensuring that the BBC retains its courage, integrity and independence – independence from any source, political, commercial or propagandist', showing awareness of the privilege and the responsibility that goes with it, and the need to be vigilant against any falling below 'those high standards' (loc. cit.).

On page four of the same document, the Director-General, Mr Michael Checkland, refers to a commitment:

... to a BBC which makes quality programmes ... and which recognises that such programmes are the result of creative people working together, who have to be motivated and rewarded fairly ... .

'Regrettably, in the process of achieving this, some jobs will be lost', such losses being approached in 'as responsible and decent a way as we can' (*ibid.*).

Independent assessment using methods of ethical analysis of the degree of achievement of these proud values is not yet available, but there are alternative viewpoints. An indirect, and by no means decisive indicator of consumer viewpoints is to be found in the 'ratings'. In 1990, when audience ratings were reported as being at a six-year low, the Chairman of the BBC was reported as claiming that the BBC not only sets the standards, but 'feeds the rest of broadcasting with a sense of adventure and invention', holding that the source of funding elsewhere – advertising – produced competitive pressures which drove people to seek low-cost popular programmes in preference for higher quality ones (*The Guardian*, 25 June, 1990). The Managing Director of London Weekend Television was reported in the same piece as regarding the BBC Chairman's remarks as 'sour grapes'.

The bullish tone of the BBC annual report from which the above quotations were taken should be considered in the context of the earlier announcement that the BBC had appointed Sir John Harvey-Jones, industrialist and consultant, to advise senior management. Reportedly, the BBC was then seeking savings of £75 million, and to introduce market-oriented pay systems to replace those based on centralized civil service models. As one reporter put it:

The BBC is so impressed with its own *Troubleshooter* series that Marmaduke Hussey, Chairman of the Governors, has called in Sir John Harvey-Jones to give senior management the benefit of his advice. Sir John, former head of ICI ... said, 'I am a very considerable admirer of the BBC, and if it calls for help I would do what I can for them. British television is very much better than anywhere else.' M. Brown. (*The Independent*, 27 April, 1990)

Some months later, in an interview Sir John is quoted as remaining a firm supporter of the Corporation, but with business advice for consideration:

Sir John said that the first objective should be to cut staff, which absorbed more than 80 per cent of running costs. He said that while the BBC needed to reduce staff costs by one third, it should halve the top management, abolishing posts from Deputy Director-General onwards . . .: 'The BBC has far too many layers and a very complex management structure. The people at the top create work for the people at the bottom . . . . I think the whole place is not run that efficiently. A decision is taken and retaken many times at different layers. The place is stuffed with people who say no . . . . Everyone is petrified of not spending money allocated . . . . There is no reward for good behaviour. The outcome of the Home Office licence fee negotiations, a retail price index minus formula . . . could be used to increase pressure on the BBC until radical change did occur' . . . . 'Output should be judged on appreciation indices, rather than ratings, measuring the degree of satisfaction derived by viewers from programmes.' (*The Independent*, 9 January, 1991, p. 5)

Later in January, Ted Gorton, a former BBC manager and producer observed, in an attempt to define the problem in relation to the BBC's services:

What are their goals and objectives? How should they be measured? . . . . How can bloated and reactionary engineering and technical operations empires be controlled? How can staff be made less complacent? It is bizarre, but true that thousands of BBC staff are going about their duties without any formal idea about the aims and objectives of their work, because no one has ever asked the question, let alone tried to answer it. Under the BBC's system of highly idiosyncratic management, your aims and objectives are what the boss says they are. The Chairman and Director-General sincerely appear to believe that the BBC is taking giant strides towards becoming a more efficient and businesslike organisation. Seen from the ranks of middle management, this is not the case. Indeed, such steps are in practice thwarted by entrenched bureaucratic attitudes . . . the perception from below is, then, not of dynamism and reform, but of confusion of purpose, of inefficient, even mindless bureaucracy . . . of senior management whose lack of formal management training and interpersonal skills contributes so much to the confusion between management and administration . . . . The BBC's senior management does not help by being paranoid about open discussion of the corporation's internal workings, ludicrously defensive about any kind of criticism in the media, and totally incapable of admission of error on its own part . . .

Predicting that, as a result of Sir John's critique, something 'might be done about it', but that:

On past form, however, it is much more likely that a witch-hunt will be launched to discover how Sir John was able to make his remarks in the first place. A head or two will roll, and that will be that.

He concludes that:

Asking for honest opinions, and listening to the answers has never come easy to self-perpetuating oligarchies, and the BBC's version is, I suppose, no different from any other. (*The Independent*, 16 January, 1991, p. 17)

A tendency by the Corporation for lavish expenditure in defence of questioned decisions was noted by Michael Leapman:

The corporation had also been criticised for wasting money by competing with the . . . [then] new ITV breakfast television programme . . . it was seen as part of a driven obsession with getting the corporate finger into every broadcasting pie, regardless of cost or reason. (Leapman, 1986, p. 14)

Attitudes to severance of senior staff were also noted by Leapman, referring to 'early retirement' as a diplomatic euphemism (*op. cit.* page 18), while in relation to more junior staff, according to Burton Paulu (1981, p. 144)

'. . . . often take the matter to industrial tribunals.

Referring to the Annan Committee which reported in 1977, Leapman comments:

Annan had detected in BBC current affairs output a fear of offending people in authority – and with the licence fee up for consideration by Parliament again in 1985, that factor would not diminish. (Leapman, op. cit., p. 14)

Turning to the late 1970s, Leapman drew attention to a battle between the BBC and ITV over football coverage. The issue concerned the ending of the BBC's exclusive right to coverage on the Saturday night; Leapman cited one BBC executive as saying, 'It looks like war'; the managing director, television, as referring to opponents as 'Mafia with cheque books very much in evidence', and the then Director-General as writing to his opposite number in the Independent Broadcasting Authority a letter in which:

He complained about the casting aside of the 'concordat' – a fine BBC word borrowed from the arcane reaches of nineteenth-century diplomacy to describe the agreement between the two channels on carving up the soccer coverage. (Leapman, op. cit., p. 22)

Claims by the BBC would suggest that the Corporation is not unaware of the requirements for skilled management. The Corporation makes the following claims in its literature advertising training videos:

Let the BBC show you the way forward in the 90s. A new decade demands a new breed of highly trained and skilled managers. Let the BBC show you how to develop your team, improve your meeting skills and enhance your interpersonal relations with our great double bill, 'Give & Take'. (BBC leaflet, undated)

Clearly the attitudes and claims quoted above are highly judgemental, no less for the executives and defenders of the Press and broadcasting media than for their critics. The BBC itself can be regarded as a special case because of the high reputation it has enjoyed throughout much of its existence and because of the high aspirations set for it by Lord Reith, and reaffirmed as recently as in the 1990 annual report. There has been, so far as I know, no independent study specifically of the ethical standards set for and achieved by the BBC. The many informative studies and reports have, quite properly, had other purposes. It does appear, though, that there is prima-facie support for Argyris's proposition that external and internal events and processes affect each other. Bureaucratic habits, market pressures, funding methods and traditions can and do run counter to the official values expressed by companies and corporations. In the BBC's case and in that of the Press and communications media in general, a number of questions appear to need answering.

Is the gap between aspirations and conduct greater or less than that in more standard service and manufacturing industry? If it is greater, is this because the formal aspirations are typically higher and thus more difficult to achieve? Or is it because the influence of moral claims on people's behaviour is everywhere so great that the institutions that propagate national values, including business values, could not cope with pluralism in moral ideas? If so, is this because there are technical limits to the variety of ideas that can be broadcast at any one time? Or is it more likely that the 'intervening processes' are simply the inevitable results of bureaucratic and hierarchical modes of thought, abetted by the reluctance to become informed about and educated in the ethical dimensions of corporate cultures, as Soler suggests in the quotation at the beginning of this chapter?

The propagation of corporate values: conclusions

1 The mass media provide good examples of the propagation of corporate values, because they are large corporations in their own right, as well as professional propagators of values to the public at large. In some cases, strong claims to ethical superiority are made before international audiences.

2 According to Deal and Kennedy (1988), 'Values are the bedrock of any corporate culture', but noting their existence has, at least in mainstream discussions, not yet led to their incorporating in ethical terms, which provide their 'natural habitat'. According to Soler (1990) the consequences of doing

so could be generally beneficial, but would involve some major shift in modes of thought as well as in practice.

3 Whose values dominate and are propagated is problematic. The notion of freedom not to join, or to leave a corporation whose values you do not approve of is appealing, but highly problematic (e.g. how can you know before joining?). In legal theory and practice, citizens have an absolute duty before the law to report law-breaking. Doing so, however, can lead to all the problems of 'whistleblowing', blacklisting, etc. Bureaucratic secrecy and the propensity to cover-up questionable decisions are institutionally well-entrenched, and are likely to remain so as long as corporate officers are allowed to remain judge and jury in their own cause in so many aspects of corporate life.

4 Company values tend to be 'winners' values. Winners are not necessarily the owners or major stakeholders, as is witnessed in the literature in economics on the 'divorce between ownership and control'. This appears to apply as much to public service broadcasting as to private manufacturing and service industries. The public's values (i.e. the owners' values) are hard to identify. Control tends towards Michels' 'iron law of oligarchy'.

5 Some latitude is allowed by the operation of myths. Examples from the the 1950s to 1970s include the myths of union power; the myth of the cut-throat market; the myth of egoistic determinism. The myths allow for considerable variation in corporate cultures and in corporate ethical stances.

6 Ailleret provides an example of how values are propagated, internally and externally. They can 'lead', as in the Electricité de France example, or they can 'lag', as seen in the numerous *causes célèbres* reported in the mass media.

Monopoly power or a guaranteed income can allow much additional latitude for idiosyncratic values and cultures.

7 Corporate values are determined, in large part, by:
   (i) the dominant beliefs and myths of a milieu/age or country (e.g. egoistic motivation; free markets, democracy);
  (ii) market demands and their interpretation; 'winners'' values idiosyncrasies; and
 (iii) a haphazard element. This can often be related to the specific concerns of pressure groups who are able to add them to the agenda. For example, the ethical issues discussed recently and in public in relation to the mass media have been different for the Press and for broadcasting. The former have been concerned with issues of privacy in relation to the public interest, and with self-control and codes. The latter have been concerned with the effects on standards of different methods of raising

revenue; bias and state interference, and the privileged ethical status of one institution, the BBC, whose internal and external standards and claims have increasingly been under investigation, review and criticism.

8 External values influence internal operations, but internal values influence product or service quality.

9 Claims to operate 'high' values or standards can be weapons for use in competitive rivalries. This is because values drive people, and are more basic than motives. If in doubt, observe the power of calls to patriotism, holy wars, the examples of loyalty to corporate values reported by Deal and Kennedy (1988); Goldsmith and Clutterbuck (1985) and the cases in the present collection, or the primitive emotions stirred at the rallies of the political parties.

Such claims can be decreasingly plausible as practice and claims diverge. 'Official' claims to operate 'high' standards or values can be destructive of realized standards. This effect is usually identifiable when retreats from reality are masked by cover-ups, corporate propaganda efforts, etc.

The genteel destruction of values and of ethical standards can be masked more easily in high-prestige organizations than in fly-by-night sweatshops, but the excuses are harder to justify.

12 FINANCIAL SERVICES AND NORMAL VALUES

Money and values

Financial services occupy a special place in the economic system. Money, their main stock-in-trade, as the economic textbooks remind us, has many facets:

1 Money is a store of value, a medium of exchange, measure of income and wealth, and much else. Money can be converted into power and influence, and back again.

2 'Sound money' is required – without it, economies are prone to rising prices, i.e. inflation. Inflation is held to be immoral because it redistributes income from the weak to the powerful, without consent. Hard-earned savings can be wiped out, sometimes overnight, if the rate of inflation is high enough. Hard-won business can collapse as a result of the authorities trying to bring down the level of inflation. Jobs and futures, indeed many of the things that people value most, can be lost through inadequate or irresponsible monetary policies. What is or could be an 'adequate' or 'responsible' monetary policy is very controversial, and the literature tends to be very technical and unsure. It is probable that more has been written on the control of money in scholarly journals and serious newspapers than on any other subject. The subject has yet to be tackled from the point of view of the systematic handling of values, and the problems of inflation remain very difficult to control; the degree of control varies between countries and over time. Bell and Kristol (1981) in an edited volume include contributions that give the flavour of the debate, which continues in similar vein.

3 The financial services concentrate very large sums of money into the control of a relatively few people and institutions. Such power can corrupt, and 'the need for eternal vigilance' is widely accepted, and incorporated into a great deal of legislation and regulation.

In discussing the ethics of financial services, three features draw primary attention. The first of these is that there is often a fervent, almost evangelical tone to the advocacy, in different parts of the

224

political spectrum, of wider ownership of financial assets. These clearly befit the importance of the subject. Ideals vary from that of a 'property-owning democracy' to the importance of saving for emergencies, for retirement, or for one's children. Financial intermediaries often stress the need for impeccable standards – 'my word is my bond'.

It has often been asserted that the distribution of income and wealth tends to narrow with economic advance. (This trend has also been denied, however, and sometimes has been declared to be in reverse.) An observation with respect to Britain is supplied in *The Guardian* newspaper:

The distribution of wealth in Britain is becoming less equal for the first time since the Second World War, according to Inland Revenue statistics published yesterday. The new trend which began to establish itself when Mrs Thatcher* came to power in 1979, reverses a half-century shift towards equality .... The broader measure [of marketable wealth] including pensions, ... shows that the top 5 per cent has stabilised its share at 25 per cent, but that the top 10 per cent has increased its share to 36 per cent and the top quarter to 57–60 per cent. The poorest half of the population have seen their share of wealth drop from 17–21 per cent in 1979 to 15–19 per cent in 1985. (C. Huhne, *The Guardian*, 13 January, 1988, p. 30)

The statistical measurement of, and the factors affecting the distribution of income and wealth are complex. As yet these important topics remain controversial. Their ethical, political and economic content is clearly of the first importance. Like many other important topics, the volume and expenditure on authentic research is very low, and perhaps displaced by less vital, but more easily researched and less controversial matters. The literature and issues and policies were reviewed by J. Donaldson and P. Philby (eds), *Pay Differentials* (1985).

The second notable feature is that, to outsiders, the jargon and the issues involved in discussion of financial services seem to be impenetrable.

The third, and to many the most exciting feature of financial services, has been the huge rise, worldwide, of financial services scandals as reported in the Press. Alongside this trend there has been a series of sustained attempts to legislate to control activities in the sector, by professional bodies as well as by governments and the EC authorities.

This chapter discusses some of the main ethical matters raised by the first two of these features, the ideals and 'best practices', and the technical difficulties and associated jargon faced by any

---

* Mrs Thatcher was Prime Minister, 1979–1990.

outsider who wishes to penetrate the topic's mysteries.

The 'normal values' in financial services, as for all business activities, are those whose presence can be seen in, or inferred from ordinary, everyday activities. Sometimes they are set down in explanatory leaflets and in codes of practice. Sometimes they amount to nothing more specialized than the standard rules of behaviour that relate to telling the truth, keeping promises, refraining from deliberate harm to others, or respecting other people's rights. They are 'normal' in the descriptive sense that they are commonly observable. They are also 'normal' in a prescriptive sense in that they express rules, principles and 'norms' and are reinforced by formal and informal control procedures.

As circumstances change, it is to be expected that practices also change, and that new rules are issued from time to time. Sometimes the rules 'lag', in that they are issued to stop or abandon new practices that have emerged and drawn criticism. Sometimes the rules 'lead' in that they are designed to raise standards to meet the requirements of first principles.

Huge changes such as those associated with the European Single Market can be expected to be accompanied by leading and lagging reissues of rules. But '1992' has not been the only pressure for change. There is much talk of 'globalization' of financial markets. There have been many changes of a domestic nature over the years. Some of these can best be explained in terms of legislation, as when the British clearing banks' control of retail banking was opened up in the mid-1980s to allow other institutions to compete. They can also be explained by government policies such as the abolition of exchange control in the early 1980s in Britain. Exchange control set limits to dealings in gold and foreign currencies, and operated in Britain continuously from the late 1940s to the early 1980s. All of these changes can be explained further in terms of a philosophical (or ideological) preference on the part of the government of the day to extend the principles of the free market to as many activities as possible, including financial services.

These, too, need to be put into context. The principles of competition were not new to Britain in the 1980s. Exchange control was essential in the 1940s because massive overseas debts had been incurred in the Second World War, and calling in of those debts could have caused a major depression, as demand would have had to be reduced to keep imports down.

The above explanations can in turn be put into a longer perspective. The development of financial services has occurred in three major phases. In the first of these, during the early industrial revolution, the principal role of financial services was to assist in the accumulation of capital and its allocation to industry to secure industrial growth. The second phase, from the 1920s onwards, was a self-conscious effort to use financial services, and banking in particular, to establish control of the general level of economic activity, or more technically, as a countercyclical means. The third phase has been more recent. In this, the services themselves provide for consumer demand to use monies for a variety of personal reasons, from borrowing for consumption to saving for retirement and for setting up small businesses, speculating on the housing market, or buying shares, to become part of the 'property-owning democracy'. Each new role has supplemented, rather than replaced the older ones. The indications are that all of these consumer purposes are problematic, largely as a result of the difficult nature of general economic regulation as well as of achieving steady growth.

In some quarters, suspicions are voiced that a main role of the monetary system has become that of making money for a few, rather than providing needed services to the public at a fair level of profit through the market.

Financial services institutions

Regulation of business practices by the EC is done through several media. The general ethical principles are those of the freedoms of movement: of people, goods and services. European Community institutions for achieving this freedom include the Council of Ministers, the European Parliament, the European Commission, the European Court of Justice, and a variety of directives specific to various industries. Subjects for regulation in financial services include the control of monopolies and mergers. At present regulation is more at the national than the EC level, as the EEC Treaty does not include measures concerning these controls. The Single European Act of 1987 does, however, provide for:

1 the liberalization of international capital movements,
2 the abolition of cross-border restrictions on the provision of financial services;
3 the removal of obstructions to the free movement of goods and services.

The European Council of Ministers is the Community's decision-making body (the Parliament being advisory to the Council). The Council and Commission are able to issue Regulations, Directives, Decisions, Recommendations and Opinions, ranging in order from the most to the least generally binding. Directives, for example, are binding on Member States as to the result to be achieved, but leave the method of implementation to national governments. By April 1990 at least eighty Directives on financial services had been issued, following the Single European Act of 1987, which amended the 1958 Treaty of Rome. Some Directives took the form of codes of conduct. These included, for example, a Code of Conduct on Electronic Payment, Directives on Motor Insurance, Mutual Recognition, Reinsurance, Banking, Life Assurance, Capital Liberalization, Insider Dealing, Prospectuses, and Takeovers (source: UK, Department of Industry, *The Single Market, Financial Services*, April and September, 1990).

It seems that preserving the freedom of the market requires increasingly heavy doses of regulation.

Financial services include a large variety of institutions whose role in the market place and in relation to each other has changed dramatically in recent years. The Draft Code needs to be set against this. The various institutions and their developing functions are discussed by Philip Coggan (1987) in *The Money Machine: How The City Works*. For present purposes, the British financial services institutions include:

- the commercial or retail banks;
- merchant banks (investment banks);
- insurance/assurance companies and societies;
- pension funds (often set up by major companies or trade unions);
- the Stock Exchange;
- discount houses;
- stockbrokers;
- insurance brokers;
- building societies (providers of investment capital and mortgage funds for house purchase);
- the Lloyds market – an elaborate structure which brings together clients, underwriters (insurers), brokers (who bring clients and underwriters together), 'names' (syndicates who provide risk capital) and their underwriting agents.

The distinctive roles of these various institutions have been changing significantly. For example, banks and insurance companies have moved into and sometimes out of estate agency and mortgage provision. One building society has become a fully-fledged bank, while most provide banking-type services, including current accounts.

It is thus against this background that the Draft Code of Banking Practice should be set.

A Draft Code of Banking Practice

In addition to the laws of the Member States, EC Directives, Regulations, Decisions and Recommendations, there are many specific practices which are ethically relevant that are covered by more specific and local codes and sets of rules. An example is provided by the British Draft Code of Banking Practice Consultative Document issued jointly in December 1990 by the Association for Payment Clearing Services, the British Bankers' Association and the Building Societies Association (Association for Payment Clearing Services, 1990, London).

The Consultative Document was developed in response to the establishment of a government committee (the Jack Committee) in 1987. The Jack Committee's purpose was to carry out an independent review of the law and practices of banking services. It reported in February 1989, and one of its conclusions was that a number of recommendations should be implemented by means of a Code of Banking Practice. The recommendation was that the banks and building societies should draw up a 'non-statutory statement of best practice'. The basic principles contained within the Draft Code are:

1 that it should set out the standards of good banking practice which banks, building societies and card issuers will follow;
2 that it should ensure a clear and fair relationship between customers, their banks, building societies and card issuers;
3 that customers should be helped to understand how their accounts operate;
4 that confidence in the security and integrity of banking and card payment systems should be maintained. Banks, building societies and card issuers recognize that their systems and technology need to be reliable to protect their customers and themselves. They will keep systems under review, introducing new technology when appropriate.

The Draft Code is in two parts, dealing with customers and their banks, and with customers and cards. The former part applies only to banks, while the latter applies also to building societies and others 'who provide financial services by means of plastic cards'. These are termed 'card issuers'.

The topics covered include:

• **security in opening accounts** – to protect customers and bankers alike from misuse
• **terms and conditions** – especially the clarity of the terms, and notice and publicity by banks to customers before any variation takes effect

230 Business Ethics: a European Casebook

- **bank charges and interest** – providing details of tariffs, interest, and when it will be paid
- **handling of customers' complaints** – using the banks' own procedures, and if necessary, appropriate ombudsman and arbitration schemes
- **confidentiality of customer information** – covering the conditions under which disclosure of information within the banks or to third parties is or is not permissible
- **direct mailing of services** – restraint to be exercised, especially in relation to marketing to minors and marketing of loans and overdrafts
- **marketing and provision of credit** – restraint to be applied, especially for prevention of young people overcommitting themselves, early handling of cases where customers are in hardship difficulty with their accounts
- **availability of funds** – the timing of the clearing cycle
- **use of cheques**
- **terms relating to foreign exchange services**
- **guarantees and data protection**.

In relation to credit cards, the code is concerned with the terms and conditions, issue of cards, security and liabilities for loss, and handling of customers' complaints.

When put into operation, the code will be the first one to be adopted by British Banks.

Many of the proposals address mounting criticism by customers of banking practices which appear to have emerged without much or any warning or consultation. One immediate response was:

On the thorny issue of unauthorised overdrafts – where customers frequently complain that banks charge a penalty rate of interest and levy other charges without warning – the Code allows banks to continue as before, but requires them to notify customers of their action. This falls short of the Government White Paper recommendation that charge could not be debited from a customer's account without notice. (M. Hughes, *The Guardian*, 8 December, 1990, p. 13)

Some observers have gone further and hold that even notice is not sufficient. The grounds for this are that such charges are not agreed in advance between the customer and the bank, and that the decision when to levy the charges is not only unpredictable from the customer's point of view, but difficult and time-consuming to correct, given that clearing times seem to be highly variable, as does liaison between departments within banks.

Ethics and the Code

In considering the ethical content of the Draft Code, one point to note is that no direct ethical claims are made. Like most others, it is a code of practice. Many ethical values are easily inferred from it. One of these is that minors and inexperienced young people should be protected from getting into financial difficulties from which they cannot extricate themselves. This could be seen as not really an ethical move at all, but more a form of prudence, to allay public suspicion or to keep a step ahead of legislation, or paternalism, in which the banks would be required to protect people from the consequences of their own actions. This does not demonstrate that the ethical principle is absent, however. At most, it demonstrates that it *might not* have been the chief motive of the drafters of the Code. Another ethical value is that the terms of the relationship between banker and customer ought to be of a contractual nature. Ethically valid contracts are mutually agreed, not laid down by one side for the other to take or leave. This implies an approximate equalization of power between the parties to the contract.

The argument has been a major feature of most moral and political theories from the seventeenth century onwards, is recognized in legal theory in the concept of 'natural justice', and in other contexts is readily accepted. For example, the European Court has held that it is contrary to the Charter of Human Rights to compel employees to join a closed shop (Brit Rail Case; Joanna Harris case), on the grounds that freedom to join a trade union implies freedom not to join. It also implies that an existing employee who is not a member of a trade union ought not to be forced to join as a condition for continued employment if a closed shop (union membership) agreement is subsequently signed by employer and union after the employee commenced work. In effect, the principle is that conditions of contract cannot morally be altered unilaterally, even if it is lawful to do so. There seem to be no ethical reasons why what applies in the labour relations sphere should not also apply in any other contractual relationship.

Even though the Draft Code does not claim to be an ethical code, the above 'ethics 1' arguments are reinforced by the 'ethics 2' argument that even if the outcome is justifiable in that the financial results of the practices are fair and would be consented to by any reasonable person, the method by which the rules are changed is a matter for ethical judgement. Thus, what an impartial observer might regard as a fair result could be held to be in conflict with the principles of autonomy and the golden rule.

The Draft Code, then, provides an example of criticisms that have been made of practices that have developed over time, perhaps in a one-sided way. It also provides an example of a process by which constructive solutions are considered, criticized in a continuing process of dialogue, which has by no means ended yet. It provides an example of normal values, moral, prudential and technical, in the process of assertion, debate and interpretation into practical rules. Whether the Code as eventually adopted shares the typical strengths and weaknesses of the other codes discussed in this book remains to be seen.

Normal values can be seen in what people say and do. They can also be seen in the policies adopted by business and in the official statements made about them. As explained in Chapters 6 and 7, the values are not new inventions for each action or policy statement. As a matter of fact, their generation and propagation are the results of much discussion within firms and within the institutions that interact with them. Few values are new, and some assessments of business values echo through the ages. At the same time, it is often said that the meanings of values change between different cultures and within the same culture over time. For instance, it is said that 'democracy' meant something different in classical Greece from what it means in Europe now. Even in the twentieth century, its meaning has varied, in that at the beginning of the century, few countries officially thought it necessary to claim to be democratic. Now most countries claim to be democratic, or aspire to democracy. Clearly, the practices under the democratic label have varied so widely that either some claims are false, or democracy has more emotive meaning than descriptive content. These ideas have some force, but it tends to go unnoticed by the supporters of such 'relativist' viewpoints that the argument applies equally within the same culture at the same time. Democracy is, logically, a compound concept, requiring basic principles, which are invariably ethical principles, and institutional arrangements by which the principles are thought to be effectively operated. As it happens, 'democrats' are to be found offering widely different moral principles and arrangements, from anarchism through to modern capitalism, via the many, usually mutually hostile, forms of 'socialism'.

A conclusion is that the fact that ethical principles (and the meanings of the words that express them) differ over time and between places is far from impressive. They also differ within the same communities at the same time. Mostly they are *ideals* which inform and guide practice. Sometimes they are vague, but contain much emotional meaning. The vaguer they are, the easier it can be for people to become committed to them, even to die for them.

At a less exalted level, values are visible in ordinary statements of company policy. They can share many of the characteristics of the general ethical expressions discussed above. The principles can be very old, and be clearly visible in one or more of the standard ethical theories. In other words, they can be analysed using the rival frameworks described in Chapter 7. These frameworks were there seen to have the useful function of acting as checks and balances against the potentially dangerous adoption of, say, a thoroughgoing utilitarianism, duty-based theory, or doctrine of the inalienable rights of man or of property. Tests of a sound ethical company policy relate to how far the policy goes in recognizing and balancing the demands of the competing ethical principles and competing claimants found in company statements.

Clearly, some succeed more than others both in principle and in putting it into practice.

Case 41 summarizes the values as expressed by one of the long-established and largest Lloyd's insurance brokers. Its inclusion here is for the purpose of demonstrating the wealth of ethical principles in ordinary day-to-day policies and practices. The author is grateful to the company for providing the material, and for explaining some of the administrative and organizational arrangements for encouraging, monitoring and improving the values and standards. The interpretations and the selection of the material are the responsibility of the author alone.

CASE 41

Sedgwick Group plc

The material in this study is taken from three of the Group's publications: the annual report for 1989; Sedgwick Group UK's Code of Practice for the Avoidance of Errors and Omission Claims (March 1988, second edition); and Sedgwick Group UK's policy statement (1986).

The annual report opens with the statement:

Sedgwick is a major international insurance broking, risk management and consulting group in the financial services industry. In more than 300 offices around the world the group measures its achievement by the return generated for shareholders, by the quality of the service offered to clients, by the skill and commitment of its staff, by speed and flexibility in response to changing conditions, and by its relationship as a good citizen of the communities of which it is a part. The group's aim is to be the leader in every field in which it chooses to operate. (Report, p. 1)

Profits before tax are recorded as £85.2 million (US$137.2) in 1989, compared with £77.9 million in 1988 (US$125.4 million).

The statement contains no claim to be a 'profit maximizer', but does refer to 'skill and competence in managing our business' (Report, p. 4).

According to the report, performance depends largely, in addition to the skill and competence, on:

... the level of insurance rates, the level of interest rates in the principal markets in which we operate, and the relative value of the pound sterling against the US dollar and other major currencies. The last two have a significant effect and contributed to our profits in 1989. The first two are of overriding importance and we have had to exercise our skills for yet another year against the background of falling insurance rates across the world. Although our proportion of fee-based income continues to increase in our consultancy business and in our retail insurance business, by far the greater part of our turnover is generated as commission related to premiums. Since 1986 the overcapacity of insurance markets has led to fierce competition for business between underwriters and between brokers. (Report, p. 4)

Hurricane Hugo, the San Francisco earthquake, the Philips petrochemical explosion and, more recently, the European windstorm losses, serve as sharp reminders to clients and to the market of the severity of natural disasters .... Our objective ... is to see that Sedgwick operates and is regarded as a truly international business owing its loyalty to clients; to produce for them the best advice and service wherever they are located, and from whichever insurance market best serves their needs. If, as we hope, London and Lloyd's offer good security and service at competitive prices then we will continue as we have in the past to be major participants and supporters of that market. (Report, p. 5)

Lloyd's has passed through a most difficult period; it has endeavoured to prevent the healthy baby of free enterprise from disappearing with the bathwater of regulation and bureaucracy. (Report, p. 6)

The Group's UK Policy Statement, signed by the company Chairman, W.R. White-Cooper, provides more detail on the company's values:

In recent years, senior management within the UK Group have been reviewing our business philosophies and practices as they affect our clients, our staff and the insurance markets in which we operate. Part of this review included a reassessment of our management policies and the role we should play within local communities. This document is intended as a summary of the UK Group's business policy; as such the various statements made will continue to play an important part in our future development. It will also serve to remind us – management and staff – of the values to which we subscribe.

The statement covers six major areas:

- **Clients** (meeting their needs and and their perception of value in doing business with the company).
- **Staff** (recognition of its added value, promotion and remuneration on merit, comfortable, yet stimulating environment, individual development, seen as having mutual advantages).
- **The insurance market** (relationships based on mutual trust, respect and confidence, 'because these relationships enhance our ability to serve our clients. We must therefore: maintain the highest ethical

standards in the conduct of our business dealings and support fully the principle of utmost good faith . . . .'

- **Management** 'We believe that effective systems of management improve our competitive edge – thus we employ proven management techniques and procedures based on the principle of decentralised decision-making with control of performance from the centre . . . . Consistent with these principles is the need for proper and on-going two-way communication between management and staff.'

- **Financial performance** 'We aim to operate at a level of profitability comparable with the most efficient in the UK broking sector, and to achieve real growth year on year of at least 15%.'

- **Community role**: 'We believe that we have a responsibility to the community in which we conduct our business and we aspire to foster good citizenship through providing career opportunities, by making use of local resources and by assisting in the development of community projects.'

The Company's *Code of Practice for the Avoidance of Errors and Omissions Claims* (Second edition, 1988) sets out principles and detailed practice. For example, the general principles include:

Duty of disclosure: It is the duty of the Insured and his Broker to act with the utmost good faith towards underwriters to disclose all material circumstances within their knowledge; and to give a 'fair presentation' of the risk to the underwriter.

These principles are followed by detailed instructions relating to such matters as confirmation in writing (to provide a demonstrable record in the event of a dispute); effective time of binding cover; dating of all documents, use of facsimile; prohibition of completing proposal forms or claim forms for clients; the role of telephone discussions – keeping adequate notes of them.

In the opening sentence of the code, it is made clear that the rules set down the minimum requirements. The second indicates that the code is not a substitute for a detailed procedure manual. The third sentence states that the code of practice must be read in its entirety and complied with without exception.

Several observations may be mentioned immediately in considering the above statements:

1 The statements themselves represent the civilized values of a major, long-established private corporation.
2 Such statements show a good deal of self-confidence, in that the forthright expression of values would expose the authors to major risks if a gap between aspiration and achievement were to be seen as significant, especially to clients. Indeed, other cases have shown

how great these risks can be, inviting not only public debate, but often, controlling legislation.

3 From the point of view of business ethics as a discipline the statements illustrate the influence of a whole range of moral and value concepts – skill, prudence and duties (Kant's distinction, made in the seventeenth century) – utilitarianism is clearly visible, and not only in the profit objectives. It can be seen in the recognition of differing interests and in the endorsement of free markets and the mutual benefits they can bring, and in the community-welfare values. The rights of the various 'stakeholders' are recognized. The concepts of autonomy are applied to staff and clients, and the recognition of competitors is a pluralist concept. About the only element that belongs to the standard repertoire of ethics that appears to be missing is a formal statement of the golden rule.

4 Also from the point of view of business ethics it is interesting that the concepts of moral philosophy appear to be more integrated into what normal business says and does, than into the traditional management and business literature.

At this point a pertinent question might be, to what extent are the 'normal values' described in this chapter really typical of industry? After all, some of the cases in this collection show a substantial gap between aspirations and outcomes. Others show considerable doubt as to what an ethically defensible course of action would be in the circumstances presented. Yet others show that even when the principles are agreed, the facts of the matter can be obscure, and knowledge of them can be within the control of some stakeholders or participants to the exclusion of others.

The question provides the starting point for Chapter 13.

13 THE SIGNIFICANCE OF SCANDALS IN FINANCIAL SERVICES

Changing images of financial services

There has been an explosive growth in financial services activities. Equally impressive has been the growth in the journal literature on the subject. This has included press comment describing and analysing current trends and advising on how to react to them, how to invest wisely, or how to keep up to date. A recent computerized literature search revealed that almost ten thousand journal and press articles relating to Europe alone have reached the list of the data base in the last four years. Clearly, to keep informed, the most dedicated researchers and the most conscientious managers could not hope to do more than scratch the surface of this mine of information. Of course, not all the material is relevant to any particular interest, scholarly or financial, and not all material is of the same standard, but the volume alone is one indication of the importance of the subject.

Another indication is the deep concern shown in high places about the growth of criticism and of dubious practices, prosecutions and convictions connected with certain activities in the financial services sector. A speech by the Duke of Edinburgh to a conference organized by the Confederation of British Industry provides an example. According to the report by Peter Large of the Duke's speech:

He likened monetary economists – in their 'cosy, closed-cycle system' to a pilot trying to fly to Australia on the assumption the earth was flat. Economic theory, he said, had to broaden its vision to include the facts of planetary life. Prince Philip reminded his London audience of business people that the City of London's reputation had been built on the basis of a man's word being his bond. Absolute confidence in honesty had not only built that unique reputation: it had increased speed of reaction and reliability in action. Lost trust was almost impossible to regain. Nothing corrodes a community more quickly or more completely than lying, cheating, corruption and double-dealing. (*The Guardian*, 1 May, 1990, p. 14)

Three years earlier, concern at inadequate enforcement of legislation in the area was frequently expressed. For example, according to Hamish McRae:

The newspaper headline in the *London Evening Standard* said it all: 'City Cheat Goes Free' .... . It is too simple to say that the majority of would-be criminals in the City will rejoice at the leniency of the sentence and carry on their insider trading unabated. That would be a rational response, for the fine of £25,000 would be equivalent to the profits on one good deal. The risk of being caught for insider trading on the evidence of the number of cases being even considered, is tiny .... . But you cannot suppose that criminals are wholly rational. If they were, this outcome would herald a giant leap in city crime. (*The Independent*, 2 July, 1987)

McRae continued to list other possible motives that constrain behaviour, such as fear of losing one's livelihood, the 'zest and the fun' of running an international securities operation, the bleakness of life as an outsider, public humiliation. He added,

There is, however, a larger force which will help keep City crime under control. This is the fact that the whole moral climate in the country is moving the other way. The Government did not stiffen the penalties for insider trading, increasing the maximum sentence to seven years because it could not think of anything else to do. It did it because it perceived, rightly, that this was what society wanted. And society wanted it not because of some leftish propaganda against the City, but rather because the whole country is stumbling towards a new social bargain. (Loc. cit.)

Three years on, the public concern, as expressed by press reports, was showing strong signs of intensifying. Particularly in what came to be known as 'the Guinness affair', this concern was taking more practical expression. It could be that corporate crime, illegal share dealing, fraud and the like are truly on the increase. It could equally be that the threshold of tolerance of it has lowered. It could be that the reporting of it reflects the context of the cases before the courts more than their content, or the fact that those who believed themselves to have been wronged were able to bring the matter to public attention, having the resources, knowledge and skills to do so. These are matters for empirical research in the social science or economic traditions. For a casebook in business ethics, the more pressing problem is where they fit into the various frameworks for the systematic handling of values. Before proceeding to compare financial services cases to ethical theories, it will be helpful to review the variety of issues that have been reported, and some of the *causes célèbres* that exemplify them. In other words, the issues and cases as raised in the literature will first be described, and the ethical, as opposed to the economic, political and legal issues can then be fitted to them. Inevitably, matters economic, political and legal overlap with matters ethical, but our concern will be with the specifically ethical issues raised. Ethical issues are matters which are uncertain or contentious. It is not an issue if someone breaks a moral rule. It is an issue if the breaking is done in support of a rival moral rule, or if the concerned parties do not know what to do about it, or are not in a position to do anything even if they do know.

To return to the major scandals, if some of the cases are major because the persons or companies are chosen as scapegoats, or are losers in some internal squabble, it is difficult to argue that any ethical gain is made from the action against them. Ethically, the motives and justification of the hounds are as important as those of the quarry. It is not necessarily an ethical issue if someone breaks the law. It is always a legal matter, by definition. The law gives practical expression to matters that are directly ethical or have ethical implications. It is well recognized in moral and political theory that people can truly believe, with justification, that a particular law is immoral or improper. There have been many cases of people refusing to pay taxes, of motorcyclists who refuse to wear helmets, or of people who refuse to send their children to school on the moral principle of the freedom of choice.

These matters are issues because there is usually a strong ethical principle in opposition to them. The responsibility of citizens to pay lawfully-levied taxes is one principle, the duty to provide a competent education for children is another, justified on the ultimate ground of autonomy, for which education is an essential precondition. Parents may doubt whether the formal education system is truly competent to teach their children. Citizens may doubt whether a tax is legally imposed, or may claim that the law itself is immoral. Legal progress often comes from refusal to support bad laws, or from the practice of ignoring them. Legislators need to be reminded from time to time where the bounds of public tolerance lie.

All of these are commonplace issues in moral and political theory. It will be seen that in some cases there is no suggestion that the companies and individuals at the centre of the case objected to the current legislation. In others it will be seen that there is at least a suggestion that the persons involved may have been selected for exemplary treatment, in order to discourage others from risking the practice of which they were accused. This is, in itself, clearly a matter for enforcement policy, but that, too is capable of analysis on grounds of ethical standards as well as on grounds of whether it is effective or not.

The image of financial services has changed over time, just as their role has changed over time. There is nothing new about financial scandals. A review in the *Financial Times* in 1990 by

Richard Lambert covered British cases from the South Sea Bubble of the eighteenth century to the ending of the Guinness Trial in August, 1990. Lambert identified some common factors, some recurring uncertainties and some variations. On the common factors:

> The most obvious common pattern among the falling business idols of the past 300 years was a forceful, even autocratic personality . . . . (*The Financial Times*, September 1–2, 1990, Section II)

Often, fellow directors were reduced to cyphers, or chosen for that amenable quality:

> Whitaker Wright, who was sentenced to seven years' penal servitude in 1901 for manipulating the accounts of the New Globe finance company, was similarly careful about his choice of directors. One of them, a General Gough-Calthorpe, was asked in a subsequent inquiry whether he had any idea of his duties as a company director. He replied thoughtfully, 'as far as I could ascertain it was to sign my name many thousands of times on share certificates'. (Loc. cit.)

Of Sir John Blunt, key figure in the South Sea Bubble, which burst in 1720, along with the collapse of Law's system of banking in France (the 'Mississippi Bubble'), Lambert quotes a contemporary pamphleteer:

> 'Twas his maxim, a thousand times repeated, that the advancing by all means of the price of the stock was the only way to promote the good of the company . . . .
> 'Then the bubble burst and squadrons of people were seen to have had their hand in the till.' (Loc. cit.)

A hundred years later, a similar pattern is discernible from a detailed description by a well-placed observer of the financial crisis of 1825, published under the title, 'Letters from a Young Lady'.

CASE 42 | Letters from a Young Lady

Well, then, I am afraid I must begin with the beginning of the story, tho' I don't like going so far back. Ten years ago I think you know that Peter Free contrived by his speculations nearly to ruin us, Down and himself. Sir R. Pole, however, an immensely rich man, came in, and since then, the profits have been immense, and the house is going on apparently most prosperously. Three years ago Henry began to serve his time there, merely to learn the trade, under the understanding that when the Partnership dissolved, which it did last Mid-summer, he was to come in. He met with some opposition from Pole – who is a mere sleeping partner and did not like his share being diminished by Henry receiving some of the profits – and from Free who did not like being watched.

However, for very shame's sake they admitted him. As soon as he was there, and let into their secrets, he found that Down and Scott were perfect cyphers, Pole never came near them, Free governed supremely, and he was not satisfied with many parts of his proceedings. There was a spirit of speculation, a love of concealing what he did, making the best of a story, which to Henry was intolerable, and they have had some lively disputes about things; on one occasion Henry set off in the night, and brought up Pole from Hampshire, to interfere by nine the next morning, because he could not make Free give up a plan which he did not think strictly honourable and therefore not prudent. (Ashton and Sayers, 1954)

A further common feature to which Lambert draws attention, is that of deciding at what point accepted business practice ceases, and actions become unlawful or criminal (Lambert, loc. cit.).

Lambert notes a feature of the Guinness case which appears to have broken new ground, that the company prospered after the acquisition of the Distillers company. The Guinness affair arose from the process of acquisition, which began in 1985.

Historically, the sums involved in cases such as this appear to have shown no strong trend towards increasing. Sentences in enforcement of the law have also varied in severity, with no very clear determining pattern.

Ethical relevance

Recent financial services scandals have by no means been confined to one country. Britain, America, Australia, Germany, France, Greece, Nigeria, Japan, Italy, Israel and the Philippines can all claim at least one such event. The issues involve a catalogue of financial pathology. The details of some of these are more readily available, and more widely-discussed than others.

From the point of view of ethics in business, a number of cautionary points must be made as a preliminary to analysis. The first is that, although there is a strong relationship between ethics and law, there is no necessary logical link that makes an 'unethical' act or practice unlawful, or vice versa. This is because the law generally enforces ethical rules, but is at all times capable of being appraised in ethical terms. In short, the law may be unjust, or unjustly applied. By definition, 'the law' cannot say so, but ethical appraisal can.

A second point on this theme is that the law sets minimum standards. Responsible citizens are expected to do more than the bare minimum. Some laws are uncertain until tested, and there is a high probability that anyone who chose to comply only with the minimum legal requirements would frequently fall below them, because of these uncertainties.

A conclusion from the foregoing is that it is neither a necessary nor a sufficient condition that an act or practice is found to be lawful or unlawful for making the judgement that it is ethical or unethical. Nevertheless, the probability is that the two categories, 'lawful' and 'ethical' coincide. That is, they coincide if by 'ethical' we mean 'justified by reference to sound ethical principles and to properly-considered evidence. It follows that if it really is the case that law-breaking in financial services is increasing, this could be more a matter of law enforcement than of business ethics. The possibility does remain that an all-round rise in ethical standards will decrease the propensity for law-breaking, or that business ethics can provide cheap ways of damage-avoidance or damage limitation by reducing the risk of civil or criminal law proceedings.

A second conclusion is that, although an act or practice may be susceptible to criticism in ethical terms, it is unlikely to be an issue, if it is simply a matter of someone breaking the law and being found out. It could become an ethical issue, if serious claims were made, for example, that the law is being applied unfairly, or in support of punishing scapegoats. It could also become an ethical issue if people came to believe that the law ought to be changed, perhaps because it was drawn up to regulate conditions that no longer apply. This suggests that a good many of the cases that have drawn direct or implied criticism on ethical grounds are of little ethical, as opposed to legal significance. Ethical issues are likely to arise not just because standards are falling, but because people do not know what to do about it, or do the wrong things to control it, or shirk the responsibility for acting when they have a duty to act.

A point to note is that the exposure of those cases that come to light can signify a variety of attitudes, not all of which are in themselves ethically defensible. The motives and the actions of whistleblowers have not always been shown to be sound, but equally they have not always been shown to be indefensible. One suggestion made in the 'Guinness' trial was that the matter became public in the first place primarily because of enmities engendered during the takeover battles, and only secondarily because there were legal and ethical issues involved. This raises some difficult questions concerning the moral psychology of industry. Traditional moral sceptics would no doubt see such an outcome as only to be expected, on the grounds that there are in principle no 'ethical' motives, only self-interested ones. Moral pessimists would typically declare that the 'right thing to do' may be known to all from the start, but that people will only do it if there is some advantage, making a virtue out of necessity. One problem with these arguments is that they are untestable. If appraisal of action is to be done in terms of motives, it would be useful to have methods for determining what the 'true' motive for any action is. But motives are unobservable to outsiders. Actions are observable, or at least some physical manifestations are, but motivations are not. The motives that people will admit to are often mixed, and frequently held to be unconscious. Sometimes they are inconsistent with actions, but this can be because people are not always aware of what the efficient way will be to achieve what they want. Reflecting on a number of investigations of fraud or suspected fraud, Rowan Bosworth-Davies makes the observation:

Greed was a fairly regular feature in most investment-related scams . . . greed on the part of the investor did play a significant part in bringing the investor and fraudsman together. I was to discover that one of the most appealing influences on the decision to invest money in a speculative scheme was where the investor believed that the particular investment was dishonest or illegal. (Bosworth-Davies, 1988, p. 5)

Bosworth-Davies notes that individual victims, including directors of large companies, often turn their anger on the investigator out of the fear of ridicule, which is a powerful enough motive to persuade people to stand a loss, rather than admit that they have been taken in (loc. cit.).

The size of the problem can only be guessed at, although the number of people involved in buying company shares is small, generally estimated at less the five per cent of the total population. That the proportion of the population from which the issues arise is small should not be taken to indicate that the problem is trivial, only that the small number of people involved in active investment makes it difficult to generalize on the causes of recent scandals from the real or alleged motivations of the participants, and even more difficult to extrapolate those motives to the rest of the population. In other words, if greed and fear of ridicule really are major motives in financial services, it does not follow that these are the driving forces that give rise to ethical issues or to variations in their intensity and incidence in other sectors, or among the enforcement agencies. The proposition that there are different base motives operating to generate issues in different industries does not seem to stand much of a chance of explaining the rise in business ethics issues. The idea that the same number of base motives explains the general rise seems even less likely. In my view, Bosworth-Davies has provided some valuable clues as to the rational reasons why people might be involved in covering up improper actions, or become involved in them. This is important both for preventive and for control purposes. But the intervening processes are discernible from the quotations – the need for secrecy, and the win-lose nature of many takeover battles, and the secretive, hierarchical nature of large organizations. The win-lose games by which people's worth is estimated, and the huge rise in opportunities as the volume, speed and complexity of transactions have increased provide a potent combination of factors. But these are still not enough. Some of the cases which conclude this chapter show many other processes at work.

One of these processes is the scope for manipulation arising from the lack of knowledge and information available to the public. Much of the jargon of the business functions very well in baffling all but insiders as to what the issues are about when they arise. This has given rise to suggestions that juries ought not be used in fraud cases, which can be too complicated, or that juries should at least be drawn from suitably knowledgeable people. What does seem to be inescapable is that the 'cultural milieu' described in Chapter 11 provides the assumptions, which in turn set the rules by which businesses operate. The secrecy, diminished role or absence of external checks and balances remain constant features in virtually all the cases where issues arise. The 'positive' cases, in which standards are made explicit virtually all provide for external and independent checks and for visibility.

Scope and variety

The range and scale of activities in financial services that have generated attention are truly impressive. During the late 1980s they attracted attention on a scale that was reserved for trade unions in the previous two or three decades, at least in some countries. The range and scope was indicated in *Key Issues*, using press headlines from the mid to late-1980s as follows:

'Dissecting the Anatomy of a Scandal' (the early stages of the 'Guinness affair')
'Bank Scandal Test for Greek Government'
'CBI Chief Attacks the City's Rush for Profit – Fund Chiefs would "Sell their Grannies" '
'Three Arrested in £60m Hill Samuel Plot'
'Row Over City Flares Again'
'New Merger body "Essential" '
'For Whom the Bell Tolls at Lloyds' (allegations of widespread fraud, underwriters with luxury yachts, villas and strings of racehorses)

'War Declared on £3 billion-a-year Pinstripe Fraud'
'Auditors May Get Crime-Busting Role'
'How Will the City's Mini Policemen Stop Tripping Over Each Others' Big Flat Feet?'
'Former JMB Staff Linked to Nigeria Fraud'
'Fraud Measures "Let Off" City'
'Minister Was Member of a Syndicate Which Made Profits for a Select Few'
'£400,000 Whistleblower on the Dole'
'Bail in £853,000 False Accounting Case'
'Whitehall Helped Company Evade EEC Law'.

A later sample

'The Investing Public is Still in the Dark'
'Judges' Panel Urged for Fraud Trials'
'Shame on All Their Houses: Gullibility and Cowardice Mark the Harrods Affair'
'A Small Victory for Ethical Investments and Honest Adverts'
'Professionals in a Catch-22 Situation'
'The Decline and Fall of a Bank That Was Not Kept in Check' (the Manx Savings and Investment Bank)
'French Watchdog Steps Up Drive to Stamp Out Corporate Conspirators'
'Complaints Over Building Societies up 63% in Year'
'EC Directives Change Securities Markets' (regulations for gaining admission for Official Listings)
'Insider Probe as AMP Eyes Pearl'
'Legal Failings Lead to Pressure for Reform'
'Days Numbered for the Pinstripe Twisters of Paris'
'New Charges in French Insider Share Scandal' (in connection with the privatized bank the Société Générale)
'The Death of the Insider Dealer: All countries Must Outlaw the Unacceptable Face of Capitalism by June, 1991'
'If This is Our Best City Standard then Heaven Help Us' (comment on the British Department of Trade and Industry Report into County NatWest (July, 1989))
'Millions Diverted in Lloyds Scandals'.

Not all the action was in Europe in the period. From Israel:

'Shamir Adviser in Bribery Scandal' (land development contracts, in which it was claimed that speculators were asked to contribute to political party funds).

From America:

'Prince of Wall Street Returns' (return of an imprisoned arbitrageur)

'America's Economic Black Hole' (bailing out of the Savings and Loans industry at an estimated cost of $500 billion dollars ('More, in real terms than the Marshall Plan') as a result of deregulation and excessive credit extended

... and back to Britain:

'Compound Disinterest ... How One Man's Debt was Overestimated by £33,000'

'City Fraud Cases are a Trial by Ordeal for the Legal System' (a look forward to 'Guinness 2', Barlow Clowes and Blue Arrow).

The Guinness affair is Case 43, below. The Barlow Clowes affair involved the failure of a large securities group, with more than £1 billion in debts. 'Blue Arrow' refers to a takeover bid by the Blue Arrow employment agency, involved in a Department of Trade and Industry enquiry, and involving the Company's advisers from County NatWest, in 1989.

The issues which have attracted greatest press coverage include illegal share dealing (usually, 'insider trading'); fraud and embezzlement; false accounting; improper use of company funds; forgery; lack of adequate control; bribery; concealing relevant facts; and breach of Covenants.

The matters appear to be considered important issues in financial services, presumably because they involve other people's money entrusted to the financial service institutions. It can be claimed also that holding such funds places a particularly important burden of responsibility upon people in financial services. Without labouring the point, it is worth asking what it is about financial services that is so important: is it the sheer size of the sums involved, the fact that by and large the owners of the sums misused often have the means to seek redress with some hope of success, or is it that as exemplars of the business community, higher standards are expected from them than from others? The questions are important because many of the matters that are issues appear to be commonplace in other industries also. Compare the description of Chernobyl or the University Case in Chapter 6, the accusations of misleading 'fake-green' advertisements, or matters of unfair dismissal in which the rules are used or abused to secure a desired result, rather than seek the truth. In terms of the principles involved, financial services are not obviously special cases, requiring special legislation on standards. This is not to say that the interest and controls are superfluous or misdirected. It would seem to be more defensible to apply the standards of probity and proper accounting across the industry and institutional board, rather than to advocate relaxation of standards in financial services. If the law sets only minimum standards, and sets them higher in financial services than elsewhere, it does provide an indication of the distance yet to be covered by regulation, codes, voluntary agreements, and in-company values programmes.

The typical ethical problems of distinguishing different kinds of values and of distinguishing values from factual beliefs or claims are present in the financial services cases with which the collection is concluded, but they do not all appear to the same degree or in the same way. The cases are presented without comment, other than to explain terms or events which appear to require this for the sake of continuity of the narrative.

CASE
43 | **The 'Guinness affair'**

This case is condensed from an MSc Report in the University of London, by Ruben Atekpe (1990, Chapter 9).

It was reported above that the 'Guinness affair' broke new ground in that the issues raised led to trial and conviction, including imprisonment and fines, although the performance of the newly merged company showed an improvement, not a loss.

A convenient starting point for explaining the events is the takeover battle in 1985 for the control of the Distillers Company, Scottish-based producer of alcoholic beverages. The image of the company had been described as 'sluggish'. Partly in an apparent attempt to throw off this image the company had made some changes in its top management. In September 1985, a smaller company, the Argyll Group, also Scottish-based, had been rumoured to be contemplating a bid to take over the Distillers Company. The British Takeover Panel required a comment from Argyll. A statement was released to the effect that the Argyll Group had no interest in bidding for Distillers 'at the present time'. This expression fuelled rumours about a possible future bid. It also prevented Argyll, under the Takeover Code, from making a formal bid for Distillers, effectively until December of that year. During this period, the Distillers share price began to rise, and the Distillers company had time to prepare a defence against the bid, making it clear that there had in fact been negotiations between the two companies, which had broken down. The bid, when it came, offered eight ordinary shares plus ten new convertible preference shares, plus £14.50 in cash for every ten Distillers shares, or £4.85 in cash for every share. At the time, it was the biggest single takeover to be launched in Britain.

Loans were provided to Argyll for the purpose of the bid by the Royal Bank of Scotland. As it happened, Distillers also banked there, and as a result of the news, changed their bankers. Once the takeover battle was joined, it was conducted in part in newspaper advertisement campaigns, with each party apparently implying that statements and figures provided by the other side were misleading. These were accompanied by reported allegations of malpractice, including accusations of bribery and of smear campaigns. The battle was finally joined when Guinness plc, in the role of a 'white knight' agreed a takeover bid with Distillers, at a substantially higher price than that of Argyll.

One consequence was that a new company on this basis would have a share of the whisky market estimated at 35–40 per cent, making a referral to the Monopoly and Mergers Commission probable. Such a referral was made, and subsequently withdrawn. A consequence of the referral was that the Guinness offer automatically lapsed; following the withdrawal, Guinness was permitted to make a renewed bid, which it did.

By March 1986, the two bids were roughly equal, and Guinness switched tactics to demonstrating its expertise in distilling, and especially in selling to the American market. The Guinness bid was ultimately successful in April 1986.

The Governor of the Bank of Scotland had been identified as the likely Chairman of the joint Board. This did not happen, and Mr Ernest Saunders, the Chief Executive of Guinness, was chosen.

The matters which had the most serious consequences related to the tactics which had been used by key personnel and advisers during the bid. Arrangements had been made with institutional and other investors to buy shares in Guinness in return for management fees, and even guarantees that the purchaser would be recompensed if the share price were to fall subsequently.

It was estimated that in the latter stages of its bid, Guinness had over £200 million of its own money supporting its own share price (*The Sunday Times*, 8 March, 1987, p. 50). Later, when the Guinness share price fell it appeared that shares were repurchased at a price above the market price and using the company's funds. It is, however, illegal for a UK company to provide cash for the purchase of its own shares, except under clearly defined circumstances. (Atekpe, op. cit.)

In December 1986, the Department of Trade and Industry began an investigation. This appears to have resulted from information disclosed to the American Securities and Exchange Commission, which had been investigating some activities of Ivan Boesky concerning insider dealing. Guinness had invested $100 million in Mr Boesky's arbitrage fund (arbitrage, broadly is the activity of making money by rapid trading, usually of large sums of money, taking advantage of different prices in different markets).

As the investigation progressed, the Guinness share price fell. The merchant bankers who had advised Guinness during the bid resigned as advisers to Guinness. The Chairman of Guinness, Mr Saunders, resigned and was later replaced as Chief Executive also. It was estimated that £25 million had been paid as fees in consideration of share-support activities.

The culmination of the affair was a trial which began in February and ended in August 1990 when the former Chairman of Guinness, the former Chairman of the Heron Group, Mr Gerald Ronson, stockbroker Mr Anthony Parnes, and financier Sir Jack Lyons were found guilty, fined and imprisoned on charges of theft and false accounting, all of which were denied.

During the trial some City solicitors, accountants and management consultants were accused of conspiring to keep details of an illegal share support operation from the Guinness Chairman, who also spoke of how he and his colleagues at Guinness had been outmanoeuvred by the 'corporate mafia' (*The Financial Times*, 13 June, 1990, p. 8). According to a press editorial:

All four defendants in the City trial of the century have been found guilty. So too have the business ethics of the 1980s. The six-month trial has lifted the lid on the seamy side of the City, exposing a sordid story of greed, manipulation and total disregard for takeover regulations. (*The Guardian*, 28 August, 1990, p. 18)

More than a hint of the 'intervening processes', gamesmanship and the powerful impact of informal, often tacit, rules was provided by the case. From the point of view of ethical analysis, as opposed to law enforcement, most of the important ethical issues arise from how the processes which eventually led to the trial were permitted to proceed. Some observers spoke of weaknesses in the takeover code, others of weakness of enforcement, and others of deliberate acts of ignoring it. A comment which provides many clues was made by Lord Alexander, Chairman of National Westminster Bank, in a different context:

They [takeovers] involve the skills, competitiveness, and sometimes aggression, which in a former age were channelled into territorial conquests or the tournament. As the conflict reaches a climax, the stakes become ever higher. The drama, heightened by media attention, makes failure almost unthinkable. The pressures on advisers are intense: their reputations are at issue, and their money – the success fee – will be much higher than the fee for trying and failing. (*The Financial Times*, 28 August, 1990, p. 7)

Returning to the possible contribution of ethical analysis to the prevention or early discovery of issues such as those described in the above case, it is clear that codes of practice, though drawn up by experts in the field, have had a limited control value. The legal and financial education of many, though not all, of the participants has been of a high enough order for ignorance to be ruled out as a primary cause. Education of individuals in the concepts of ethics has no obvious promise in this respect. There are no reasons why ethically well-educated persons should be immune to the temptations or pressures described. It would appear that control of the informal and intervening processes holds out some promise, but as is so often the case, the bureaucratic systems which allow only for control from the top downwards, and which provide for control by limiting information to underlings, have a major role to play. So too does the absence of juridical processes in the large bureaucracies, public and private. Where they exist in codes of practice, employee handbooks and working rules, they still leave much scope for manipulation. In the case of City scandals, the appointed watchdogs tend to operate through codes supported by informal networks or informal rules, and safeguards such as the system of independent auditors have proved to be problematic. This is recognized by the evidence that professional associations are considering or operating hot lines or extensions to indemnity insurance. (Detailed arguments on this topic appear in *Key Issues*.)

Thus, the lack of visibility, the informal rules and rarely acknowledged win-lose 'games' in many of the operations in the sector provide a recipe for the generation of issues and scandals. The value of takeovers and mergers to shareholders and to the economy in general in terms of improved efficiency has yet to be demonstrated, although it was claimed as a benefit by some commentators on the Guinness affair. As is so often the case, the ethical issues are deeply enmeshed with the assumptions and the factual claims and counter claims. This appears to be yet another area in which specific research, using explicit ethics concepts, including those of criteria for improvement, has much to offer. It has rarely been tried, and never on a large scale.

The cases in the final group have all attracted public attention, and include plans and actions aimed at improvement, as well as practices that were questioned. They are included so that it can be seen whether they confirm the idea that there are common patterns in these matters, or instead, indicate that the variations are so large that any control policy measures would necessarily face severe limitations.

CASE
44 | **Insider dealing and controls in France**

In June 1990, two French financiers were charged with insider trading, two others having been charged earlier. The matters concerned the French bank, Société Générale. The issue concerned allegations of selling shares at a profit in the period leading up to a takeover bid, which did not in the end succeed. The matter became public in early 1989 when the Commission des Opérations de la Bourse (COB) referred it to the judiciary. The charges were denied (Source: *The European*, 22 June, 1990, p. 20). Convictions led to fines and a suspended prison sentence. Insider trading had been a crime in France since 1970. The COB subsequently tightened regulations to cover anyone who uses information relevant to the issue, even if it is acquired outside their work.

CASE
45

Some life assurance sales methods

In July 1990, in Britain, the Life Insurance and Unit Trust Regulatory Organization (LAUTRO) criticized a Mutual Insurance Society in connection with the operations of one salesman. The criticism was that the Society

. . . failed to have and to maintain adequate arrangements for the monitoring of the performance of its company representatives,

and

Did not deal adequately with a number of complaints received about certain business conducted through the same appointed representative.

The ruling was based on 'unauthorised entry to student hostels and halls of residence, aggressive behaviour, non-disclosure of important information', and the giving of poor advice.

LAUTRO held that adequate compliance or product training was not given. The Society preferred not to comment on the ruling, except to say that the procedures had been improved and that the contract with the agent had been cancelled. No information was forthcoming on the ways in which the procedures had been improved.

A speaker for the Consumers' Association commented that

It is very difficult for the public to see if the monitoring is adequate. One has to take it on trust that the companies are monitoring their representatives properly. (*The Independent*, 7 July, 1990).

CASE
46

Problems of regulatory bodies

Reactions to the rising tide of financial services scandals included the establishment of regulatory agencies. One issue concerns the reasons for deciding in a particular case whether regulation should be by statutory body, or voluntary code. One variant of voluntary codes is known as 'industry self-regulation'.

How does a regulatory body know that a problem is brewing at one of its charges when all the external signs suggest that nothing is wrong? The question is taxing the minds of financial regulators and in particular the Financial Intermediaries Managers and Brokers Regulatory Association in the wake of the collapse ... of Dunsdale Securities. (Richard Waters, *The Financial Times*, 13 June, 1990, p. 9)

The issues were:

1 The collapsed firm was an authorized trader under the regulations.
2 The firm had recently passed a FIMBRA inspection.
3 FIMBRA was not aware of the existence of a problem until several days after clients had begun legal action to recover money from the firm.
4 FIMBRA at the time had authorized over 1,000 firms.
5 FIMBRA had only thirty compliance officers.
6 Firms seeking authorization are subject to checks to establish that they and their proprietors are 'honest, solvent and competent'. This includes references and checks on the personal histories of those principally involved.
7 FIMBRA was understood to have carried out checks on audited statements and on internal management accounts.
8 Some unease had been expressed to FIMBRA about the company, but checks were not made.
9 There was no statutory provision for recourse for investors against regulatory bodies. Such provision had been discussed and eventually rejected in the 1986 legislation which covered the case. (Source: Richard Waters, loc. cit.)

CASE
47 **The Blue Arrow affair**

In August 1987 the Blue Arrow employment agency made a takeover bid for the firm Manpower, with a £837 million rights issue planned. That September, the rights issue was recognized as unsuccessful, and the balance of shares were placed with investors. A press statement was released claiming the rights issue to have been a success, however. In October, in the Stock Market crash, there was a £65 million loss on NatWest's Blue Arrow involvement.

A subsequent report by the British Department of Trade and Industry subsequently criticized the deal:

The Stock Market was deliberately misled through the concealment of important information, the Companies Act was broken and there may have been insider trading ... the Report is unprecedentedly critical of Britain's biggest High Street Clearing Bank and its dealings in the City. (*The Guardian*, 21 July, 1989)

Some top executives from the bank were criticized, some for

misleading the Bank of England, for 'conduct well below that to be expected from a responsible executive', 'deliberate evasion of disclosure', 'placing misleading advertisements'. Some directors of the bank's stockbrokers, Phillips and Drew, were accused of 'conduct well below the standard expected from a responsible executive'. A report from the bank's deputy chairman attempting to explain the affair was accepted as 'bona fide', but as presenting 'a confused picture', and containing 'inaccuracies'.

Blue Arrow were cleared of any involvement in the actions that were criticized.

CASE 48 | **Barlow Clowes**

Under the heading, 'DTI breached rules over new Clowes' licence', Lawrence Lever wrote in *The Times*:

The Department of Trade and Industry renewed Barlow Clowes' licence to trade as a securities dealer without first obtaining an auditors' report, which is a statutory requirement. Moreover, it wrote to a Barlow Clowes investor on March 25, 1988 – four months after inspectors had been appointed – implying that it had obtained an auditors' report. (*The Times*, 22 July, 1988, p. 21)

Two Barlow Clowes funds collapsed in June 1988, putting nearly £190 million of investors' money at risk. (Source: *The Guardian*, 12 September, 1988, p. 10)

Conclusions

The interim conclusions outlined earlier in this chapter appear to stand. In summary, it can be said that:

1 Ethical issues in financial services are not new, not confined to any one country, stage of development or legal system.

2 The legal problems of enforcement and control still appear to be formidable. The balance between statutes and policing on the one hand, and voluntary self-regulation seems capable of no definitive solution, but restriction of the possible kinds of controlling action to just these seems difficult to justify in ethical terms, especially in the light of the evidence of very many 'intervening processes' which operate at a level and in ways which cannot be controlled effectively, except by means of detailed examination of how they operate, and the unwritten values that underpin them.

3 The ethical issues in the sector are not different in kind, as

opposed to degree from those in other sectors. The prominence of issues in the sector no doubt reflects that people who object to the various practices have resources, including those of skill and knowledge, not always available elsewhere. To some extent, this is manifested in the suspicion that the events reflect private quarrels: observers even discuss the matters in terms of 'victimless crimes'.

4 The fact that the transgressions occur is evidence either of low values or of confused ones. That objections are raised is evidence that defensible ethical values do help to drive people. The case for asserting that ethical standards are low or do not exist would be strong if the objections were never raised, or if no action were taken at all, rather than being of limited effect.

5 The scale of the issues in the 1980s suggests that the opportunities for malpractice were greater then than they were during earlier periods of stricter control through the gold standard, exchange control, and fixed currency values.

6 The need for collaborative research, based on ethical as well as legal, political and technical expertise, is as strong in financial services as elsewhere.

14 PROCEDURES FOR IMPROVEMENT – A DIALOGUE

Speakers: Peter Davis; John Donaldson; David Huddy; Diana Robertson

John: Many people now believe that ethical reasoning and procedures could help to improve standards of business behaviour and performance. For instance, many companies are adopting codes of ethics or codes of practice, whereas ten years ago, in Europe at least, they were typically confined to the professions – medical and legal, for example – and to some forms of legislation, such as prices and incomes codes, industrial relations codes of practice or the highway code.

Do we really believe that they can improve performance and prevent disasters? Even if they can, are they really *ethical*, or are they merely methods of staying one step ahead of the law? How different are 'ethical' codes from straightforward competent business practice? Are codes the only way to get improvement and maintain standards, or are they the best among several ways?

Peter: Well, John, as you indicate, even in the relatively underdeveloped management area of business ethics there are quite a few examples of codes of practice, and in some quarters a great deal of emphasis is placed on them. I am sure that codes are a constructive and realistic strategy but we must remember that the existence of a code is only the first step. I have three questions to put concerning any code:

1 Does the code improve matters for the consumer – does it improve choice, quality and service?
2 Does the code support the weak against the strong, i.e. small businesses against large ones; individual consumers; employees; persons in third world economies, and the natural, and all too fragile environment?
3 Is it enforced? Is the commitment of management in training and communication being actively followed through?

Interestingly, we can see as soon as we raise questions exactly the kinds of real conflicts of interest, and dilemmas that only a clear analysis, based on the factual content can hope to resolve.

255

As you say, there are choices. There are greater or lesser evils, but of course, these choices are often far from easy in practice. The main strength of codes is their ability to turn ethical principles into routines. It is unlikely that they could even in principle provide adequate guidance in the presence of some of the most serious, and perhaps the most common of moral dilemmas, as opposed to rule-setting.

Diana: A code of ethics is a signal from senior management that ethics deserves corporate attention. A code can also be used as a public relations effort to announce to the outside world that the corporation is serious about ethics. But these are not the functions that most people see and expect from a code of ethics. People tend to see a code instead as a form of social control by the corporation, that is, an attempt to influence the behaviour of employees in the direction that the corporation deems desirable.

Perhaps we are paying too much attention to this question of whether or not codes of ethics 'work' to control or direct behaviour. Certainly it is an empirical question, but it is a very complicated one. Early studies trying to draw some conclusions about the effectiveness of codes have suffered from the problem of first, defining effectiveness, and second, holding all other variables constant. In fact, trying to hold all other variables constant seems counter-intuitive. Surely a code of ethics is likely to 'work' in a corporation in which the entire corporate culture is supportive of ethics, rather than in one in which the culture is not supportive. This suggests that while corporations should institute codes of ethics, they should be paying attention as well to the messages conveyed to employees through their compensation system, their corporate mission statement, their organizational structure, indeed every facet of the corporation. Business ethics theorists like to emphasize that ethics is integral to corporate activity, that every organizational decision has an ethical component. If this is true, it is unlikely that the specifics of any code of ethics will be able to guide every decision, but the corporate spirit behind the adoption of the code of ethics can. A code of ethics can be considered to be one aspect of an overall corporate ethics initiative. Other aspects include ethics training for employees, the addition of responsibility for ethics to certain job titles, e.g. ethics officer, examination of how performance pressures on employees affect their ethical behaviour, analysis of reward systems and their compatibility with ethics, and the ethical tone set by senior management.

Codes of ethics can perform a valuable function. But they are not a panacea that will ensure ethical behaviour, and it is unfair to expect that of them. The danger is that a corporation will think that once it has a code of ethics, it has sufficiently addressed the topic of ethics and can move on to other more pressing issues. Corporate attention to ethics must be ongoing and constant.

John: I have no difficulty in going along with both of these responses. It is clear from what you say that proper attention to standards, or ethics, is much more than bolting on or patching in some codes, and leaving the rest of the system untouched and unexamined. Peter emphasizes the breadth of cover of the codes, and the importance of getting the commitment of the most influential people in the firm. Diana's emphasis is on the influence that existing rules and expectations can have on the quality of the work done by codes. I am sure that both of these perspectives are vital. I wonder, Diana, whether you would say a little more on the problems of defining and identifying the effectiveness of operation. Is it, for example, mainly that the interactions that you mention make cause and effect difficult to distinguish, or is it that the various code writers find it difficult to sort out matters of skill and competence, and prudent use of resources, equipment and privileges and to distinguish them from general ethical principles?

Diana: It seems to me that the major problem is neither the difficulty of distinguishing cause and effect, nor that of differentiating competence and performance from ethical outcomes, although these certainly are problems. The major problem is that in the field of business ethics we don't as yet have sophisticated means of determining what the desired ethical behaviour is.

We know how to measure legal violations, and we have some sense of the well-publicized disasters that seem to indicate lapses of ethical behaviour, but we don't have a clear idea of the incidence of unethical behaviour in day-to-day activities. As a field, business ethics needs to be able first to define exactly what ethical behaviour is and is not. Then we need methodology that assures that unethical behaviour is accurately reported, and not underreported as it undoubtedly is in many ethics surveys.

On the matter of the reasons why individuals may be inclined to subordinate codes to career ambitions: codes of ethics seem to be most effective in regulating employee behaviour directed against the best interests of the firm, for example, employees cheating the company on their expense accounts, or using company time and resources for personal business. In fact, studies analysing the content of codes demonstrate that they are most likely to include guidelines about potential behaviour against the firm.

But when you begin to think about unethical behaviour resulting from so many pressures to perform, you're talking about a different category – that of unethical behaviour perpetrated on behalf of the firm's interests. Dangerous products that are brought to market, unsafe working conditions in a plant, reporting procedures that inflate company per-formance, are all examples of areas in which codes of ethics alone are inadequate. In those cases, employees are receiving two conflicting messages: one, that profitability is important, and two, that ethics is important (through the existence of a code), and it is not surprising that employees are savvy enough to discern which of the two messages they should heed.

John: Yes, it is clear that attention to the various systems that Diana identifies does pay off in many ways, but perhaps we need to say something more about the basic reasons why some companies should wish to introduce codes, and why there is pressure for others to follow, and for 'industry self-regulation' and other industry-wide codes?

Peter: I would like to pick up on Diana's point about the importance of the corporate culture in supporting ethical behaviour and ethical codes. Diana said that firms need to pay attention to other areas like the corporate mission statement. This is an important point. If the objectives of the firm are not ethical and the whole cultural context is not supportive of ethical behaviour then no code of practice can make an impact. But even firms who do adopt ethically defensible mission statements and try to operate their businesses on ethical principles still have to confront the realities of the market-place. It is here that I believe a code of practice can make a really positive contribution. When ethical codes are adopted at industry level they provide a common framework within which managements know they can operate on an equal footing. However, industry-wide codes need to be adequately policed and sanctions must be in place for breaches that are real, and the sanctions must be enforceable.

I believe that it is in the competitive pressures of the market-place that much of the motivation as well as justification for 'unethical' practices originates. The myth of the survival of the fittest interpreted as an individualistic competitive process has done much to provide the value framework to justify 'unethical behaviour' – it is the 'let's do it to them before they do it to us' mentality. Responding to 'market pressure' becomes the commercial equivalent to 'I was only obeying orders'. Industry-wide codes are the best means for the regulation of the market-place, short of legislation. Ethics is about keeping to the spirit as well as the letter. This cannot be legislated for, but it can be created by discussion and prior agreement. The creation of industry-wide codes of ethical practice can only evolve following discussions between management from the leading firms and, for example, the trade or industry associations that have existed for a long time to regulate pay and conditions. This process may prove to be the best way of moving away from the notion of markets as places for individualistic cut-throat competition to the notion of markets as places where people communicate complementary needs, and cooperate to exchange mutually required necessaries. (I have expanded on this theme in my forthcoming book, *The Cooperative Challenge*.)

If the really pressing ethical issues of distributive justice in the world and the preservaton of our natural environment are to be addressed, then we need ethical codes that transform our notion of the objectives of industry from capital-centred to people-centred. Capital remains crucial as the means, but the enrichment and empowerment of people are the ends. Markets that tend towards the concentration of capital and power are in my view distorted and fundamentally unethical in their processes. If monopolies draw up codes to restrain themselves to avoid intervention, there is little or no ethical content in it.

Industry-wide codes should be able to answer positively the three questions I listed earlier, relating to improving matters for the consumers, for improving protection for the weak against the strong, and for the protection of the natural environment against destruction. Even though the world does not operate in an ideally logical and methodical way, the codes are to be welcomed, despite their faults, as pointers towards fully justifiable behaviour.

David: For my benefit, would you mind, John, summarizing the key points in the discussion, in case I have misunderstood what has been said?

John: Gladly. I think we have agreed that there is a need for external validation, so that individuals or companies are not entitled to be 'judge and jury in their own cause', to use a standard phrase.

Maldistribution of power can permit manipulation or cynical flouting of codes which, as they stand, are impeccable. Diana draws attention to problems in deciding what the content of the codes ought to be: who speaks with an authentic voice for all? Peter sees a need to replace the myth of the cut-throat market with a recognition that competition and cooperation are both proper, but need to be kept in balance. Only then can the major issues of distributive justice be tackled. I think we are agreed on the need for pluralism – there is not only one way to operate business or to establish the ground rules. Codes can represent an improvement, but do not always do so, and they are rarely sufficient, if the legitimate values of all persons who have to do with a firm or industry are to be given due weight.

We have taken it for granted that firms have good reasons for wanting to introduce codes. We have not yet addressed the question why they want to do so, or what pressures exist that persuade them that they ought to.

David: I agree that ethics need not be in opposition to the market. Indeed, I suggest that ethics can easily be incorporated directly and explicitly into the market-place. You do not have to trade with, work for or buy from, a firm whose ethics you do not like. My proposed register [see Case 23] is not offered as a panacea, but as a step forward.

John: Yes. Perhaps before we discuss the Register it would be useful to remind ourselves of the very large variety of ways in which standards have been raised in the past, and are still used. These include the use of 'ombudsmen', the law, arbitration and conciliation, small claims courts and the like. On the whole, it is difficult to claim that they have not produced improvements, but the rise in interest in business ethics serves to underline their limitations. Self-interested or ideology-bound groups can still amass enough distorting influence for the problem to remain serious. Opportunities for mutual gain can be lost nationally and at company level by a mixture of lack of effective checks and balances and the depressing influence of stale ideologies (whether pro- or anti-market). Some robust defenders of 'business' still see, or claim to see, any criticism of current practice as an attack on business itself. Some circles still see 'business' as an unworthy field for honest and intelligent people to become embroiled in. Yet others see business ethics as both hopelessly idealistic and as a cynical piece of business propaganda, 'whitewashing' what they see as essentially a dog-eat-dog world of business. We might look for business education in ethics, but if it is provided by educational bureaucracies, it will share their characteristics, become institutionalized, and ultimately become as much part of the problem as the key to its solution. Does 'public opinion' really want to be bothered with ethics?

Peter: There is clearly a link between our discussion of codes and David's proposed Register. I would like to hear David's view of what that link is.

David : I don't want to enlarge in any way on any theory of ethical standards. My ideas are offered as a practical approach to bringing day-to-day business dealings within public jurisdiction. Business ethical standards are not meeting the needs of the twentieth century and will even less meet those of the twenty-first. It may even now be that present practices are threatening Western civilization.

There is an amusing Wall Street saying that demonstrates this disregard in which the public interest is held: 'When in doubt, do what's right!' Confidence and contact between people and corporate business have failed to the extent that they are different citizens in the same culture, living to different standards and different ends. How long will this continue and what will be the medium of change?

A company has three attributes that are central to our discussion – what it does (objects); how it does it (articles) and its responsibilities in doing so (ethical standards). The Company Acts require a statement of the first two but say nothing about the third. It is this omission that needs to be corrected.

A statement of ethical standards should be required in the same way as it is required for the other two. It is unlikely that such a statement could be legally binding, and therefore it would not carry such obligations. Legal sanctions are not the only sanctions that can be applied, nor are they necessarily the easiest or the most effective.

Market forces are a well understood and practical alternative. At present they are ineffective because there are no adequate means of public awareness. Given the information, a company with good ethical standards will prosper. Indeed, such companies are already known as 'good' companies. The reality of this approach cannot be better exemplified than in a letter to a newspaper in March 1990:

Sir, The Government may not have a method of dealing with businessmen who tell lies, but the customers do. I have this evening written to [a named company, then in the news] closing my account. Yours, etc.

For such judgements to be made the statement of ethical standards must be a readily available public record, and so also must be a company's performance in relation to those standards.

How can this be achieved? It can be achieved in many ways. One example might run as follows: the statement of ethical principles is made part of company formation documents. A copy of the statement is filed with a Registrar for public companies, or with the local library for private companies. Alleged breaches can be referred to the Registrar or the Local Registrar for private companies (perhaps the local Chamber of Commerce?). At the discretion of the Registrar the companies are invited to reply and the correspondence filed for reference. The Registrar would not be a medium for redress.

Diana: It might be useful to remind ourselves what the social control mechanisms are that operate to result in ethical behaviour. First, there are regulatory or legal controls, which David mentions. Secondly, there are organizational controls, including codes of ethics and ethics training. Finally, there is personal control which operates at the individual level as an employee decides whether or not to behave ethically. To these mechanisms David would add a market force 'control', prompting firms to ethical behaviour. David mentions possible implementation issues concerning his idea and I think he offers a reasonable solution to those issues. I would like to back up a step and instead look at the underlying *rationale* for market force control. David's proposal fits very nicely into the argument that 'ethics pays' or 'social responsibility pays'. His Registrar would make available to the public the social responsibility or ethics 'track record' of firms. His proposal may test how much the public does care about the ethics of a company and whether or not that public concern translates into differences in consumption patterns.

The major difficulty that I see with his proposal is that of sorting through and weighing what may well be contradictory evidence of a company's ethical stance. For example, a company may have an excellent record of treatment of employees but a poor record of product safety. The types of ethical 'screens' used to evaluate the overall ethics of a company may be problematic.

David: I think it vital to confront this issue which Diana has so rightly raised. It is not seen as any part of the Registrar's function to decide between issues or referee any exchange of argument. The Registrar will be there to receive complaints, to decide whether they are mere carping or well-founded, and if so to invite the chairman of the offending organization to respond, and to close the issue when he or she feels that fair representation has been made by both sides. Regarding the other issue: where there is, for example, a good employee relations record, but a poor one on safety, the Registrar will exert pressure on the second. As regards the first, companies have not been noticeably reticent about their virtues and I think we can leave any promotion of these to them. Two things are needed to make the idea effective: feedback (the Registrar) and a control (public response), which continuously adjusts the ethics towards the target (informed public acceptance). There are many codes and the eclectic nature of public response would distil from them a general reservoir of standards to the then current *mores*.

Peter: But there is still a need for individual initiatives where there is no pool to base general codes on. Competitive companies can and should agree to use, for example, catalytic converters where such a needed benefit exists, so that competitive advantage could not be gained by having unacceptable standards – a cooperative element within the competitive framework. The public does not always have the expertise to demand these mutual benefits.

John: We shouldn't forget that there is already a great deal of cooperation among competitive firms, through learned societies, through standards committees, professional qualifying bodies. Sometimes such cooperation is at a less respectable level in cartels. Either way, it establishes that cooperation and competition are not mutually exclusive in all dimensions.

David: What the public needs is a continuous overview of corporate behaviour with an effective means of applying sanctions.

Peter: Agreed. But the public may choose a low-cost option, transferring the risks to other people.

John: To what extent should people be protected against their own folly? The principle of autonomy suggests that, if they are properly aware of the issues, or if they have no excuse for not being so aware, they (or we) should be allowed to get on with it. Everyone else should be protected against individual folly or greed. This brings us back to the mechanisms or methods for adjusting between different wants, aspirations and principles, i.e. back to the codes, Register, etc.

Peter: There are times when the public cannot tell, as when a company uses brand names that do not identify the company. The 'simple-minded' or 'foolish' may have others in their care, such as children, who have a right to protection, provided it is properly done. Possessors of specific knowledge have a duty to inform those others who are affected.

John: This brings us back full circle. It is one thing to have a code, but is it honoured, and if not, what should be done?

David: We could turn it round. Why doesn't it work? Each code could be an element in a distilling process.

John: Someone has to draw up the formal codes as opposed to those that are powerful, but unofficial, or informal. There is a case for formalizing, or formally rejecting some of the informal elements. But there is the persisting problem of who has the right to impose their codes and their values on others, and what confers that right?

David: A changing code is a sign of life. There is no reason why every code should be got right at the first attempt.

Peter: The challenge in David's proposal is how the spirit can be translated into practice.

David: It has to be made worth people's while. The consequences of not living up to what is required should be serious.

Peter: Perhaps the problem is not that individuals have no ethics, but that the industrial system has grown up without it. Some codes simply do not protect the weak against the strong. They should not be used to legitimate the powerful against the weak.

John: ... or at least, it has grown up without any formal treatment of ethical matters, so that their incorporation has been unsystematic, if not apologetic, or even clandestine.

Peter: Part of the knowledge problem is that a firm may have good relationships with consumers, but unethical ones with suppliers. The consumers could be seen to have a right, if not a duty, to know and act on the information.

John: We seem to be agreed. The codes are as good as their enforcement procedures. But I would add that unless there is a voluntary element, visible or genuinely implied, then a 'code of ethics' – or a set of ethical rules or principles, is no more than the imposition of one person's or group's values on others.

David: This reminds me of an example of an employer who dismissed a man who had cancer, on the grounds that the company could not afford to support a growing list of widows. I have never knowingly bought their product since.

To return to Diana's comments, my proposal *is* in the 'ethics pays' category. It doesn't pay often enough, but it should be made to do so. The (now abandoned) 'fair wages clause' in Britain was an example of properly enforced ethical standards. The word 'fair' was a clear indication that there was a major ethical component.

John: Certainly. In the case of its abolition, a different set of beliefs about what was 'fair' was substituted. But it was not the principle, but the most effective method of bringing it into operation that was called upon. To my mind, it was another example of the entanglement of facts and values. Different sides attached ethical values to the facts, so that what people preferred to be the 'facts' were taken as tests of loyalty to one or other group preference in relation to policy. But can we summarize, why *do* we think codes, or David's Register, might work?

David: A British Member of Parliament, in response to the idea of the Register, claimed that: 'We do not consider ethics to be a matter for the law.' We noted earlier that this has not been a typical 'legislator's view'.

Peter: Yes, that is a quite revealing statement. A problem is that companies' *real* values are to satisfy the demands for growth. Maybe firms do make decisions on 'quality' and values, but only if they think they are instrumental in securing growth. These universal 'growth values' need to be replaced. The necessity for survival in modern economies drives the values that firms actually do adopt.

John: In the end it will be difficult to show that the conduct of business is quite as determinist as that. For instance, some companies and institutions have secure incomes, because of monopoly powers or privileged status. An example of the latter is provided by the universities. Some of their income may sometimes be under threat, but the likelihood of the market closing down the ones that fail to grow is quite low. The evidence on takeovers is that although growth is the ostensible motive, very many do not achieve the end, and it leaves open that when managers say they are hard-nosed growth maximizers, or are held to be, other values are at work. One of these is power. Another is status. A third is the need to play the business game according to what the 'captains' of industry believe it to be, rather than according to what it really is. My own view is that industry is neither single- minded nor systematic, nor very consistent in what it does. It could become so.

David: Ethics in business is a desirable thing. We are all agreed. But there is room for cowboys and down-market operators operating services at different costs and responsibilities. They, their competitors and customers can recognize each other for what they are and accept the business environment. But they need not be allowed to set the standards for the rest.

John: Back to the question, why do we need business ethics?

Peter: Because without it the market imperatives do tend to drive it out. This is not because the 'hidden hand' does not work, but because we have a political/economic system, not a purely economic one. We need standards to regulate political and economic progress. Business ethics is needed as a regulator to market forces. The general consensus, David's distilled 'code of codes', could be the regulator that provides the consensus.

David: That is a big step. But there is no reason why a start should not be made.

15 CONCLUSIONS

Values drive business. Values determine business performance. Values determine how customers, employees and public react to what business does. Firms and institutions spend much time, effort and money propagating values, internally and externally. Advertising, public relations and internal communications provide obvious examples of this, but values are continuously transmitted by conduct in industry, and by what is said, or left unsaid.

The central position of values contrasts sharply with a reluctance to handle them systematically, or even to discuss them. Propagation, it seems, is all. This reluctance to handle systematically the values that dominate people's working lives has consequences, all of which are amply brought out in the studies in this casebook.

The consequences can be summarized as follows:

1 **Because values can be propagated, but not easily discussed, a gap inevitably occurs between what is aspired to and what is achieved by business.** Opportunities are therefore lost for innovation in product, process and administration, for peaceful and low-cost settlement of industrial disputes, and for smooth adaptation to changes in the market-place. The habit of not discussing values leads to the development of myths, some of which can easily become excuses for living with a low-productivity, low-morale environment. One of the important myths is that of the 'hard-nosed profit-maximizing' nature of business. If all of business were really 'hard-nosed', it would not so easily be dissuaded from examining the myths that so effectively depress its performance.

2 **The gap between claim and reality is highly variable between firms and industries and over time.** This demonstrates that results can be affected by choices and policies. The use of formulae, and short-lived 'quick-fixes' and techniques in the search for steady growth in profits and reputation has delivered relatively little, but is still often conducted with great energy. Systematic handling of values can narrow the gap on the average, and reduce the extreme differences.

267

3 Some of the reluctance to discuss values openly appears to be connected with the underdevelopment of a 'language for analysing business values'. This is partly due to the mistaken belief that values cannot be analysed for consistency with each other or for their implications and consequences. My own view, from discussions with business people, researchers and academics is that there is still a widespread belief that to express an interest in business ethics is at the same time pretentious and imprudent. It seems pretentious in that business ethics seem (in bad taste) to offer a claim to moral superiority. It appears to be imprudent because a manager or firm claiming to be 'ethical' is inviting brickbats when the inevitable (possibly imaginary) skeleton is found in the cupboard. The cases show that business is a system of ethics. Business operates according to rules, within an ethical system. As a discipline or research method, business ethics is not entitled to prescribe what rules firms ought to live by. Firms can and will make their own choices. These are increasingly being questioned by the rest of the community, and occasionally by business people in the absence of external pressure. Students of business ethics are entitled to point out what the consequences are when one set of rules is used rather than another, or when the rules are confused, inconsistent, or incompatible with aspirations. Industry always has the choice, but is sometimes prevented by its own myths and practices from exercising it.

4 On the constructive side, the reluctance to discuss business values openly, and the underdevelopment of a suitable language for doing so, provide plausible means of explaining the rise of value issues in business. Value-concepts provide more scope for constructive action than the old-fashioned beliefs that the demands of the market-place and the (allegedly) inevitable mean-mindedness of human motivation wholly detemine what happens in industry. Not all values are ethical in the sense of expressing moral imperatives, but all values are morally relevant. When put into operation, values are often mistaken for the imperatives of the market place or of human nature. Claims to factual knowledge can be true or false, confused, unwarranted, cynical or honest. Much the same applies to expressions of values. They are normally thought of as not being amenable to rational analysis, or to amendment in the light of evidence, but their interrelationships with evidence makes it clear that action is almost always based on interdependent beliefs, factual and moral. This makes possible rational moral argument in business.

Public concern about ethical issues in business increased dramatically in the 1980s. There is no single source of this awareness. Well-publicized scandals (often in the financial services industry, or in labour relations), the visible environmental deterioration, the juxtaposition of different practices and beliefs in the EC, the decline of 'positivist' academic outlooks (with no clear replacement to fill the gap) can all be seen to have been at work. Possibly, writers on business ethics may have helped in a small way to raise this awareness. What was clarified in the 1980s was that conviction and strong will are not enough to satisfy people's industrial aspirations unless they are based on an understanding of the complexity of consequences. False economic dawns have succeeded one another. Widely-accepted assertions that we have seen the end of depressions, the end of incomes policies and of trade union influence, claims to the 'greening' of public life, have all been accompanied by the reappearance of these problems. Disappointments from well-drafted legislation bear witness to this, in Europe and elsewhere.

It is against this background that the case studies provide at least some clues to the complexity of the practical problems of dealing with the ethical issues raised in and by business. Effective action requires adequate description and analysis of events. This in turn requires sound and objective descriptive and analytical methods and concepts. It is arguable that the rising awareness of the scope and seriousness of ethical issues in business has too often been accompanied by actions based upon impressionistic perceptions of both causes and cures. The proliferation of codes is one indication of this. Another is the shortage of detailed case studies of the kind that were undertaken, especially in America, from the Hawthorne studies of the 1920s onwards. No doubt part of the reason for this shortage has been the absence of 'research paradigms' that can handle such potentially explosive matters as fundamental values.

5 **The cases show that the normal values that drive business are widely-shared and rarely criticized.** Typical business behaviour *does* honour contracts, pay wages on time, employ technically-qualified people for key jobs, and it secures some degree of consumer loyalty. Most products are generally what they are claimed to be, and of reasonable standards of quality. Most people *do* try to do a competent and conscientious job. If improvement in the ethical behaviour of business is indeed called for, it will be effective only if based on adequate concepts and evidence. The rise in interest in business ethics

does not appear to have been based upon any innovative fundamental ethical concepts. The traditional ones, indeed may be seen to be adequate, if applied. The problem, as the case studies clearly show, does not relate to the value-related aspirations expressed in, by and on behalf of business. It is more applicable to the (highly variable) gap between aspirations and actual outcomes.

6 The evidence from the cases points to the need for much more than proceeding directly from an identified problem to a code of practice. The additional elements are related to what have been called 'intervening processes'. The intervening processes can be recognized and used constructively, but this is unlikely to happen without some in-depth research that uses the traditional and emerging concepts of business ethics, in addition to the detailed knowledge and experience of industrialists themselves. This would appear to require much more than the traditional division of labour between industrialists and academics. The development of a common language is likely to be one element. The kind of cooperation that requires access to information and resources, and time to process the information and discuss it, seems to require different kinds of division of labour, and perhaps different institutions from the traditional ones. The shortage of case material that involves such cooperation is testimony itself to this. It is not only that more research needs to be done. Different kinds of research are required. These are unlikely to be cost-free, but their prospects for improving performance are very great and are largely untapped.

The process of working towards procedures for improvement may now be summarized. The actual stages in the modern development of business ethics were:

1 awareness, through papers and conferences;
2 provision of codes and legislation;
3 setting up of teaching courses and of 'business ethics propagating' institutions.

It could be that there are some more stages and elements that might help.

In the European context, actions to identify and improve ethical standards in business, and to maintain the improvement, seem to have consisted mainly of provision of legislation (e.g. on matters relating to the physical environment, financial services and labour market matters) codes, courses and counselling. Research and consultancy paradigms have rarely been developed, or if they have, knowledge of them has been hard to come by. Methods for institutionalizing whistleblowing have been tried in America, as has the institutionalizing of ethics officers. Consultancy models have been developed there, as the quotations from Laura Nash (Chapter 7) show. These models and methods address the major areas of securing support and commitment to the activities of an enterprise or corporation from the various stakeholders. Much can be learned from this experience. There does seem to be scope for further development on these lines. Additional lines of development would seem to be dependent upon drawing together the experience from general actions (such as legislation, or industry-wide or professional codes), assessment of new levels of expectation arising from public awareness, and the development of criteria for improvement and procedures for improvement.

New standards

In a particular case it may be judged that standards are high, for example, on the grounds of the extent to which they satisfy the legitimate aspirations of those who have to do with the business. This is not a mere question-begging formula. Identification of the 'legitimate aspirations' themselves is a matter of satisfying agreed principles and processes, and of ensuring consistency with standard general rules. For instance, rules imposed upon people 'for their own good' may, in fact, be able to satisfy a utilitarian principle, but the imposition could itself be a breach of the principle of autonomy, or of other basic rights. Whether this is so, and is justifiable, depends upon yet other principles, such as the traditional ones of keeping promises and telling the truth. Thus, the judgment that standards are high is one that can defensively be made. It is neither a simple judgment, nor one that can be properly made simply by casual inspection or the presence or absence of a simple rule.

There are signs that business standards are not as uniformly high as they could be. Symptoms include the activities of pressure groups (whose standards are not necessarily higher than those of the target companies or institutions), litigation, and public criticisms. There are also signs that the standards are not as uniformly attuned to modern aspirations as they could, and perhaps should be. Symptoms are the renewed calls for participative activity, for more professionalism in management, and the permanent vulnerability of managers to streams of 'quick-fix' management systems and catch-phrases. The minor impact of, say, the 'participation' movement in America and Britain, by contrast with Germany, and the disappointments associated with quality circles, may well have provided some of the impetus for the development of codes of practice. But codes of practice often leave major ethical gaps in content, design, application, enforcement and monitoring, indicating that at best, they are partial solutions to ethical issues.

A speaker at the European Business Ethics Network conference in October 1990 drew attention to the fact that there is little controversy among those who have an active interest in business ethics in Europe. This is so. One possible reason is that there appears to be an instinctive determination to avoid it at the present stage of development. To an extent, the business ethics community is 'all in the same boat' – viewed with (albeit decreasing) scepticism, incomprehension and suspicion by many colleagues, with few of the standard trappings of a discipline that is accepted. Another possible reason is that the business and academic community are not well-equipped to debate the major issues. The agenda-narrowing tendency of organized group intellectual effort is evident in the case studies on incomes policy and on innovation, and on the concentration on codes as the principal procedures for improvement in ethical standards in business.

Where intellectual, academic and business controversies do occur, they tend to be narrow rather than broad in scope, as was observed long ago by the student of administrative behaviour, C. Northcote Parkinson (1981). In Britain, for example, the debates on 'participation' were long run on the lines of the form that would most conveniently fit into existing bureaucratic and hierarchical structures, and culminated in a short debate in the 1970s on the formula '$2x + y$'. This merely represented a view that boards of directors in large firms should contain one-third representatives of shareholders, one-third representatives of employees (voted through trade unions) and one-third from outside nominees. In the event, nothing happened, and most other experiments in 'participation' quietly faded.

Another example, also from Britain, is the narrowing of the public debate on economic and industry policy in the 1980s to discussions of whether M1, M2 or M3 provided the best definition of money from which the general control of economic and industrial activity could be exercised. Admittedly, the question was one that was of great significance at the time to a properly-elected government, but most other European countries survived very well using a slightly wider agenda. This suggests that the narrowing process in agenda-setting does not take a unique form. Since economic policy has profound implications for income distribution, it is therefore a major ethical matter. There is scope for much wider agendas. The processes of business debates rarely seem to allow for this desirable widening. The absence of controversy could thus be a feature of the unspoken conditions of public debate, but there could also be other reasons. Some of these appear to be to do with the concepts available to the business ethics community. The language of business as taught in the business schools and used in middle management is of technical methods for success and survival. 'Responsibility' there means little more than 'being in charge of something', and having to answer to a superior. The language at the top is replete with concepts of 'integrity', 'trust', 'honesty', 'impartiality', 'truthfulness', 'scrupulously refraining from any form of illegal, dishonest or unethical behaviour', 'positions of trust', 'avoiding conflicts of private self-interest and the interests of the employer and customer', 'fidelity', 'self-respect', 'courtesy', 'corporate values' and much more.

The cases presented in this book show that many companies are deliberately seeking to raise standards of business behaviour, and that the gap between aspiration and performance is variable. There is some confirmation that high aspirations at the top of organizations are often genuine and effective. This is a positive development. There is confirmation that the standard forms of hierarchical and bureaucratic organizations can sometimes render such aspirations unworkable. The problem is not so much that high-sounding language at the top is cynical and manipulative, but that the history, structure and financing of the companies or institutions can make the aspirations impossible to achieve. Some cases show this, too. This can be because the structures and 'intervening processes' ensure that the demands placed on people in different parts of the company allow the luxury of strong ethical aspirations only to the top management. It is often seen as presumptuous of lesser functionaries to hold such values, or at least to express them.

Ethical issues can arise from or grow out of secrecy and confidentiality. These values, in turn, are highly prized, and sometimes imperative. Bankers are expected not to disclose information which would be damaging to their clients. Timing of release of product information is important in the competitive game in industry. But confidentiality, and restriction of information from the lower reaches of the company, create many dilemmas for business people, giving rise to issues of whistleblowing, and providing opportunities for corporate crime. As is often the case, 'unethical' behaviour (in the sense of 'ethics 1') thrives in the dark. The challenge is to reconcile genuine needs for secrecy with proper checks and balances on conduct. In another form, trust accorded to persons in positions of responsibility needs to be reconciled with the need to provide proper redress for grievances of employees, customers, shareholders and others. Many formal codes and procedures are very seriously lacking in this respect.

Business ethics has grown partly as a reaction to safety disasters, financial mishandling and environmental pollution. Although rarely included in business ethics, conduct of labour organizations, and labour relations generally, raises issues that are just as serious both in principle and in their practical consequences.

Criteria for improvement

In *Key Issues* I offered three criteria for improvement in ethical standards in business. These were the golden rule, autonomy, and pluralism. These are by no means original, and have been in the literature of ethics and politics for many years.

Major obstacles to the operation of these criteria have been apparent in the case studies. These include the assumption that ethical standards in business can be consistently raised and maintained, while leaving the traditional bureaucratic and hierarchical structures of business intact. This is despite considerable research from Gouldner, Burns and Stalker, Argyris, Parkinson, Bennis and many others from the 1950s onwards that such structures are highly vulnerable to the games of office politics, and to ossification. This has historically been mitigated from the point of view of survival by periodic shocks, sometimes delivered by the market, and sometimes by legislation, or succession crises. This area has been intensively researched by students of 'business policy' or 'business strategy', but rarely, if ever by the use of standard ethical concepts.

A second, but related, obstacle, is in the operation of what have been called in this collection 'intervening processes'. These involve hidden and unspoken codes that can conflict with overt ones.

A third reason is the paucity of suitable language in which to express ethical concepts to and within business. The standard rhetoric of business is that of profit, efficiency, market disciplines, pragmatism. This is in contrast, it is true, with the loftier statements from annual reports with which this book opened. Both modes of discourse can be seen to be influential, and they are not necessarily incompatible. There is a third rhetoric, of responsibility ('to' and 'for'), duties and 'missions', and a good deal of persuasive labelling: from 'efficiency' and 'effectiveness' to 'profit', 'wealth creation' and 'excellence'.

These terms are often applied with justification, but not always. Much of the language serves to mask the difference between intention and performance. Wide latitude is often allowed to functionaries in private and public appointments. This has the merit of permitting inspired leadership to function, but also of permitting, sometimes on a long-term basis, firms and institutions to be vulnerable to duffers in influential places. The relative incidence of these types of functionaries is difficult to ascertain, if only because they often hold the keys to access to the kind of information which would shed light on the issues.

As it is, the underdevelopment of the language of business ethics permits many misunderstandings. Companies are naturally loth to admit an interest in business ethics, in case they are accused of adopting a sanctimonious attitude, or in case they might be vulnerable to unspecified accusations in the future. The persuasive power of values such as 'responsibility', 'authority', 'competence', 'competitiveness', and 'excellence' is attested to every time executives or commentators use them. Their legitimate application is not always obvious.

Procedures for improvement

Some elements in programmes for improvement may now be suggested:

1 **Visibility of action.** The Register suggested by David Huddy (Case 23, Chapter 3) is one way in which companies could be encouraged to think deeply about how the high aspirations exemplified in the case studies can be enacted in ways which permit due corrective action to be taken whenever the 'intervening processes' begin to assert themselves in the 'wrong' direction. Independent statements of values and of proposals for improvement by relevant groups and individuals can be recorded, as can the consequences of disagreeing with the official line.

2 **Systematic identification of the intervening processes.** Once recognized and understood, it can become possible to work with them (rather than to ignore them, or to try, perhaps vainly, to mitigate their effects).

3 **Reformulation of codes of ethics (codes of practice) to incorporate:**
   (i) Explicit treatments of how conflicts of duties should be handled (conspicuously missing from so many of the codes described in the cases studies).

(ii) Explicit incorporation of encouraging, enforcing and monitoring procedures into codes. These will, of necessity, contain education and training on their use, and in concepts such as 'natural justice', as well as understanding of the basis for the principal ethical theories.

(iii) Incorporation of provision for external validation of the codes, through publication of any disputed cases, of monitoring, enforcement and revision procedures. The external validation requires that some members of drafting committees and enforcement bodies should be chosen from outside the institution, and acceptable to the parties concerned.

(iv) Development of detailed cases, not only for use in training, but also for use in a constant process of revision and improvement of the codes and their operation. The cases should be chosen to illustrate the operation of the values that drive the business, and need not necessarily be adversarial, or geared to occasions when something goes wrong. The scope for manipulation and subversion of codes can be wide, and appears to be widest in the most hierarchical and authoritarian contexts.

The manipulation of codes is not always deliberate. There are many specific ways in which codes can be rendered ineffective. In some situations, an operating cycle can occur in which people are driven by circumstances into modes of action that reinforce ethical lapses, and into modes of linguistic evasion that mask, or even exacerbate them. One example is the 'cover-up' syndrome. Another is the 'win at all costs' syndrome evident in some of the cases concerning financial services, and from the labour market, for example.

Some businesses operate according to defensible and consistent values and some do not. An important role for business ethics is to identify, from argument and evidence rather than from assumption, the factors that make the difference. Another important and legitimate role is to develop agreed procedures for improvement, and methods for monitoring them. This is unlikely to occur if the division of labour requires researchers to remain in their ivory towers reading second-hand reports of what business is doing. If the other side of the division of labour is to require businesses to issue streams of codes, in addition to getting on with their business, progress will be slow, if it occurs at all. Some of the cases show clearly the interdependence of different organizations and industries. Simple declarations of faith in old-fashioned, as opposed to ethically-informed, concepts of competition have been shown to be inadequate. A mix of cooperative and competitive relationships is already a reality in industry. Lasting improvement is likely to come from cooperative relationships between industrialists, researchers and observers, so that authentic information, based on shared experience and explicit ethical concepts can inform practice. This can replace the speculation and after-the-event damage limitation that characterizes so much current activity.

Thus operated, the agenda for ethics in business might appear to be full, but it is also manageable, both for business and for business-related institutions.

Bibliography

(References in square brackets denote the chapter(s) in which the reference is made)

Adams, S. (1985) *Roche Versus Adams*. Fontana, Glasgow. [7]
Ailleret, F. (1990) 'Ethical Decision-making in a National Utility: The Electricity Industry in France'. In Enderle, G., Almond, B. and Argandoña, A. (1990) *People in Corporations – Ethical Responsibilities and Corporate Effectiveness*. Kluwer Academic Publishers, Dordrecht, Boston and London. [11]
Argyris, C. (1974) *Behind the Front Page*. Jossey-Bass, New York. [1]
Ashton, T. and Sayers, R. (1954) *Papers in English Monetary History*. Oxford University Press, Oxford. [13]
Association for Payment Clearing Services (1990) *Draft Code of Banking Practice – A Consultative Document*. With the British Bankers' Association and the Building Societies' Association, London. [12]
Atekpe, R. (1990) 'Mergers and Acquisitions' (MSc Report). University of London. [13]
Atkinson, A. (ed.) (1980) *Wealth, Income and Inequality*. Oxford University Press, London. [9]
Atkinson, D. (1990) *The Guardian*, 17 April, p. 22. [1]
Automobile Association (1990) Summer Newsletter: 'The Car and the Environment'. Basingstoke. [1]
Ayer, Sir A. (1936) *Language, Truth and Logic*. Gollancz, London. [7]
Barclays Bank PLC (1987) Annual Report. [1]
Beauchamp, T. and Bowie, N. (1988) *Ethical Theory and Business*, fourth edition. Prentice-Hall, Englewood Cliffs, New Jersey. [2, 4, 7]
Beecham PLC (1987) Annual Report. [1]
Bell, D. and Kristol, I. (eds) (1981) *The Crisis in Economic Theory*. Basis Books Inc., New York. [9]
Bennis, W. (1972) 'A Funny Thing Happened on the Way to the Future'. In J. Thomas and W. Bennis (eds) *The Management of Change and Conflict*. Penguin, Harmondsworth. [5]

278

Bosworth-Davies, R. (1988) *Fraud in the City: Too good to be True*. Penguin, Harmondsworth. [13]

Bowie, N. (1990) 'Empowering People as an End for Business'. In Enderle, G., Almond, B. and Argandoña, A. (1990) *People in Corporations – Ethical Responsibilities and Corporate Effectiveness*. Kluwer Academic Publishers, Dordrecht, Boston and London. [3]

Boyd, C. (1990) 'The Responsibility of Individuals for a Company Disaster: The Example of the Zeebrugge Car Ferry'. In Enderle, G., Almond, B. and Argandoña, A. (1990) *People in Corporations – Ethical Responsibilities and Corporate Effectiveness*. Kluwer Academic Publishers, Dordrecht, Boston and London. [1, 3]

Bradley, K. and Hill, R. (1983) 'The Quality Circle Transplant and Productive Efficiency', *British Journal of Industrial Relations* Vol. XXI, No. 3. [6]

Braid, M. (1990) *The Independent*, 12 December. [6]

Bready, J. (1926) *Lord Shaftesbury and Social-Industrial Progress*. Allen & Unwin, London. [6]

British Telecom (BT) (1988) Annual Report. [1]

Brown, M. (1990a) 'BBC's trouble is too many chiefs, Harvey-Jones says', *The Independent*, 9 January. [11]

Brown, M. (1990b) 'BBC gives Sir John new troubleshooting role', *The Independent*, 27 April. [11]

Brown, P. (1990) *The Guardian*, 24 August and 28 December. [8]

Buckingham, L. (1990) 'Lloyd's of London denies asbestosis cover-up', *The Guardian*, p. 15. [1]

Burns, T. and Stalker, J. (1961) *The Management of Innovation*. Tavistock, London. [4, 5]

Cadbury, Sir A. (1987) 'Ethical Managers Make Their Own Rules', *Harvard Business Review*, Sept-Oct. [2]

Carmichael, S. and Drummond, J. (1989) *Good Business*. Hutchinson, London. [2, 7]

Cartwright, D. and Zander, A. (1962) *Group Dynamics*. Row, Peterson and Co., Evanstan, Illinois. [5]

Castle, T. (1990) 'All EC countries must outlaw the unacceptable face of capitalism by June 1991', *The Independent*, 15 June, p. 21. [4]

Checkland, M. (1990) BBC Annual Report and Accounts, London. [11]

Chng, J. (1990) 'The Structure and Control of Financial Services – Analysis, Review and Prospect' (MSc Report). University of London. [13]

Coggan, P. (1987) *The Money Machine*. Penguin, Harmondsworth. [12]

Cohen, K. and Cyert, R. (1975) *The Theory of the Firm* (second edition). Prentice-Hall, Englewood Cliffs, New Jersey. [7]

Cole, R. (1990) *The Independent*, 7 July. [13]

Commission of the European Communities (1990) *The Community Charter of Fundamental Social Rights for Workers*, London. [9]

Crequer, N. and McLeod, D. (1990) 'Universities reject MPs' allegations of poor management', *The Independent*, 7 September, p. 2. [6]

Crozier, M. (1964) *The Bureaucratic Phenomenon*. Tavistock, London. [4, 5]

Daily Express (1990) 27 July leading article, 'BBC boss warns: cut out bias', p. 1. [11]

Davis, P. (1991) *Environmental Policy: Standards and Development*. Report, National Materials Handling Centre, Cranfield. [8]

Davies-Gliezes, F. (1990) 'Eco-labels fool the Greens', *The European*, 8–10 June, p. 20. [1]

Davis, P. and Donaldson, J. (1990) 'Ethical Structures for Large Organisations: Review, Prospects and Proposals'. Paper to the third European Business Ethics Network Conference, Milan, October. [5]

Dawson, H. (1990) *The Guardian*, 31 August (letter). [11]

Deal, T. and Kennedy, A. (1988) *Corporate Cultures*. Penguin, Harmondsworth. [1]

De George, R. (1989) *Business Ethics* (third edition). Macmillan, New York. [2]

De George, R. and Pichler, J. (eds) (1978) *Ethics, Free Enterprise and Public Policy*. Macmillan, New York. [3, 7, 10]

Donaldson, J. (1989) *Key Issues in Business Ethics*. Academic Press, London. [2, 7, 10]

Donaldson, J. and Davis, P. (1990) 'Business Ethics? Yes But What Can It Do For The Bottom Line?', *Management Decision*, Vol. 28, No. 6, pp. 29–33. [1]

Donaldson, J. and Philby, P. (eds) (1985) *Pay Differentials*. Gower Publishing Co., Aldershot. [9]

Donaldson, T. (1989) *The Ethics of International Business*. Oxford University Press, New York. [3]

Drucker, P. (1981) 'What is Business Ethics?', *The Public Interest*, spring. [2]

Dunfee, T. and Robertson, D. (1988) 'Integrating Ethics into the Business School Curriculum', *Journal of Business Ethics*. Vol. 7, pp. 61–73. [2]

Dunfee, T. (1990) 'To Encourage or Repress? Corporate Policy and Whistle-Blowing'. In Enderle, G., Almond, B. and

Argandoña, A. (1990) *People in Corporations – Ethical Responsibilities and Corporate Effectiveness*. Kluwer Academic Publishers, Dordrecht, Boston and London. [4, 7]

Enderle, G., Almond, B. and Argandoña, A. (1990) *People in Corporations – Ethical Responsibilities and Corporate Effectiveness*. Kluwer Academic Publishers, Dordrecht, Boston and London. [2]

Financial Times, The (1990) 13 June (editorial). [13]

Flew, A. (1976) *Thinking About Thinking*. Fontana/Collins, Glasgow. [7]

Flew, A. (1984) *A Dictionary of Philosophy*. Pan Books in association with the Macmillan Press, London. [7]

Fox, A. (1974) *Man Mismanagement*. Hutchinson, London. [2]

Frankena, W. (1963) (second edition 1973) *Ethics*. Prentice-Hall, Englewood Cliffs, New Jersey. [7]

Freeman, R. (1984) *Strategic Management: A Stakeholder Approach*. Pitman, Boston. [2]

Frederick, R. (1989) 'Business Ethics and the Environment'. Report, Bentley College, USA, October, p. 2. [8]

French, P. (1984) *Collective and Corporate Responsibility*. Columbia University Press, New York. [2]

Fritzche and Becker (1984) 'Linking Management Behavior to Ethical Philosophy', *Academy of Management Journal*, March. [3]

Galbraith, J. (1958) *The Affluent Society* (second edition). Mentor Books, New York. [8]

Galbraith, J. (1967) *The New Industrial State*. Hamish Hamilton, London. [4]

Glasgow University Media Group (1976) *Bad News*. Routledge and Kegan Paul, London. [11]

Glasgow University Media Group (1980) *More Bad News*. Routledge and Kegan Paul, London. [11]

Glasgow University Media Group (1985) *War and Peace News*. Open University Press, Milton Keynes. [11]

Goldsmith, W. and Clutterbuck, D. (1986) *The Winning Streak*. Penguin, Harmondsworth. [1]

Goldsmith, W. and Clutterbuck, D. (1986) *The Winning Streak Checkbook*. Penguin, Harmondsworth. [1]

Gorton, T. (1991) 'BBC: bloated, bureaucratic, confused', *The Independent*, 16 January, p. 17. [11]

Gotbaum, V. (1978) 'Public Sector Strikes: Where Prevention is Worse than the Cure'. In De George, R. and Pichler, J. (eds) (1978) *Ethics, Free Enterprise and Public Policy*. Macmillan, New York. [3, 7]

Gouldner, A. (1954) *Patterns of Industrial Bureaucracy*, Free Press, New York. [4, 5]

Gouldner, A. (1954/5) *Wildcat Strike*. Free Press, New York. [5]

Grayeff, F. (1980) *A Short Treatise on Ethics*. Duckworth, London. [7]

Griffin, R. (1987) *Management* (second edition). Houghton Miflin, Boston. [2]

Griffiths, I. (1990) *The Independent*, 3 May, 1990, p. 32. [4]

The Guardian (1990) Editorial, 28 August. [13]

Habermas, J. (1981) *Moralbewusstsein und kommunikatives Handeln*. Heinemann Educational Books, London. [10]

Hare, R. (1961) (revised edition) *The Language of Morals*. Oxford University Press, Oxford. [7]

Hare, R. (1963) *Freedom and Reason*. Oxford University Press, London. [4, 5, 7]

Hare, R. (1981) *Moral Thinking, Its Levels, Method and Point*. Clarendon Press, Oxford. [5]

Harrison, M. (1989) 'CBI defends high pay awards', *The Independent*, 20 November, p. 22. [9]

Hencke, D. (1990) 'Brittan Deadline for Sweeteners', *The Guardian*, 21 July, p. 2. [1]

Henry, G. (1990) *The Guardian*, 25 June and 28 December. [11]

Hospers, J. (1978) 'Free Enterprise as the Embodiment of Justice'. In De George, R. and Pichler, J. (eds) (1978) *Ethics, Free Enterprise and Public Policy*. Macmillan, New York. [10]

Hughes, M. (1990) *The Guardian*, 8 December, p. 13. [12]

Hughes, R. (1985) 'European Court awards damages to Adams', *The Financial Times*, 8 November. [7]

Huhne, C. (1988) *The Guardian*, 13 January, p. 30. [12]

Hume, D. (1739/1965) *A Treatise of Human Nature*. Clarendon Press, Oxford. [6]

Hussey, M. (1990) BBC Annual Report and Accounts, London. [11]

Independent Broadcasting Authority (1983–84) Annual Report. [1]

Industrial Relations Review and Report (1988) 'Business Ethics Codes: A Moral Majority?', No. 422, 16 August, London. [4]

Institute of Personnel Management (c.1990) 'The IPM Code of Professional Conduct', *The IPM Codes of Practice*, London. [4]

International Labour Office (1988) *Summaries of International Labour Standards*. ILO Office, Geneva. [1]

Irvine, J. (1988) 'Professionals in a Catch-22 Situation', *The Independent*, 12 January. [4, 7]

John, D. (1990) *The Guardian*, 12 September. [13]

Johnson, C. (1988) 'Desperately seeking sounder statistics', *The*

Independent, 26 June. [9]

Kellner, P. (1988) 'I see no armies of unemployed', *The Independent*, 27 June. [9]

Kenny, T. (1976) 'The Asbestos Situation, or Whose Safety First?', *Personnel Management*, August. [4]

Keynes, J. (1936) *General Theory of Employment, Interest and Money*. Macmillan, London. [6]

Knight, H. (1987) 'Financial Services Legislation and Control' (MSc report). University of London. [13]

Kotsokis, S. (1990) 'Telecom giants named in Greek phones probe', *The European*, 10–12 August, p. 18. [2]

Lambert, R. (1990) 'Three Centuries of Scandal', *The Financial Times*, 1–2 September. [13]

Large, P. (1990) 'Duke attacks City failings', *The Guardian*, 1 May. [13]

Leapman, M. (1986) *The Last Days of the Beeb*. Allen & Unwin, Hemel Hempstead. [11]

Leapman, M. (1990) *The Independent*, 28 March. [11]

Lindblom, C. (1959) 'The Science of "Muddling Through"', *Public Administration Review*, Vol. 19, No. 2. [9]

Lipsey, R. (1963 and various editions) *An Introduction to Positive Economics*. Weidenfeld and Nicholson, London. [9]

Lupton, T. (1964) *On The Shop Floor*. Pergamon Press, Oxford. [4]

Lustig, R. (1990) 'A recipe for learning to love the law', *The Guardian*, 29 January, p. 23. [11]

Lydall, H. (1967) *The Structure of Earnings*. Oxford University Press, London. [9]

McGill, M. (1989) 'Why Managers Buy the Quick Fix', *Best of Business International*, Vol. 1, No. 3, summer.

McGregor, D. (1960) *The Human Side of Enterprise*, McGraw-Hill, New York. [7]

McHugh, F. (1988) *Keyguide to Information Sources in Business Ethics*. Nichols Publishing, New York. [6]

MacIntyre, A. (1985) *After Virtue – A Study in Moral Theory* (second edition). Duckworth, London. [7]

McRae, H. (1987) *The Independent*, 2 July. [13]

Mahoney, J. (1990) *Teaching Business Ethics in the UK, Europe and USA*. Athlone Press, London. [2, 6, 8]

Margerison, T., Wallace, M. and Hallstein, D. (1976/1978) *The Superpoison*. London, Macmillan. [1]

Mathison, D. and Boje, D. (1991) 'What Worries New Europe's Chief Executives the Most? A Study of Social Attitudes and Mixed Priorities'. (Paper presented to the American National Academy of Management.) [10]

May, L. (1987) *The Morality of Groups*. University of Notre Dame Press, Notre Dame, Indiana. [3]

Milne, S. (1990) 'TUC wants green stewards at work', *The Guardian*, 21 August, p. 2. [8]

Mishan, E. (1967) *The Costs of Economic Growth*. Penguin Books, Harmondsworth. [8]

Moore, G. (1903) *Principia Ethica*. Cambridge University Press, Cambridge. [7]

Nash, L. (1990) *Good Intentions Aside: A Manager's Guide to Solving Ethical Problems*. Harvard Business School Press, Boston, Massachusetts. [7]

Nash, L. (1981) 'Ethics Without the Sermon', *Harvard Business Review*, November/December. [7]

Newbiggin, E. (1984) *Stanley Adams*. Case Clearing House, Cranfield. [7]

Nowell-Smith, P. (1954) *Ethics*. Penguin Books, Harmondsworth. [7]

O'Riordan, T. (1990) 'The Legacy of Chernobyl' (Review). *Times Higher Education Supplement* 8 June, London. [5]

O'Toole, J. (1985) *Vanguard Management*. Doubleday and Co., New York. [3]

Paulu, B. (1981) *Television and Radio in the United Kingdom*. Macmillan, London. [11]

Parkinson, C. (1981) *The Law*. Penguin Books, Harmondsworth. [8]

Pen, J. (1971) *Income Distribution*. Allen Lane, London. [9]

Peters, T. (1987) *Thriving on Chaos*. Harper and Row, New York. [11]

Peters, T. and Austin, N. (1985) *A Passion for Excellence*. Random House, New York. [7]

Peters, T. and Waterman, R. (1981) *In Search of Excellence*. Harper and Row, New York. [7]

Phelps Brown, Sir H. (1977) *The Inequality of Pay*, Oxford University Press, Oxford. [9]

Pierce, J. and Newstrom, J. (1990) *The Manager's Bookshelf* (second edition). Harper and Row, New York. [3]

Pinchcome, S. *The Independent*, 3 July, 1990, p. 17. [1]

Plato (ed. H. Lee) (1955) *The Republic*. Penguin Books, Harmondsworth. [7]

Plender, J. (1990) *The Financial Times*, 28 August, p. 7. [13]

Procurement Weekly (1991) 14 March. [8]

Rawls, J. (1971) *A Theory of Justice*. Harvard University Press, Cambridge, Massachusetts. [7]

Rehbinder, E. (1989) 'US Environmental Policy: Lessons for Europe?' *International Environmental Affairs* Vol. 1, No. 1, Winter.

Roethlisberger, A. and Dickson, W. (1939a) *Management and the Worker.* Harvard University Press, Cambridge, Massachusetts. [4]

Roethlisberger, A. and Dickson, W. (1939b) *Management and Morale.* Harvard University Press, Cambridge, Massachusetts. [4]

Rosenbaum, A. (1990) 'New charges in French insider scandal', *The European,* 22–24 June, p. 20. [13]

Ross, Sir D. (1989) *The Foundations of Ethics.* Oxford University Press, London.

Rousseau, J.-J. (1762/1984) *The Social Contract.* Penguin Books, Harmondsworth. [7]

Ryan, A. (ed.) (1973) *The Philosophy of Social Explanation.* Oxford University Press, Oxford. [3]

Schoon, N. (1990) 'Gas guzzling cars could be in the next budget', *The Independent,* 26 September. [8]

Sedgwick UK Group (1989) *Annual Report,* London. [12]

Sedgwick UK Group (1988) *Code of Practice for Avoiding Errors and Omissions Claims,* London. [12]

Sedgwick UK Group (1986) *Policy Statement,* London. [12]

Sen, A. (1987) *On Ethics and Economics.* Basil Blackwell, Oxford. [4]

Silverman, D. (1970) *Theory of Organisations.* Heinemann, London. [3]

Singer, P. (1986) *Applied Ethics.* Oxford University Press, Oxford. [7]

Smith, A. (1766) *The Wealth of Nations* (Everyman Edition, 1962). J.M. Dent, London. [4]

Stevenson, C. (1937) 'Persuasive Definitions', *Mind,* 1937. [7]

Soler, C. (1990) 'Management as the Symbolisation of Ethical Values'. In Enderle, G., Almond, B. and Argandoña, A. (1990) *People in Corporations – Ethical Responsibilities and Corporate Effectiveness.* Kluwer Academic Publishers, Dordrecht, Boston and London. [11]

Sunday Times (1990) 8 March. [13]

Tawney, R. (1922/1961) *Religion and the Rise of Capitalism.* Penguin, Harmondsworth. [6]

Taylor, F. (1910) *Scientific Management.* Harper and Row, London (1947 edition). [7]

Thomas, T. (1990) 'Going green to stay out of the red', *The European,* 13 May. [8]

Thomas, D. and Riddell, P. (1990) *The Financial Times,* London 13 June. [8]

Thompson, Lord (1990) 'Economic and political change in broadcasting', *Royal Bank of Scotland Review,* No. 168, November. [11]

Thompson, Lord (1990) *The Guardian* (letter), 31 August. [11]

Titmuss, R. (1960) *The Irresponsible Society*. Fabian Tract 323, the Fabian Society, London. [8]

Titmuss, R. (1970) *The Gift Relationship*. Allen & Unwin, London. [10]

United Kingdom: Department of Trade and Industry (1990) *Single Market News*, autumn, p. 11. [5]

United Kingdom Department of Trade and Industry (1990) *The Single Market: Financial Services*, April and September. [12]

United Kingdom: National Economic Development Office (1987 and various editions) *British Industrial Performance and International Competitiveness*. NEDO, London. [9]

Unilever (1981) *The Responsibilities of Unilever*. Unilever Information Division, London. [4]

Usborne, D. (1990) 'EC launches enquiry into overseas phone charges', *The Independent*, 11 May, p. 1. [1]

Velasquez, M. (1988) *Business Ethics: Concepts and Cases* (second edition). Prentice-Hall, Englewood Cliffs, New Jersey. [3, 4]

Warnock, G. (1967) *Contemporary Moral Philosophy*. Macmillan, London. [7]

Wassermann, U. (1989) *Journal of World Trade Law*, Sept-Oct, Vol. 15, pp. 410–30. [1]

Waters, R. (1990) *The Financial Times*, 13 June. [13]

Watkins, J. (1973) 'Ideal Types and Historical Explanation'. In A. Ryan (ed.) (1973) *The Philosophy of Social Explanation*. Oxford University Press, Oxford. [3]

Weber, M. (1920) *The Protestant Ethic and the Spirit of Capitalism* (Tr. Henderson, A. and Parsons, T.) (1947). In *Collection of Essays*. The Free Press, New York. [6]

Webley, S. (1988) *Company Philosophies and Codes of Business Ethics: A Guide to their Drafting and Use*. Institute of Business Ethics, London. [4]

Williams, O. (1987) 'Business Ethics: A Trojan Horse?', *California Management Review*, Vol. XXIV, No. 4. [1]

Wittgenstein, L. (1963) *Philosophical Investigations*. Basil Blackwell, Oxford. [2]

Wolf, J. (1990) *The Guardian*, 15 and 16 October. [2]

Wolmar, C. (1990) *The Independent*, 22 June. [11]

Woodward, J. (1965) *Industrial Organisation – Theory and Practice*. Oxford University Press, London. [4]

NAME INDEX

287

SUBJECT INDEX

291